Mind Over Machine

Psychology of Riding Motorcycles

A deep insight into the Mental Side of Riding and Racing Motorcycles.

Authored by Can Akkaya, Head Coach of the Superbike-Coach Corp in Sacramento, CA.

❊ Mind Note – How you know?!

"...of course I've been there myself. How else would I even know?!"

— *Can Akkaya*

Copyright and Imprint

Copyright:	Copyright © 2025 Superbike-Coach Corp
Rights Reserved:	All rights reserved. No part of this book may be reproduced, distributed, or transmitted in any form or by any means, electronic or mechanical, including photocopying, recording, or by any information storage and retrieval system, without the prior written permission of the author, except in the case of brief quotations embodied in critical reviews and certain other noncommercial uses permitted by copyright law.
ISBN (Paperback):	979-8-9942445-0-0
ISBN (eBook):	979-8-9942445-1-7
Publisher:	Superbike-Coach Corp
Author:	Can Akkaya
Location:	Sacramento, CA United States
Edition:	First Edition
Website:	www.moto-psych.com
Cover Artwork and Interior Design: Illustrations and Graphics:	Dean Lonskey and Can Akkaya Can Akkaya (Created with Adobe Photoshop and Macromedia)
Quotes:	Attributed to Albert Einstein; used for educational purposes by permission/license of the Hebrew University of Jerusalem, Ann-M. P. (Yelp review)
Editorial, creative collaborator:	Jill Akkaya
Statistics:	Insurance Information Institute
Dedication:	This book is dedicated to the entire Superbike-Coach Corp team and their tireless, selfless dedication, whose unwavering commitment to each student's growth and safety makes true mastery possible.

Legal and Safety Disclaimer

This book, *Mind Over Machine: Psychology of Riding Motorcycles*, is presented strictly for the reader's personal education and self-improvement of mental skills. It is essential that the reader understands and acknowledges the following conditions:

- **Assumption of Risk and High-Risk Acknowledgement** Motorcycle riding is an inherently high-risk activity that carries a significant and unavoidable risk of serious injury, disability, or death. The concepts, techniques, and opinions discussed in this book are based on the author's personal experience and decades of professional coaching; they are not infallible. They are not a substitute for certified, hands-on physical training from a qualified instructor, nor do they guarantee safety or accident prevention. The information in this book is provided on an "as is" basis without any warranties, express or implied. By reading and applying the information in this book, the reader voluntarily assumes all risks associated with motorcycle riding.

- **Release of Liability** The reader agrees that they, and not the Author (Can Akkaya), the Publisher (Superbike-Coach Corp), Dean Lonskey, or any affiliated entity, are solely responsible for their actions, decisions, and safety. The reader hereby releases, waives, and discharges the Author, Publisher, and their respective designers and contractors from all liability for any personal injury, death, property damage, or loss resulting from the use or misuse of the information contained within this book.

- **Age and Licensing Restriction** This book assumes the reader is a legally licensed adult operating a motorcycle in full compliance with all local, state, and national traffic laws. The author strongly advises against the application of any advanced concepts by unlicensed, inexperienced, or juvenile riders.

- **Voice and Tone Disclaimer** The author utilizes a direct, passionate, and challenging tone intended to provoke critical self-assessment and promote truth in riding instruction. Readers should understand that any language that may be perceived as rough, controversial, or critical of other programs is born from a professional commitment to rider safety and the exposure of inadequate training methodologies. Such language is intended for educational impact and is not intended to harass, offend, or ridicule.

- **Commentary on Rival Methodologies** Any critique, assessment, or comparison of other riding schools, training programs, or teaching methodologies contained within this book is based solely on the author's personal professional experience, observation, and expert opinion. This commentary is intended to promote rider safety and truth in instruction. All such statements are protected as fair comment on matters of public interest and should be interpreted as subjective professional opinion, not as actionable false statements of fact.

- **Limitation of Psychological/Medical Scope** The author, Can Akkaya, is a professional riding coach and former racer, but is **not a licensed mental health professional, psychiatrist, physician, or therapist.** The psychological analysis and advice contained herein is for informational and educational purposes only (focused on performance and skill enhancement) and is not a substitute for professional clinical diagnosis or treatment.

The services and information provided are complementary to, and not a substitute for, healing arts services licensed by the State of California. If you believe you are suffering from a medical or mental health condition, you must consult a licensed healthcare provider.

- **Intellectual Property and Commercial Use** The concepts, methodologies, proprietary terms, and psychological frameworks presented in this book (including the "Mind Over Machine" framework) are the exclusive intellectual property of the Author, Can Akkaya. Reproduction, teaching, or commercial utilization of these methods, in whole or in part, without the express written permission of the Author is strictly prohibited and constitutes a violation of copyright. This material is provided for the personal education and self-improvement of the reader only.

- **Use of AI-Assisted Content and Artistic Attribution** The base visual elements for the Cover Artwork and internal Graphics/Illustrations were initially developed using generative digital tools, including Gemini AI. However, the Author, Can Akkaya, and Designer, Dean Lonskey, have applied substantial and original human modification, editing, and arrangement to these base elements using professional software. The Author hereby claims and asserts full copyright protection over the final edited compositions and the unique artistic contributions applied to these visuals. These works are human-directed, hybrid-creative works and are not "AI-generated" in their final form.

- **Referential Use of Public Figures** The inclusion of names belonging to professional athletes and public figures (e.g., Valentino Rossi, Marc Márquez, Peyton Manning, Albert Einstein, or others) is strictly for the purpose of factual, editorial commentary, performance analysis, and educational illustration. This use is protected under the doctrine of Nominative Fair Use and the First Amendment. It does not imply any form of sponsorship, affiliation, endorsement, or approval by the referenced individuals or their associated organizations.

- **Use of Quoted Material (Fair Use)** The inclusion of short, attributed quotations from public figures, published works, or personal anecdotes is strictly for the purpose of commentary, education, and analysis, and falls under the doctrine of Fair Use in copyright law. Extended use of copyrighted material has been intentionally avoided or secured by express permission where required.

- **No Endorsement** Any mention of third-party products, services, organizations, or individuals (including motorcycle manufacturers or racing gear brands) in this book is for informational purposes only. Such references do not constitute an endorsement, recommendation, or affiliation by the Author or Publisher, nor does the mention of these entities imply their endorsement of this work.

- **Governing Law and Jurisdiction** Any legal action or proceeding relating to this book or its content shall be brought exclusively in the courts located in the State of California, County of Sacramento. You agree to resolve any disputes on an individual basis and waive any right to participate in a class-action lawsuit or class-wide arbitration.

READ THIS ENTIRE DISCLAIMER BEFORE PROCEEDING. Your use of this book confirms your understanding and agreement to these terms.

Content

Foreword by Jeremy G.	7	Nuts n' Bolts	93
Introduction	9	Rethinking Learning Curve	97
PART I: Self-Critique		That Thing About Progress	103
Die Hard Honesty	13	**PART II: Understanding**	
Learning to Learn	16	That Rear Brake Thang	108
The Right Order	20	Brake at All Times	113
Ego and Emotions	26	That ABS Thang	116
Hopes and Wisch-Thinking	30	Hurt, Pain, and Dying	121
Being a Talented Rider	34	About Commitment	127
'Body Positioning' Hype	38	Reestablishment the Hurt	129
The Power of Ignorance	43	Growing Balls	133
'Sensei' Has to Be Old	48	Fear Tradeoff	135
The Rookie Effect	52	Protective Reactions	138
Your Skill Bubble Pops	55	Anxieties	142
Excuses	59	Self-Imposed Pressure	148
Being Unlucky	62	Pressure	152
What's Really Wrong Here	67	Being Desperate	156
Don't Be a Fool	73	Chaos Control	161
The 28 Bux Suicide	76	Negative vs. Positive	166
Statistics and Its Data	79	Confidence	170
The European Odyssey	80	What Bad Feels Like	176
Listening to "Experts"	83	Awareness	181
Dragging Knee Makes Fast	90	Why New Riders Don't 'See'	185

"Car Awareness" Class	188	Yin and Yang	241
Paradox of Speed	192	Addicted to Perfection	246
Getting Lost in Electronics	197	Own the Damn Candy Store	251
PART III: Intelligence		Being the Underdog	255
Competitiveness	201	Favoritism	258
Beast Mode	205	Track Days for Better Riders	262
Being Gung-Ho	209	**PART IV: The Long Game**	
Physical Aggression	216	Expectations Are Good	266
Mama Bear Effect	221	Living in Denial	270
Race Intelligence	225	Celebrate You	275
The Mastery Loop	230	The Decline	279
A Child's Heart	233	Final Word	283
Learning Fast	237	Bonus Material	285

※ **Mind Note – Memorize**

"Mistakes are always forgivable, if one has the courage to admit them."

— Bruce Lee

Foreword

There are as many different starting points to learning to ride a motorcycle as there are motorcyclists, but mine was my first track day. An aspiring street rider, I signed up in hopes of leaving the track with a newfound sense of confidence in cornering at speed. I reasoned that all those repeated laps with no cars, no pedestrians and no speed limit would be the perfect place to figure out the skills that had been making every corner at speed on the street feel like a roll of the dice. I thought by eliminating the risks and variables of the street, like a child learning to ride a bike on a tennis court, my cornering ability would blossom. The reality of the day itself was a blur of excitement, adrenaline and sheer terror. Unfortunately, not only did I leave the track without the newfound sense of confidence I was seeking, I left with the feeling that I could do a thousand more track days and never attain my goals. Along with my brutal reality check, I left the track with something else. A burning desire, a holy mission, to learn how to truly ride a motorcycle. Not to learn how to work the controls, or how to wrestle the machine into submission, but how to attain the kind of easy, confident, free flowing speed I saw in evidence among the fastest of the "A" group riders out on the track. A mission to learn the whys behind the how's, the psychology behind what was holding me back. A mission to learn abilities I could use on the track without limitation, but that I could also use to make my street riding safer and feel like less of a gamble. That mission ultimately led me to Can Akkaya, or simply "Coach" as he's known to his students.

A very few times in my life, I have been lucky to meet a mentor like Coach. Someone who has experiential knowledge, knowledge based on a lifetime of doing, of wins and losses, of successes and mistakes. Someone who has empathy, that can put themselves in the shoes of others, a prerequisite to being able to relate knowledge to them. Someone who is analytic, who knows things deep in their guts, but can use their mind to reverse engineer the why of every how. Someone with a passion for connecting and sharing what they know with others, out of a love for people as much as for knowledge. Someone that can deliver uncomfortable truths plainly, telling you what you need to hear, without getting caught up in what you want to hear.

While I have no aspirations to be a racer, my journey to Coach came from a belief that racing is the highest form of expression of riding a motorcycle. In every mental and physical skill I've learned from Coach, comes the choice of using newfound mental or physical margins for speed or for safety. From Coach, I have learned that at every level of motorcycling, among the hardest challenges to overcome are psychological. But just like with physical challenges, there are concrete strategies, tactics and skills that can be learned and applied to honing your mental skills. What a luxury to be able to learn from a man who has climbed to the peaks of the mountains that I was hoping to scale the foothills of! Reader, be warned. The mountain climbing analogy is apt not just due to the gulf between the dizzying heights aspired compared to the lowly starting point, but also because the honest truths you'll find on the climb will leave you exposed and bitterly sting your ego. While Coach will show you the path, he will not hold your hand, and he will not sugar coat the time, work and risk involved in the ascent. While it's true that there's theoretically no limit to the heights you can climb, I have learned from Coach that in reality few riders are psychologically prepared or able to do what is necessary to reach the highest peaks. Most of us also need to consider the practical limits imposed upon us by mother nature and father time when picking the heights for which we strive. The mental and physical skills you can learn from Coach apply to all forms of motorcycle riding from casual street riders, to weekend track warriors, to serious racers. While the psychology and skills that follow may take a lifetime to master, I can speak first hand to the fact that in their essence, they're immediately applicable to riders at the start of their journey.

I didn't know it when I met him, but the knowledge Coach would share with me would change my life, set me down a path of lifelong learning and deepen my love of motorcycling. I hope in the chapters that follow you will find the same!

Jeremy Gordon, November, 2025

Introduction

I feel like it was all meant to be. Looking back on my childhood in Europe—growing up half Turkish and half German—I went through years marked by racism, bullying, and confusion. Bloody noses and fights were almost routine. In this mess, I was constantly searching for my place in the world. Standing up for myself, for the people I cared about, and for what I believed was right came naturally to me. It still does. Being direct and calling out what is wrong became second nature. Over time, I learned not to suppress my feelings, and that honesty, while often uncomfortable, is necessary. Everything had to go my way. Always. I've made mistakes. I've made choices. Some I regret, but I'd regret it far more if I had never tried. I have come to terms with the fact that mistakes are part of growth. As a teenager, I did what society expected. I finished school, learned a trade, and got a job. But I had no clear goals, no structure, and no direction. I was floating, and let the current take me wherever it wanted. What I did have were dreams. I have always believed that everything great begins with a dream. Riding a motorcycle on the street became my escape. It was therapy. Freedom, if you will. It also got me into trouble more than once, until I finally discovered racetracks. I'll keep this short, because the story is long. I was scouted at Zolder Circuit in Belgium and began racing. That was the moment my life found direction. I found purpose, and in many ways, I found myself.

Being scouted isn't common, so yes, I had *it*. But talent alone doesn't get you far. There was still an enormous amount to learn, and I had to figure most of it out on my own. I gave sweat, heart, soul, blood, and a few broken bones to become a professional FIM licensed racer. I went from an amateur forced to run slicks in the rain 'cuz I couldn't afford rain tires, to a high-level international competitor earning a living doing what I love. Most importantly, I did it on my own. Why does that matter? You will see soon enough.

Coming to America

When I first came to America to chase a new dream, I was genuinely shocked. The first time I commuted from the East Bay to San Francisco on a motorcycle, California hit me all at once. Lane splitting, constant honking, potholes, unpredictable traffic, and the Oakland Bay Bridge. It was chaos compared to what I was used to. The DMV written exam and circle test were easy, but they prepare you for paperwork, not for real California roads. I adapted quickly. That's part of being a racer. But as I thought about what it takes to ride safely here, something became obvious. I'm a European Championship racer and coach. I've got the tools, the experience, and a mindset that adapts in a heartbeat. But what about the rider who just passed their license course? They're out there on their own, falling for whatever garbage social media is feeding them. They've got to follow people who think that just because they ride and learned how to talk, they're qualified to teach.

Anyway, my first Sunday ride through California's canyons should have been pure joy. I was ready to let the bike breathe. To my surprise, most car drivers were polite and respectful, very different from Germany. Then came the reality. Fallen trees, deer, gravel, and potholes big enough to swallow a wheel. After nearly losing the front end a few times, I pulled over, helmet still on, and stood there staring at the road. That was me. A racer who had bent rims flying through gravel beds while chasing lap records at Zolder. I'm used to chaos. Still, the thought wouldn't leave me. What about a new rider? Someone without those instincts and reflexes. Someone who crashes alone on a mountain road, slides into a ravine, breaks a leg, and sits there with no cell reception while a bear starts licking off his blood. It sounds absurd, but it's closer to reality than most people want to admit.

As my circle of riding friends grew, I experienced some incredible rides. Highway 1, Skaggs Springs, Redwood Road, Lake Berryessa. I love the atmosphere here—the enthusiasm, the openness, the passion. But I was also confronted with something else. Group riding, where risk is buried under ego. Jeans instead of leathers. Music in helmets. Endless videotaping and phones on handlebars. Wheelie contests. Ego races on public roads. It's a reflection of society today; most seem to worry more about the show than the skill. Everyone has an ego. I do too. The difference is knowing when to back off. After enough close calls, after hearing too many riders laugh and say, "Damn, that was close," the pattern became obvious. Experienced riders know when to disengage. Inexperienced riders don't—and they'll crash. I've seen it happen. Friends scrambling to pick up bikes and broken parts. Days that were supposed to be fun ending in tickets, or worse... dead riders.

The root cause is always the same. Lack of experience. Lack of knowledge. Poor judgment. Insufficient skill—but truckloads of ego. Two of those can be taught. The other two only come with time. Push beyond what you truly understand, and you may spend your summer staring at hospital walls instead of riding into the sunsets.

That realization forced a decision. There's almost no meaningful rider education. I expanded what I had done in Europe and began educating riders in California. But I quickly realized something else. There's far more to pass on than any course can contain. That's *why this book exists*.

Universal Rider's Psyche

I didn't want to write another generic riding manual. This book takes a deep and sometimes uncomfortable look at the role the mind plays in riding and surviving on a motorcycle. It isn't limited by discipline. Whether you ride a sportbike on track, cruise the streets, or explore off road on an adventure bike, the psychological foundation is the same.

Fear, doubt, hesitation, overconfidence, and mental blocks don't care what you ride. How we think, feel, and learn follows the same pattern. If you stay open minded and connect the dots, mastery becomes possible.

My goal is to clear away myths, misinformation, and invented theories that have worked their way into mainstream riding education. This book challenges what you believe you already know. It applies common sense and hard logic to every maneuver and mental influence, not to confuse you, but to expose what's maybe holding you back. This isn't only about riding technique. It's about flawed learning systems and habits that prevent true skill development.

An Uncompromised Voice of Experience

You may feel that I shine a harsh light on other schools and books. That's intentional. Respect must be earned. Everything you read here is grounded in decades of first-hand experience. Riding, racing, failing, teaching, and learning. I've never relied on borrowed curricula or recycled theories from other schools. What I teach comes directly from lived professional experience. If you're willing to engage with that honestly, this book will change how you think, on and off the bike.

Proof in Practice

References to my riding school are not promotional. The school is fully booked through word of mouth alone. These references exist for one reason only. Proof. They provide real world examples of the psychological principles discussed here. Drawn from daily interactions with riders and from the experiences students bring with them from other programs. Every anecdote exists to reveal how deeply mindset shapes behavior. That's the real intent here.

Red Thread

Don't expect a traditional textbook structure. The flow of this book mirrors the way the brain actually works. Nonlinear. Interconnected. Repetitive when necessary. Certain subjects appear more than once because repetition reveals connection. Fear affects braking. Poor braking reinforces fear. Understanding one without the other is incomplete.

There won't always be a neat solution at the end of every chapter, but some solid takeaway sections for sure. Sometimes awareness itself is the solution. Recognizing an unseen mental influence is already a step toward competence.

My language may feel rough at times. That isn't aggression. It's honesty. The goal is never to belittle riders, but to serve the truth. Pointing out what's wrong is my life. I'm not blaming you. I blame the system. Growth rarely comes from comfort. Let's jump right into it…

PART I: Self-Critique

Die Hard Honesty

You know what makes truth so much more efficient than a coat of sugar?

There are many layers of lies, and thousands of reasons for them. Just like having a reasonable 'white lie' in order not to hurt the one you love that just gave you a present you actually don't like. You accept it and say thank you. But let's imagine you have that friend, Paul. Paul's armpits smell like he's been on a constant marathon through the Baja California desert. He's an outstanding guy, a real friend, and you love him. You might ignore it, or be afraid to hurt his feelings, so you keep your mouth shut.

Now Paul didn't make it in the job interview. He lost some other friends, and he has a hard time connecting to that girl in the bar. Sure, it's Paul's hygiene, and you gave careful hints, but you're the actual problem here. You are the selfish one. You are the one that didn't let him know that he smells like a mountain lion cave, straight up with truth. That might come hard on Paul, but he's also getting a chance here. A chance he wouldn't have without that honesty. You are equally responsible for his failures, don't you?!

Professional's Ethical Responsibility

See, throughout my career as a head coach, I got blamed for being mean. That goes along with a 'they like believing that' and name it this way. I'm aware. In fact, though, it's caring and worrying, as I only do the best I can to help. And that means a solid mentor also has to be able to walk the uncomfortable way. How much would it be my professional fault if I kept telling a student how good he/she looks? Constantly, just to make that student 'feel happy' and to ensure they 'like me'?! How much would covering the truth extend their learning curve?! How much of it would be my fault when that rider gets hurt in a crash, just because I went the commercial route, instead of standing up for what I truly believe as a professional who has seen it all? I'd feel equally responsible.

I truly believe, if a teacher tells a rider things like "you look so good out there," while it isn't true or not deserved. And that this teacher is either incompetent or operating purely on an 'easy money' model. What's your best pick?! Are you a teacher and you feel a tiny bit offended by my statement? If yes, you better put this book aside because you won't like the rest of it much. Feeling addressed means... you're addressed.

Confronting Cognitive Dissonance

How to address the truth? Well, that's the importance here, and how to get the truth across without breaking trust or confidence. That's the real challenge. I know how, but I truly reject sharing this here. There's no 100% way to do this anyway. Can I reach everyone and successfully steer their boats the right way? No. Because how they respond to it is mostly depending on their ego-level as an individual, and the level of cognitive dissonance protecting their self-image. They engage in wish-thinking and denial to maintain the comfortable picture they have of themselves. Maybe also because of how often they have been lied to about 'how good they look.' You know... the more people are saying it, the more it matches what one likes to believe! There, I said it!

A Rider's Self-Assessment Bias

Now what does all of this have to do with you as a motorcycle rider? A whole lot, 'cuz you'll need to have that kind of honesty, at least to yourselves, to become the rider you're visioning to be. The moment you start telling yourself these lies, you engage in a performance-limiting self-assessment bias:

Group denial. The track day rider who makes a booking for A group, while he denies the truth to be lower B group material.

Education stagnation. The brand-new rider who just got a license, but denies the need for continued education.

Knowledge ceiling. The experienced rider who is lying to him/herself that he knows it all.

Defensive blame. The amateur racer who covers a lie with an excuse.

Causality reversal. The rider who puts the car driver at fault for not seeing him, while he was riding in a blind spot for three miles.

Amnesia. That you 'don't know why you crashed.'

Skill exaggeration Lying that you know how to counter steer, or properly manage throttle.

Emotional concealment. Denying that you're actually scared when riding!

Ego protection. When you say your experience was all crap, while actually your ego doesn't allow you to see the lesson.

If you, instead, are die hard honest at least with yourselves… it will open up another world. You actually begin to help yourself.

Psychological Takeaway

The human brain is wired to choose comfort over the truth. This is self-preservation bias in action. The ego lies to avoid the temporary sting of being wrong. The moment a rider mutters, "The tires were cold," instead of admitting, "I was lazy with the throttle," they have committed a selfish act of self-preservation. It's an attempt to protect feelings at the expense of progress.

A lie is a barrier to growth. It's a wall that breaks the essential connection between an action and its result. When a rider refuses to let the raw, painful truth enter the system, the problem can't be fixed because it's never truly seen. Denial is the fastest way to shut down the natural ability to learn. It's the equivalent of turning off a GPS and wondering why the destination is never reached.

This is a mandatory system overhaul. It requires forcing raw data, such as "I was scared" or "I missed the apex 'cuz I was not looking far enough," directly into the mind as something actionable. This closes the loop. The truth is painful data, but it's the only currency that buys real speed and safety. Honesty is the price of admission to a rider's actual potential.

Learning to Learn

Being a Dumb Animal Gets You Killed

I wasn't always this analytical. Far from it actually. Back when I was an amateur, I thought I knew it all. I believed racing was about guts. The bigger your balls, the faster you'd go. That was the mindset. And with that mindset, it's easy to drown in excuses.

Sure, courage is what it takes to explore the limits, but sooner or later you realize that learning—not just daring—is what actually makes you fast. To learn is a mindset. This chapter is about cracking open your brain and accepting that the emotional thrill of speed needs to be replaced by the cold, hard logic of growth. Without that brutal honesty, you're just a dumb animal on two wheels.

Racing and riding became a philosophy for me, and that's what I try to teach today. Once you truly grasp it, it changes everything. Not just how you ride, but who you are in that moment of speed, in that slice of time and space where everything else disappears. Without that transformation, you'll never become the rider or racer you imagine yourself to be.

It took me years to understand that the learning process itself is the real joy. I used to set my goals too high. Always chasing results, always trying to "arrive". But when you focus only on the destination, you miss the brutal beauty of the journey. Not enjoying the little steps forward just builds pressure. You rush, you skip things, you burn out trying to "arrive." This is the amateur's mindset: focused on glory, blind to the grind.

Learning should feel like a road trip. Long, winding and unpredictable. It's not about the destination; it's about everything that happens on the way there. The hot dog you ate sitting on your truck bed. That weird-looking guy who told you a story at a gas station. The piss you took under flickering neon lights. It's never about lying on some beach pretending you've "made it." That's the dreamer's fantasy, not the pro's reality.

My Wake-Up Call

By the end of my amateur days, I was genuinely fast. All-out, no fear. In a class with 120 riders fighting for 45 grid spots, I was the guy to beat. And then came the shock: the following year, as a semi-pro, on the same track, in the same category, the fast guys were six seconds quicker per lap. Six seconds! That's an eternity. Me, the hotshot from last season… getting lapped. The amateur in me was screaming.

Halfway through that season, I started pushing even harder. Crashes, pain, sweat, blood. The usual recipe. I doubled on physical training because I believed that physical strength is mental strength, and vice versa. Every day I hit a 30-kilometer mountain bike loop, punishing myself into focus. But one day, while mountain biking, a memory looped in my head: me sliding out of a turn, wild and dramatic, while one of the championship contenders passed me calmly outside on the curb. Smooth, precise and unbothered.

I stopped my mountain bike right there, standing in the mud, and it hit me: I was pushing way beyond the limit. Not because I was brave, but because I was blind. I dropped the bicycle, sat down, and decided to be brutally honest with myself. Why wasn't I that good? Why didn't I look that composed? Then it clicked. I was competing against other riders instead of mastering the track. That's the Ego Trap at work, focused externally, missing the internal game.

The Matrix

That realization cracked something open inside me. I began to really see. Every turn, every movement, every flick of the wrist started to mean something. I began to listen to my body, to the bike, to the silence between moments. I learned that control wasn't about force; it was about smoothness**.** That relaxation opened new levels of reaction, like a cat landing effortlessly on its feet. My senses sharpened. I could feel the tension in the handlebars before it happened, sense the rear tire sliding before it broke loose.

I learned to read other riders, not as enemies but as moving pieces of a puzzle. Each with patterns, tells, weaknesses. I learned to influence them, to let them feel my presence until they made their own mistakes. And for the first time, I realized that dominance didn't come from aggression. It came from clarity. This is mental aggression applied with surgical precision.

As I calmed the storm inside, everything else slowed down. Corners opened wider. Time stretched. I could sense the bike's rhythm, the tires' conversation with the asphalt, the pulse of the race itself. My aggression became precision; my chaos turned into control. I wasn't just racing anymore. I was seeing the matrix. This is where the internal locus of control truly takes hold.

True Joy

Learn to learn, and you'll find joy in every step. You'll notice the details others overlook. The higher you climb, the more meaning each subtle improvement holds.

My grandmother used to tell me, "Learn to laugh about yourself. It makes life easier." She was right. It takes the pressure off. And when things got tough, she'd remind me, "You learn more from losing than from winning." I didn't understand that back then. But now I do. Every loss, every crash, every bruise was just part of learning to learn. It's about turning every setback into crucial feedback for your system.

Psychological Takeaway

The primary mental hurdle is an external locus of control. This occurs when a rider operates like a dumb animal, driven by ego, external competition, and the desire to perform for others. Focusing on external outcomes or trying to look impressive creates a volatile, unsafe, and inconsistent environment. It's a trade of true proficiency for a temporary ego fix.

Rider Reboot

The path to mastery requires a mental reboot where a rider takes command of the internal locus. This switch happens when a rider accepts that safety and progress are entirely within their own control and that every failure is simply data. Success comes from moving away from chasing specific outcomes and instead becoming obsessed with the process, the inputs, and continuous growth. This shift allows for the transition from reacting to anticipating. Learning to read patterns and the environment transforms chaos into a predictable and manageable flow. This proactive mindset is the only way to increase both survival and overall riding proficiency.

The Goal

The objective isn't just about going fast. It's about unshakeable control, maximum smoothness, and the deep enjoyment that comes from owning every aspect of the performance. Moving away from riding for the show and instead owning the internal game is the only path to mastery on the street or the track.

※ Mind Note – Coach's take

"Progress doesn't come from chasing perfection; it comes from surrendering to the process. The moment you stop forcing it, the flow finds you. In that stillness, speed is no longer something you create — it's something you become."

- Can Akkaya

The Right Order

Starting Your ABCs with the Letter P

I already gave some hints about this. Learning all physical skills in the right order isn't optional. Done right, it's got a snowball effect. Positively speaking.

Imagine this: you'd be learning the ABC's starting with a P back in school, and there were no teachers around to tell you this was the wrong order. Sure, you'd eventually learn to read and write, but skipping the correct sequence makes everything harder, right?! According to mentalfloss.com, nobody knows exactly why the alphabet is ordered this way. To me it makes sense, as the sequence creates a natural, easy-to-memorize flow.

Now, riding a motorcycle isn't about sounds. Unlike the ABC's, learning to ride is about snowball effects, safety, and above all, mental growth.

I mean... imagine coming straight off that DMV parking lot with a new moto license, and the next thing you try is trail braking. Two endings: hell or hospital. See the point about order?

When you learn in the right order, you gain mental strength. You become more "available" to understand complex physical skills. You grow bigger balls. And you brave up to learn the really bad-ass stuff.

So, what is the right order- and why am I not listing them up here? Because that would carry you away from the point I'm trying to make. I also want you to think about it, not just read it. I just hope the school you pick knows about the right sequence as well as we do.

Mental Before Physical

The mental steps must always precede and govern the physical steps. I've seen too many riders crash because they tried to learn the physical "P" (e.g., trail braking) before mastering the mental "A" (Vision). This book is your blueprint, and it's built on this sequence.

The right order is a non-negotiable loop where your mind must complete the psychological checks before the body can execute the physical task. To illustrate this, here is the Unified Sequence:

Rider Levels and Lie of Self-Assurance

Yep, I can literally sense you might think I'm sales pitching. I'm not, but I need you to look objectively at an ongoing problem, so let's see what I've seen over all the years coaching countless 1-on-1s and running tons of classes on road and track.

I hate doing this, but let me categorize riders and their level, and what their general thinking process is regarding education. This goes deep already, so bear with me.

The Beginner Rider

Beginners… you know the type. Friends who just got their motorcycle license, and probably shouldn't have yet. Two days in a parking lot, a couple hundred bucks, and suddenly they're "ready." This kind of "training" is basically useless, and often counterproductive. It creates anxieties around braking and leaves a hard-to-remove picture of what "schooling" looks like—keeping most people from seeking better options. I end up having to un-f*** almost everything they were taught.

The Intermediate Rider

They've finally gotten through the minor operational essentials, so basic skills don't block learning anymore. But then they spend nights watching YouTube: "Bad car drivers vs motorcycles, volume 155", and suddenly professional schooling doesn't seem necessary. Their riding buddies, who all think they're experts, reinforce it. Bad habits start forming, self-taught or copied. Fast doesn't equal skilled, and experience alone doesn't make a proper rider.

The Advanced Rider

These riders have miles, maybe read some riding books, and are more selective with their videos. They begin looking for professional schools, but most end up in an "advanced riding clinic" for $350—tiptoeing in a parking lot again. Advanced? Honestly, I still don't know what counts as advanced there.

The Advanced-Plus Rider

Now it's all about track time. "One track day beats a year on the road," they think. Exciting? Sure. But often overwhelming. We can't admit we're overwhelmed in front of friends, so we keep going and eventually crash many times. Professional schooling loses impact because instructors give quick praise— "You look good out there... just stick your elbow out more", without actually teaching the fundamentals.

The Expert Rider

At this stage, speed becomes a badge of honor. Drag knees, elbows out. They think they've arrived. But mastery isn't about how low you lean. True expertise is awareness, anticipation, and control under pressure. Many go back to books because they're stuck on a plateau. Years and miles alone aren't enough. Real skill comes from mental control, sequencing, and understanding your limits, not just flashy body positioning.

The Expert-Plus Rider

These riders think there's nobody left who can teach them anything. They keep crashing, getting frustrated, and losing the fun. They think years and miles equal knowledge, but they don't. Specific, structured training is what's missing.

The Racer

This is where a coach really matters. But a coach doesn't have to be physically faster. They have to be mentally sharper. At high levels, riding is more mental than physical. Think of a high school football coach: he can't outrun the players, but he knows exactly when to push them, and how to make them perform beyond what they thought possible. Riding and racing works the same way.

Be honest. Can you see yourself in one or the other category? Did you run through the same thinking process?

Schools, Videos, and Buddies

So, if any of those wonderful things really worked like people think they should… shouldn't I see a bigger percentage of riders where I could honestly say: "Sorry, you wasted your time with us. Good job."?

Now, what does all this make of these books, schools, and rock star videos? Does this still look like a way to go? Yep, you don't know me, and maybe you think I'm lying or trying to fill classes. Trust me, that's not me. In fact, this is exactly how it is. It should make you ask questions, just like I do. After seeing all this, I'd like to walk you through why these things actually can't work.

There's nothing else to learn on a damn parking lot once you can shift gears and execute basic operations like throttle and brake control. And the outcome of learning "advanced slow maneuver techniques" in all those schools? Minimal, 'cuz that's all they actually allow you to do. If you still believe otherwise, you might be living in denial. You'll find a more detailed discussion later in this book.

How about your riding buddy? He doesn't really know much himself. Maybe he's naturally faster than you, so it seems like he's a good free resource. When he offers to "help" and leads you around the street or track for a few minutes, while he actually needs help himself. What do you get from that? Imagine getting a guitar lesson from someone who held a guitar in their hands just a day before you. That's what it's like. He has no clue how to hold the ropes. Tough truth, huh?

Reading books doesn't help much either. Sure, most of the information is technically correct. But it's just information. This isn't algebra, which a smart kid could learn from a book without a teacher. Algebra doesn't kill you, but attempting trail braking on Highway One could. It's like reading a book about climbing Mount Everest and then going there to die without a guide.

Watching videos is slightly more feasible than books. But even then, who can say whether you're doing it right or wrong? Who validates your learning? What about the quality of free YouTube content? How do you even classify it as right or wrong?

Missing the Sequence

And here's the bigger problem: nobody out there seems to know the proper sequence of teaching. You can't randomly try to learn trail braking. Your eyes, brain, and body might not be ready for higher entry speeds yet, and many foundational skills must be corrected first. Taught in the right doses, in the right way, at the right time.

Same goes for that B-Level racer who "works" for a free meal or track time as an instructor. Some call them professionals, but they're not. They tell you: "Stick those elbows more out", then go off to race the other instructors in C-group. That's reality. You take that instruction 'cuz you want to be a 'racer'. His instruction supports only your wishful thinking. But in fact, you've just been taught the ABC's starting with the letter P.

So... not everything that glitters in the sun is gold. All those things you believe in—books, schools, videos—are extremely limited in regard to physical learning outcomes. Why? Because there's no quality control, no last-instance authority to tell you whether you're doing it right. All of these things leave the final judgment to the rider... the one who doesn't know. And it's not even the rider's fault. I blame the system, the media, and our "everyone's-a-winner" culture. Hope you see the point.

In all these years of teaching, I've learned that riders often believe: "Years and miles are all it takes to know it all." Honestly, that doesn't match what I see almost every day.

Psychological Takeaway

The biggest obstacle to growth isn't a lack of talent but the Dunning-Kruger Effect. This is where a rider with very little competence actually believes they're a pro. Having a few miles under the belt tricks the ego into a dangerous intermediate phase, creating a false conviction that the fundamentals are already "done."

This is the peak of mount stupid. It's a mental trap where a rider thinks they're beyond basic training when, in reality, they're just beginning to build a foundation. It's a lie the brain tells to feel superior, and it gets people hurt.

Cognitive Overload

Trying to learn advanced tricks like trail braking before mastering the basics is mental suicide. If foundational skills like straight-line braking are not 100% subconscious, the brain is too busy screaming and managing basic chaos to learn anything new. Following the correct sequence is the only way to free up mental capacity. When the basics are handled correctly, the mind finally becomes available to handle sophisticated techniques without falling apart.

The Seat-Time Myth

Racking up miles and years on the road isn't the same thing as mastery. Simply repeating the same mistakes for a decade just reinforces bad habits. That isn't experience; it's just practicing how to fail. True progression requires a structured sequence and objective feedback to keep the ego in check.

Relying on "miles" alone is just a way for the brain to avoid the hard work required for real safety and proficiency. Expertise is built on solid ground, not on how many years a rider has been sitting on a seat.

※ Mind Note – Coach's take

*"If I'd have a favorite track, it only would mean that I f*ck something up on all the other tracks!"*

— *Can Akkaya*

Ego and Emotions

Our Worst Enemy... and Our Most Potent Fuel

Everyone possesses an ego. Some more, some less. But let's be clear: a healthy ego isn't inherently negative. In fact, a goal-oriented, channeled ego can be the very substance that drives personal achievement. It's the engine that made massive projects possible. When it comes to competition, especially at the professional level, a calibrated ego isn't just helpful. It's essential to win.

Nothing is wrong with your ego as long as it's well-channeled and expertly managed. It's a fundamental part of human nature and the necessary component of any Alpha mentality. When dosed correctly, it creates great leaders. But look around the world, and you'll find that most of the toxic, destructive actions you see. Whether in politics, relationships, or on the track are the product of an unleashed, malignant ego.

My world, the hyper-competitive. High-stakes, and often violent environment of professional motorsports, is where I channeled my own ego. I had to, 'cuz I was born with an ego 'big as the Rockies.'

I was forced to learn control because an unleashed ego has a precise, negative, and immediate consequence in this sport: over-shooting turns, irrational passing attacks, unnecessary crashing, and so- getting unreasonably hurt. That outcome meant I couldn't do what I was paid for and what I loved: to race. When an ego-based, mostly bad decision leads to another spectacular screw-up, the inevitable next step is an emotional overload of anger, frustration, and recklessness.

If you're driven by these volatile feelings, you're what I call an 'out-of-the-stomach rider'. Out of my own hard-won experience with myself and my work with countless professional riders, I can tell you this truth: you might look good here and there. You might build a devoted fan base with spectacular, close-calls. But you will never win titles on a larger scale.

To achieve true, sustainable excellence—the kind that stacks championships—you must channel and dose your ego and emotions wisely.

Why I Have Zero Tolerance

I have an extremely sensitive sensor for ego-driven riders and students, specifically 'cuz I've been that guy. I know the tell-tale signs. And their problem instantly becomes my zero-tolerance approach.

Why? Because I know that an ego-fueled rider won't take anything I say. They arrive because, subconsciously, they know they have skill issues and a lack of knowledge. But consciously, their ego locks the door. That's the fundamental conflict. If they do make progress under my guidance, they will immediately and disingenuously score the credit for that improvement to themselves. They knew it all before, apparently. That's the toxic signature of the unleashed ego.

But I have also worked with those who possess that same monumental ego, yet who are willing to hold back and listen. These riders—the ones who check their baggage at the door—are the ones who forget arguments like, "This is just a small track," or, "I'm too fast for you anyway." They were willing to bite their lip, silence the inner noise, and let me decide what to tackle next, based purely on what my experienced eye saw they actually needed.

Guess what? Wonderful things happened. They didn't just become faster; they became safer, smoother, and transformed from male and female riders into disciplined souls who stopped throwing away their bikes and careers at every corner.

Tame that ego, and you will 'see' the truth that you're not perfect, no matter how many years you've been riding. Acknowledging that you still lack something. That you have a gap, a blind spot, or a plateau, is the first step of improvement. It's the key that makes you coachable, which is the only real path to mastery.

Change Who You Compete Against

Your ego loves to win, so give it a target it can actually hit. Stop letting it chase other bikes or the imaginary stopwatch in your head. That's chaotic.

Redirect your competitive drive. You're not competing against the guy next to you; you're competing against The Old You. Make the goal of every session to achieve a perfect, technical victory over the mistake you made last time. Use that aggressive, win-at-all-costs energy to hit that exact brake marker or hold that perfect throttle position. When you point your ego at technical excellence instead of just raw speed, it becomes your greatest asset.

By consistently applying this "counter-ego discipline," you clear the clutter from your mind, and the machine becomes an extension of a calm, hyper-focused rider.

Final Distinction

The most important psychological realization for any rider chasing mastery is this: ego is a long-term goal; emotion is short-term fuel.

Your ego is fundamentally obsessed with status and outcome. It wants the championship title, the praise, and the flawless reputation. This desire to win is what you must channel into technical discipline.

Your emotions (anger, fear, frustration), however, are only concerned with immediate validation or escape. They're like a chemical dump in your brain following a mistake.

The rider who fails is the one who lets the emotion hijack the Ego's goal.

Bad rider. Makes a mistake, feels a rush of anger (emotion), and lets that anger force an immediate, reckless pass to restore his pride (ego's immediate, toxic demand).

Master rider. Makes a mistake, notes the rush of anger (emotion), and instantly redirects that intense energy into a hyper-focused effort to perfectly hit the next brake marker (ego's channeled, disciplined goal).

The choice is yours: Will you allow volatile emotion to drive a toxic ego, or will you use the energy of that emotion to fuel a disciplined, goal-oriented ego?

Psychological Takeaway

When the ego starts craving status more than skill, you have hit ego misdirection. For the street rider, this engine often runs on the need to look "pro" in front of peers or the refusal to let a faster rider pass. The ego values the image of being experienced over the reality of being safe. It hates the temporary status drop of admitting a lack of knowledge, which makes a rider uncoachable and blind to their own plateaus. This mental noise is just the ego desperately trying to stay comfortable in its own lies. True mastery is impossible without the humility to be a student.

The ego should be viewed as a long term goal. A street rider must channel the hunger for proficiency toward technical discipline by giving the ego a clean, measurable target, like perfect lane positioning or flawless rev-matching. On the other hand, emotions like anger at a distracted car driver or frustration with traffic are short term fuel. They provide a sudden burst of energy, but directing that fuel at "teaching someone a lesson" or riding aggressively to reclaim pride leads to out-of-the-stomach riding that ends in a hospital.

The competition must be shifted to an internal locus. It's you against the version of you that rode yesterday. The goal is a technical victory over the small mistakes made at the last intersection. When anger spikes after a close call with a car, that intensity must be used to perform an instantaneous cognitive override.

Instead of chasing the car down, that fuel should be channeled to hyper-focus on the next technical objective, such as scanning further ahead for the next hazard or refining braking pressure. This clears the mental clutter and transforms raw, volatile drive into disciplined mastery of the environment.

Hopes, Dreams and Wisch-Thinking

Enemy of the Process

The chase for the knee-drag is the perfect example of how wish-thinking, hopes, and dreams can directly lead to dangerous, wrong-headed actions.

Your ultimate goal—to be a masterful rider—is fueled by powerful emotions. You see your hero's dragging parts and you hope to emulate that. You dream of the perfect, effortless corner.

But when you substitute the dream for the necessary process, your brain enters a dangerous shortcut mode:

Your dream of the knee-drag becomes the immediate priority, displacing the actual essentials: Finding the correct braking marker, maintaining smooth throttle control, or choosing the efficient line. You invert the entire learning hierarchy.

The intense desire to feel like "Superman" overrides the logical warnings from your body and your bike. Your fear (which should be informing your control) is temporarily suppressed by the euphoria of the wish. This leads directly to the wrong action. The exaggerated lean angle, the compromised line, and the stiff, pointed knee. All driven by the emotional need for the *look* of mastery.

When you finally get the knee down, your brain registers the dream achieved, giving you a powerful dose of confidence (the mental boost). But since this achievement was reached via a false process (poor line/forced lean), it creates a dangerous gap between your fantasy (I am fast) and reality (my technique is broken). This gap ensures you're riding far beyond the bounds of actual competence.

Your wishes and dreams are what get you into the saddle, but discipline and objective analysis are the only things that keep you safe and progressing. Don't let your greatest hopes lead you to your biggest mistakes. The focus must remain on the unglamorous process that makes the dream an eventual reality.

Pressure of Wanting It So Bad

The intense pressure of "wanting something so bad" is the engine that drives every stupid mistake in this chapter.

You want that knee-drag (just an example), that championship, that feeling of flow. That's fine, but when that "want" hits a fever pitch, it stops being motivation and starts being a time-bomb of self-sabotage.

This pressure pushes you to do the dumb stuff instead of the work:

It demands a cheat. That "want" can't handle the boring grind of the Mastery Loop (suck, click, reset). It wants the win *now*. So, you look for the fastest, shiniest cheat—the false expert's promise, the quick high of a forced knee-drag—'cuz the pain of waiting is worse than the risk of being wrong.

It blinds you to facts. When you want something that much, you become a liar to yourself. The pressure to succeed makes you blind to the truth.

It makes rebuilding hell. My statement—"It took even longer to rebuild it!"—is the brutal cost. That intense emotional drive to look like a master causes you to build a flawed house. The more emotion you pump into that flawed structure, the deeper those bad habits sink. Getting good means you have to tear down the whole damn thing, including the massive hope you built on top of the lie.

You need to take that killer desire and point it somewhere useful. Stop wasting that intensity on chasing the *glamour* of the result. Point the intensity at the process.

Wish-Thinking vs. Reality

Wish-thinking is the ultimate lie you tell yourself. It's the gap between the speed you *feel* and the speed the *clock* proves. On a motorcycle, that gap doesn't just cost you a trophy; it can cost you your skin.

Wish-Thinking creates an Illusion

You wish that one YouTube video gave you the six months of technique you needed.

You wish you'd look like Marc Marquez after taking only one class.

You wish to be able to wheelie within only an hour.

Reality delivers the Truth

Reality is the cold, hard fact that skill is measured in hours of disciplined repetition, not minutes of watching videos.

The more you're wish-thinking- the harder reality is going to hit you in the head. Stop living in the fantasy where effort is optional.

Keep Dreams in Check

You can't kill the dream, and you shouldn't try. Chasing dreams is a strong element. But you need to keep them in check and chase realistic dreams, before they turn into wish-thinking.

Psychological Takeaway

The core mental failure here is wish-thinking. It's the trap of substituting a glamorous result for the hard work required to actually earn it. Whether it's the obsession with dragging a knee on a canyon road or the dream of looking like a pro after one track day, this emotional need creates a "pressure of wanting It so bad" that acts as an engine for every stupid mistake a rider makes.

A rider commits Priority Inversion when the dream of the result displaces the unglamorous essentials. Finding the correct braking marker, maintaining smooth throttle control, and choosing a safe, efficient line are tossed aside to satisfy an immediate emotional craving.

This is a demand for a "cheat" because the ego finds the slow grind of mastery psychologically painful. This forces wrong-headed actions—exaggerated lean angles and stiff body positions—purely to feed a fantasy.

Fantasy vs. Reality Gap

Wish-thinking is the ultimate lie. A rider might force a result and get a temporary mental boost, even while reality—the slow pace or the sloppy line—proves the technique is broken. This creates a dangerous gap where a rider is operating far beyond their actual competence. By ignoring the facts to preserve the comfort of the fantasy, the rider becomes a liar to themselves.

Cost of the Lie

There is a brutal price for building a house on a flawed foundation. The more emotional intensity a rider pumps into these bad habits, the deeper they sink into the subconscious. Fixing this eventually requires tearing down the entire structure, including the massive hopes built on top of the lie.

This is a massive psychological and physical cost. Mastery requires closing that gap today and choosing the boring, unglamorous process over the shiny, fake outcome.

※ Mind Note – Emotions

"Emotion can be the enemy, if you give into your emotion, you lose yourself. You must be at one with your emotions, because the body always follows the mind."

— *Bruce Lee*

Being a Talented Motorcycle Rider

The Myth of the Gift

I hate the word 'talent'. 'Nobody is born with a 'riding DNA.' Just because your dad rode bikes really well or even raced doesn't mean "you got it." They might be able to teach you, but that's not the point. Let's take a deeper look at what that word might be doing to you.

You see a professional rider or watch a MotoGP race and go: "Man, this guy is talented!" You, however, don't feel such mystical medical phenomena running through your veins. You're not even confident enough to lie to yourself that you have some kind of "talent". And here you go: Your block to learning is set. Because you don't believe you have talent, you're not even trying to get there. You might think this all came naturally to those who are "talented."

To be honest, you didn't just extend your learning curve, and you put a crack into your own confidence. Oh, and you also just took away the credit of all those racers who dedicated their lives to become what and where they are. They gave their blood, sweat, and tears to learn everything you might see as naturally gifted.

That's not right, 'cuz some have even died in the attempt to get there. Nothing good comes for free, naturally, or in a nice gift box in this sport. Everything you see is learnable. Stop hiding behind the fancy, lazy, and mystically glowing word of talent.

True Edge

Though, there are two physical traits that do help: those who have great eye-hand coordination and those who have a great feel for distance and speed. A person with these skills is probably good at other sports, too. If you have this, you might pick things up quickly.

If you don't? Don't worry. Don't hide behind the word; just stand up and say, "I can get there too, no matter how long it takes." You just need self-honesty and the allowance to have a less steep learning curve. If you can arrange that with yourself, then you're actually on the healthier path. Let's see why.

Too Fast, Too Early

Now let's say you *do* have excellent eye-hand coordination. Everything seems to get to you easier and quicker. Being a quick learner sounds incredibly positive, doesn't it? In the 'Learning Fast' chapter, we already discovered that this might not be a good thing, so we leave this here and shine a light on how you might shut off your potential the moment you discover 'talent.'

Consequences of the "Talent" Myth

The belief in innate "talent" creates an automatic barrier for anyone who doesn't perceive themselves as having it.

The problem. The amateur's self-diagnosis is, "I don't see talent in my veins, so this level is unreachable." This is where you state, "you didn't just extend your learning curve, you also put a crack into your own confidence."

The deeper issue. This mindset provides an excuse for failure. The rider can quit or plateau and tell themselves (and others), "I just don't have the natural talent," rather than facing the truth: "I haven't put in the necessary time and repetition." It makes the pursuit of mastery feel like a futile genetic lottery.

Lazy Narrative

When you label a professional racer as "talented," you are doing two things: minimizing their dedication and maximizing your own perceived gap.

The problem. You are "taking away the credit" of those who gave "blood, sweat, and tears." This is the lazy, mystical narrative that makes the pro's achievement seem like a gift from the heavens, rather than the result of years of brutal, disciplined work.

The deeper issue. By refusing to see their success as learnable and earned, you remove the path of progression for yourself. If it's innate, there's no system to follow. Your chapter's philosophy (Chaos Control, Yin and Yang, etc.) is only valuable if the rider accepts that everything is learnable, not gifted.

Arrogance of Quick Gains

This applies to the rider who does have great hand-eye coordination and picks things up quickly.

The problem. Because initial physical skills come easy, the quick learner often skips the mental work. They don't value the "blue line" of instinct and experience because they haven't been forced to earn it. They become too fast not just for their reaction time, but for their humility.

The deeper issue. This quick-learner type often becomes immune to learning from loss because they rely on their initial physical gifts to overcome errors. They haven't had enough "bad line" or "stressed-out bike" experiences. They're mentally fragile because they lack the deep, physical wisdom. The "muscle memory from feels, sounds, and smells", that only comes from slow, hard-won experience. Their talent becomes their biggest blocker when they eventually hit the pivot point.

Psychological Takeaway

The word "talent" is a dangerous lie. Believing that high performance is the result of a genetic lottery is a form of self-sabotage. It creates an automatic barrier, convincing a rider that mastery is unreachable unless it's already running through their veins. This myth provides a lazy, instant excuse for failure or plateaus. It's much easier to say, "I just don't have the natural gift," than to face the truth: "I haven't put in the brutal time and repetition required." The reality is that every single skill is learnable. Success is forged by unwavering dedication, not luck.

Coordination vs. Wisdom

What people mistake for "riding DNA" is usually just hand-eye coordination and a feel for distance and motion. While these traits might help a rider pick things up quickly, they often create a dangerous gap. This occurs when rapid physical speed outpaces mental and instinctive development. A rider might have the coordination to go fast, but they lack the deep, physical wisdom—the muscle memory born of feels, sounds, and smells—that only comes from hard-won experience. When things go wrong, the "talented" rider is often the most fragile because they haven't learned how to earn their way out of a mistake.

True Cost

Labeling a pro as "gifted" is an insult to their sacrifice. It minimizes the blood, sweat, and tears they gave to reach that level. More importantly, it maximizes your own perceived gap. By refusing to see their success as something earned, you remove the path of progression for yourself. If you believe it's innate, there's no system to follow.

You must ditch the myth and accept that experience is the only currency that buys mastery. You're the only one holding yourself back. Stop carrying the weight of perceived failure and start the disciplined work.

▓ Mind Note – Coach's take

"Someone gave their blood and bones to become what they became. They make it look easy, which might come through as talent. Don't take their credit away!"

- *Can Akkaya*

The 'Perfect Body Positioning' Hype

Vanity vs. Vital Skills

We confront another pervasive illusion: the belief that copying a MotoGP rider's body position is the key to faster, safer riding for the average enthusiast. This isn't just about technique; it's a profound psychological trap. It prioritizes vanity and perceived mastery over the foundational skills of actual riding. By chasing the look of speed, you ignore the mental and physical building blocks that create speed, leaving you with a compromised machine and a mind full of dangerous misinformation.

Illusion of Instant Mastery

It actually amuses me to see the huge amount of attention other schools, books, forums, and videos spend on the subject called 'the perfect body positioning' for street riders. Glancing over to what MotoGP riders like Marc Márquez performs on TV, must be good for the Redwood Road in the SF East Bay. As this is also a never-ending subject around sport bike riders, you personally might not like what I have to say about it, but hear me out.

If you don't hang-off just like a Rossi... You'll be damned as being 'crossed-up' and some rookie rider who was proud showing his first hanging off pics will be scoffed at by some keyboard jockeys who know it all better. But are they really qualified to tell somebody what to do and what not to do? Especially when they actually don't know the skill set of that particular rider?! Good question, huh?!

Don't get me wrong, because yes, there's a perfect body positioning, but this one has another purpose, and that's to find another tenth of a second on a prototype race bike in MotoGP. The rookie street rider has different purposes, of course, and one of them is to stay alive, and secondarily to be in harmony with the bike, as long as he/she is dealing with essential things of riding a motorcycle. Like even to shift. The simple things. The reality is, though, that even brand-new riders already have an eye on the subject, actually even prioritizing it. Why? Because everyone makes such a big deal of it and there are hopes and dreams involved.

What 'Perfect Body Positioning' Demands

Let's have a quick overview of what advices like "you gotta smile in the mirror" and "touch the gas tank with your elbow" actually mean for a newbie:

A totally different weight distribution

An extreme hanging off demands higher corner speeds because centrifugal energy helps carrying body weights

Professional racers are extremely fit to perform this exercise

Lever, brake, shift, and throttle control are way harder to operate

90% of body weight have to be lifted over to the other side on chicanes

Center gravity while braking is totally different

Connection to the bike is off / feedback response time delayed

Very much in the way when you can't counter-steer properly

All of this is happening while they haven't learned to ride a sport bike properly yet. Line choice, trail braking, and especially to counter steer. I have a theory in regard to other schools and some B-level racers who 'teach' track day riders, but I'll keep this for myself. This subject here is already controversial enough. Again, I'm not questioning that this is all wrong. It just became too much of a big deal and that misleads the riders who are 'not there yet'.

I know you have visions and dreams, and I don't want to take that away from you. But if you put this subject first or even don't see what I'm talking about, then all of this will slow down the learning process of the one who's hoping to find an "easy" answer to all of his/her riding problems by ignoring what really the issues are. So, there are hundreds of dollars into books, videos, and riding schools which seem to have no clue what they actually take away from the riders by an 'overdose of body positioning'. Instead, they're just confusing riders, and the result is even worse as before the new 'wisdom'.

Proof in the Pudding

The proof is in the pudding, so let me point out some high-profile gentlemen.

Mick Doohan, 'crossed-up' to five MotoGP titles! The man was a missile.

Kevin Schwantz, 'crossed-up' to one World champion title!

Joey Dunlop, multiple TT winner by being 'crossed-up'.

Jean Philippe Ruggia dragged his elbow in 1988—by being in a 'perfect body position'. He never made it to a world champion title!!!

Wild, huh?!

Sure, I hear you... that was a different time back then, and tires and chassis need a lot more elbow these days. Right. The biggest difference is actually that the riders are way more athletic nowadays, but they also had qualities back then which got lost today. What never changes, though—that's physics—the line and a possible speed/lean.

Yes, I agree. The more you hang off the faster your mid-turn can be. But is it a priority for the low-experienced rider on the street? Is this how the 35-year-old office worker with the pizza belly makes his commute? Is this what the rider who attends track days three times per year should think of, when his lines are so bad that it causes people to crash around him (I've seen it many times enough).

I know I'm risking losing your trust right here, but this is what other teachers do. They know that you 'like to believe' that this is right, which makes riders look like circus clowns. Just like in this illustration: Right arm long reach, so a hard to operate brake lever. Right wrist tension, so hard to operate throttle. The right shoulder is to be pushed down to the tank, and only God knows what that's for but causes tensions. Neck muscles under high tension, but probably still not enough so that your eyes need to be tweaking up. Left shoulder tension. Left wrist totally crooked and heel against the lower bike so that the knee can't point out properly.

AND ALL THIS… while there isn't enough kinetic energy to actually hold you in place! You'll be only wearing yourself out physically, and then mentally.

Look, the true benefit of being that far off the bike is fighting center gravity, which causes the bike to be more upright. That means you can run through a turn with less lean, which is more potential/resource for more corner speed. Experienced riders, especially racers, have the abilities to actually turn these resources over. You very likely not yet.

Your eyes and brain have dialed in to 'your' comfortable entry speeds. That won't change overnight just because you hang aside the bike entirely unreasonably. This is all in your way to learn more important things first. It has to be all in the right order. When time comes, then you'll have the physical and mental capacities to get to it.

Psychological Takeaway

Focusing on extreme body positioning too early is a massive prioritization failure. It happens 'cuz the ego hijacks the learning process, chasing social validation instead of actual skill. The riding community has turned MotoGP aesthetics into the ultimate symbol of "competence," making riders more afraid of being mocked on a forum than of being unsafe on the road. This forces a rider to prioritize the look of mastery over the reality of control. It's a performance for the camera, not the corner.

Illusion of Mastery

Copying a complex physical pose creates a dangerous Illusion of Mastery. Because it looks like skill, it provides an immediate ego boost. This superficial validation is far more appealing to the brain than the tedious, unglamorous work of perfecting throttle control or line choice.

This is the "easy answer" fallacy—clinging to a tangible physical gimmick to avoid the harder mental work of understanding physics and precision inputs.

Cognitive Overload

The human brain has limited processing power. Fixating on extreme body gymnastics while entering a corner causes cognitive overload. Instead of focusing on survival fundamentals like shifting, braking, and counter-steering, the mind is busy managing a precarious pose. This draws critical mental bandwidth away from vital tasks.

For the street rider or the casual track enthusiast, this tension actually blocks the body from receiving feedback from the machine, delaying reaction times and making the bike harder to operate.

Foundation Failure

Pushing for "perfect" positioning before mastering basic controls is a Foundation Failure. It's premature specialization that actively harms the learning loop. Without a solid base, the hang-off is just a circus act that disconnects the rider from the bike. Until a rider learns to prioritize vital skills over looking like a pro, they remain stuck in the illusion. Mastery isn't found in how much you hang off the bike, but in how much mental capacity you have left to manage the ride.

※ **Mind Note – Step by step**

"Before you can be a great player, you have to be a good player. Before you can be a good player, you have to be a player."

— Kobe Bryant

The Power of Ignorance

Entering the Zen Zone

Imagine you had the ability to shut literally everything off which has a direct or indirect negative influence on you. Mentally and even physically. Even better, imagine you could turn it on and off just like a light switch, precisely when you want and need it.

Consider the power of this mental freedom:

The dog barks all night, yet you're able to mentally shut him off and have a good night's sleep anyway.

You get an extremely expensive ticket for a traffic violation, but you mentally ignore the costly consequence. You still have a good day.

A car cuts you off, inches from being dead. Your mental state makes you literally ignore your own anger about it, allowing you to move on immediately.

There is a world where there's no hunger nor thirst. There's no yesterday nor tomorrow. No consequences for damage. A state of mind that makes you forget you're racing with three broken ribs, and the pain isn't even subconsciously registered. It's the ability to live in total inner peace with the possibility of falling at 150 mph, because you're living completely in the moment.

Sounds nuts, doesn't it? Is it really, though?

Razorblade Focus

I am not saying you should disregard the damage and pain you do to yourself or others, or that racers are on a suicide mission. No, they just enjoy life a little more when on the edge. They're more afraid of the consequence of not being able to race anymore than breaking their bones.

What I'm talking about is the ability to step in and out of the 'Zen Zone' at your demand. It's the ability to mentally shut off any distraction; in whatever form it comes at you. Right off.

This is a razorblade-sharp focus that can relax every muscle in your body, down to your eyebrows and ears. When your body and soul begin to melt with that bike, speed, time, and space become one.

Everything only floats. You're not moving at 150 mph towards the slowest turn on the planet anymore. It feels like you're in a time-lapse, and the turn is coming to you, just like in a video game where the graphics flow your way. It feels as if you're sitting on the sofa and watching a movie.

Turning Off the Volume

This isn't just Hollywood. Think of the movie *For Love of the Game*, where Kevin Costner's character, the pitcher, gets "in" by turning off the volume mentally of the entire arena, making everyone disappear until he's ready to make that final, perfect pitch.

How about something more real? How about I take your imagination out with me on a prototype race bike in high-level competition racing? Let's try to deeply envision what this is going to look, feel, and sound like just for half a lap...

We are in pole position. Red light comes on. Forty race bikes revving at high volume in launch control. The ground is shaking. Even the air is vibrating. Just that would make a regular person say, "F... this," and walk right out. YOU would hold your breath... I'm calm. Lights off, but we came off the clutch too fast and your bike wheelies. The delay angers YOU... while I'm cool. Opponents are so close around that your front wheel almost comes down on someone. YOU look at it... I don't. Your missing pace down the straight makes you easy prey now. You are all tucked in and one of the opponents rubs elbows with you. YOU look at it... I don't.

We're in 7th position when we come to our braking marker, and all YOU think is that all the hard work to get on pole was for nothing... I'm not. Now we brake so hard and late out of 270 km/h down for a 60 km/h turn and the rear wheel is up. There seems to be nothing more we could do there, but someone is passing you on the curb. YOU are confused about it... I'm not. We are entering that turn now and get into a 60-

degree lean, while we see in our peripheral a front wheel. An opponent is passing us on the inside. Our ears are literally at his engine, and you actually feel the steam and vibrations. YOU look at it… I don't. The guy slipped through at the apex. Our front tire is about an inch away from his rear. YOU stare at it… I'm not. The guy loses his front grip and goes down in a split second. YOUR eyes follow the crashed rider… mine do not!

See what I mean? You know what that is?!… This is POWER!

A power that offsets Superman abilities. I can become one with the environment. This is time and space bending stuff, and it's quite more valuable than all that "body positioning hocus pocus." This is what made a Casey Stoner, an Ayrton Senna, and a Bruce Lee.

This is what can make you the leader of a Special Forces team. This is the ability to be above the survival instincts that plague the regular human being. Consequently… This is what makes even a regular street rider might find escaping gaps, and not just end up in protective reactions.

Slow Motion for the Mind

There are slow-motion videos of Casey Stoner throughout a turn. He's on the inside curb in a 60-degree lean, and his front tire lifts off. Zero grip. You'd expect a survival response, but no. He doesn't even close the throttle or stand the bike up. His body motions are in a state of flow to regain control without losing time.

What you see in that slow-motion video is what Casey feels about this entire event happening. Just like in a slow motion for mind and soul.

This is exactly the stuff that professional racers are truly masters of: Total Ignorance of all distraction and fear.

Street Rider's Urge

You, the street rider, will be fine if you can achieve and be like this for just a fraction of the time. You might never fully "arrive in the Zen Zone," but just to know that such a place exists and to have the high URGE to arrive there... that will set you apart from all other riders already, 'cuz they don't know that such a place exists.

You can't chase something you don't know about. But you will from here, and one day, it might give you just that much 'extra space' to make it around that damn car.

Imagine now, you'd have a fly sitting right on your eyeball and you wouldn't even blink... Well, everything has limits.

Ultimate Freedom

The effort required to achieve "this" is immense. It demands the ultimate expression of the over-thinker's control and the contract of commitment's peace. But the payoff is the most profound freedom a rider can experience.

This freedom isn't just about going fast; it's about eliminating internal conflict:

By mentally accepting the risk before the action, you're freed from wasting energy on fear during the action. You're liberated from the tyranny of "what if."

The distractions of opponents, the roar of the crowd, and the constant demand for a faster lap time are rendered irrelevant. Your entire focus is on the perfect execution of your established pattern, freeing you from external pressure and validation.

Your muscles are relaxed, your mind is clear, and your inputs are surgically precise. You're no longer fighting the bike or your own protective instincts; you're operating at the peak of your human potential, achieving a rare state of peace on the very edge of chaos.

This ability to turn off the volume and live in the moment is the final, hard-won reward of the master. It's the moment where the intellectual struggle ends and pure, effortless motion begins.

Psychological Takeaway

The greatest thief of performance is cognitive noise. This is the mental sewage that clutters the brain, from the fear of a wreck to the ego-driven anger at a distracted driver. Peak performance is the cold, calculated execution of filtering out every stimulus that does not help make the next move. This isn't about being a daredevil; it's the highest form of cognitive control. Ignoring the noise kills internal conflict and transforms chaos into a seamless, lethal flow.

Extreme Selective Attention

Every input must be categorized instantly as either a relevant pattern or irrelevant noise. An opponent rubbing elbows or a car cutting you off is noise. The line and the apex are patterns. Ignoring the noise frees up massive amounts of mental bandwidth that most riders waste on panic.

This leads to time dilation, where the mind operates so efficiently that the world seems to slow down. The turn stops attacking and starts coming to the rider like a movie, providing the extra space needed for surgical precision.

By using the contract of commitment, the risk is accepted before the rider ever thumbs the starter. This prior decision overrides primal survival instincts that are designed to make a human tense up and fail. When the consequence is accepted upfront, the rider is liberated. Muscles relax, the heart rate drops, and the mind gains the freedom to act with absolute, unhurried precision.

Ultimate Safety Mechanism

The Zen zone is the ultimate survival tool for the street. Even a fraction of this mental power allows for the instant shut-off of destructive emotions like road rage or blind panic during a crisis. This rapid emotional reset creates the mental clarity to choose the right tools, such as a decisive counter-steer or a controlled emergency stop, instead of falling victim to a protective reaction that ends in a wreck. Tuning out the volume of the circus is the only way to finally hear the truth of the machine.

'Sensei' Has to Be Old

The Mind's Misguided Filter

You've learned that mental aggression requires eliminating excuses and embracing harsh truths. The final filter many experienced riders and racers put up is the misconception that their teacher must be actively competing at a higher level than them. This belief is pure ego defense. By dismissing a potential mentor based on age or physical performance, you're engaging in a self-sabotaging behavior that cuts you off from the wisdom. The true coach doesn't need to out-muscle the linebacker; they need to see the play before it happens.

As explained in the beginning, there are a few things which hold back the more experienced track riders and racers from looking for education. This goes directly to that problem.

It seems that there's a wrong picture of what a teacher has to look like and be capable of. Sometimes I hear things like "Coach is too old," or "He raced in the 80's; that was different back then." The conclusion seems to be that because I'm older, I can't teach them anything. This is wrong and misguided, so let me throw a light into the dark tunnel for you.

Of course I'm not as fast as I once was, but I actually still have the fire of a thousand suns in me when I'm on track, and I can rip lap times at Laguna Seca Raceway that would make active racers quite nervous, even when the years on me have replaced my six-pack with a one-pack. Even when I'm a little hip-lame... I still know what it takes to achieve pole positions, International pro racing victories, and even lap records. And here's the deal... Besides technology and tires, we're still fighting the same old element... gravity.

Wisdom of the Sensei

Still not convinced?

Remember Karate Kid's Mr. Miyagi? How about Yoda? Or Panda's Master Shifu? They're all old, and they mentor their students to become heroes anyway. Yea... I know. That's all Hollywood?

So what about reality—like coach Bill Belichick and his New England Patriots for example? He's old and he keeps creating winning teams.

Just recently I saw a documentary about Peyton Manning's Super Bowl-ending career. Here's a multi-million-dollar NFL player who got hip-lame himself and loaded with mental blocks. This man had a QB coach on his side, a 72-year-old Sensei!

Does that mean that his sensei was expected to throw the damn ball further than record holder Manning? Was it necessary for his sensei to be quicker out of the pocket? Should his sensei have been mentally and physically strong enough to get past a 280-pound linebacker and throw a touchdown anyway? NO. But his sensei helped him on a different level, and all that that $100 million-dollar MVP and multiple record holder was replying to his sensei was… 'Yes Sir' and 'Yes Coach'!

Still not seeing the comparison? How about a basketball coach who is two feet smaller than his player? Or a hockey coach who can no longer skate fast and handle a puck like a 20-year-old? They may not be able to play the game anymore, but they know what it takes to be a success in the game. Good coaches know what to say—when to say—and how to say it!

Fast Does Not Equal Teacher

Another issue is that you only fool yourself when 'working' with an instructor for a session who is seemingly faster than you. Someone who's fast isn't necessarily also a good teacher.

They might be able to do the lap, but they can't deconstruct the process, identify the mental blocks, or communicate the required changes in a way that you can internalize. True instruction is an act of translation. It's taking highly complex inputs and outputs and making them simple and actionable for the student. The fastest racer maybe running entirely on instinct, which is impossible to teach.

Lost Logic of Coaching

So here is the logic, which I believe got lost with all those track day instructors who believe that a 10-minute 'workout' and a succinct tip in regard to 'body positioning' is all that it takes to be a good teacher. At a certain level of an athlete, a coach on the sideline is working just fine. I, as a coach, see weak spots to delete, strengths to develop, tailor a race strategy, find details to improve in the skill set, and most important, to mind-set a competitive nature, 'cuz I know what to say—when to say—and how to say!

For this, I don't have to be with the racer on the track to 'skate faster' to prove credentials. Though, I bet I even can help a Top-Gun racer to drop lap times also with his riding skill set, 'cuz I've been there too. Look at MotoGP. Even some of those guys have coaches too. Are they riding with them?! No, because how should that be even possible?!

Final Mental Barrier

You're asking why I put this on the mental side and so into this book?... Well, you might shut yourself down with that type of thinking, and might miss out on something that finally could get you on the path you always wanted to be on... the path to success on the race track.

If you still don't see that the problems are between your ears, then you keep fighting windmills and just go balls out. But if you're ready—then look out for the right Sensei.

Psychological Takeaway

A massive roadblock to progress is the idiotic belief that raw speed equals deep understanding. Amateurs often equate flashiness with mastery, which is nothing more than an ego-driven filter. This isn't logic. It's a fundamental misunderstanding of how skills are actually transferred. Many fast riders operate purely on instinct. They're fast, but they have no idea why. Because they can't deconstruct the process, they can't teach it.

Your mind gets caught in the trap of thinking that if someone can perform the act, they can explain the mechanics, overlooking the analytical and communicative skills required to actually fix a rider's broken habits.

Concrete Thinker's Trap

Less experienced riders often fall into the trap of being concrete thinkers. They demand to see the coach rip a lap time right now just to validate the lesson. This is a failure to grasp abstract concepts like strategy, mental fortitude, and nuanced feedback, which is the actual high-level currency an experienced coach provides. A true Sensei sees the play before it happens. They identify the weak spots to delete and the strengths to develop from the sidelines. A basketball coach does not need to out-jump the player to know the player's form is garbage, and a riding coach does not need to out-brake you to see that your entry line is a suicide mission.

Cost of Ego Defense

Dismissing a mentor based on age or physical performance is a symptom of immaturity. It's an ego unwilling to prioritize genuine growth over superficial validation. This mental barrier is an excuse to avoid the discomfort of being coached. By judging the "one-pack" instead of the decades of hard-won wisdom, a rider cuts themselves off from the exact information that would stop them from plateauing. Genuine mastery requires looking past the physical show and seeking the analytical mind that can translate complex physics into actionable change. Ditching the excuse and accepting that the problems are between the ears is the only way to find the path to success on the street or the track.

※ **Mind Note – Coach's take**

"Put me in a 'nothing to lose' scenario, and you'll have a massive problem."

— *Can Akkaya*

The Rookie Effect

Free Mistakes

This subject is primarily for track riders and racers. Oh well, you might find it interesting enough to know the mental side of things even more. If so, then you just found the value for you.

Let me start with examples out of life and other sports.

You have a new job. Yes, all eyes are up on you, but you also have quite a large mistake-forgiveness-contingent. You can ask the dumb questions, fumble a task, or mess up a report. You're excused 'cuz you're the "new guy." Well, but not for very long.

Here is that rookie Quarterback in an NFL team stepping on the field. Way underpaid, he plays like a seasoned top-level QB. Next thing you know is that fans and press declare him to be 'the next Joe Montana.' Quite some weight there.

The one-year-old toddler, who grabbed dad's stereo on the way down... forgiven, but not for many times more.

See where this is going? I'm sure you have way more examples to add when you think about it.

The Phenomenon

There are a few right now, but let's just mention Pedro Acosta because he is in his second year in premier class MotoGP as of 2025. That's a great example for where I want to go with this phenomenon.

His performance and fighter spirit in Moto3 and Moto2 were outstanding, and when he came to MotoGP in 2024, all eyes were upon him. That's quite an ego-pushing momentum, plus the pride of having 'arrived'. This gives one a real opportunity to shine like a star from the get-go. Way underpaid for who he was, but with the freedom of forgiveness, he pushed some amazing races throughout 2024. The fan base goes up, and the press calls him 'the next Marc Márquez,' by constantly mentioning that he's 'just a rookie.'

For me, it makes me sigh, because Acosta is in fact a Moto3 and Moto2 World Champion, so not a rookie *per se*. For Pedro though, it has another ego-boosting effect. BUT... there are big shoes to step into for the next season, while the forgiveness-contingent is slowly fading.

Reality Drop

2025 season. Big factory contracts put quite a success pressure on his game. The shoes everyone has put you in—you also liked to believe would fit—are actually still too big yet. The higher you fly, the deeper you fall, and so he crashes many times. Frustration and disappointment take over, performance goes down. Ego got bruised up and the forgiveness-contingent is almost up.

In 2026, there will be even more expectations, from himself and the outside. The back-to-reality experience can trigger both, success or failure. A strength-growing, or weakening effect. I'm sure his coach will get him on the right path.

Takeaway for Every Rider

The rookie effect is the brief, precious window where external expectations are low enough to neutralize internal pressure.

For any rider, whether you're stepping onto the racetrack for the first time or simply joining a new, faster riding group on the street, this is your lesson:

Use the initial grace period to be bold. Take the extra risks to explore the limits, knowing that the cost of an error (ego, embarrassment, judgement) is discounted.

Your rookie success must translate immediately into self-belief, 'cuz the true mental battle begins the moment everyone, including yourself, expects you to repeat the performance.

The moment your skill is acknowledged, the forgiveness-contingent closes. You must prepare mentally to handle the inevitable setback not as a catastrophic failure, but as the expected reality of a now-established competitor.

The rookie is given the freedom to fail. The champion must *earn* the right to fail.

Hope this insight gives a little conclusion on this phenomenon, and where things can go if you're in this time of your riding career. If you're beyond that, you may find triggers that allow you to step mentally into the rookie's costume, and you'll find forgiveness from yourselves. In there, there's quite some wiggle room for exploration and pure, unpressured learning that your ego has blocked for years.

Psychological Takeaway

The brain performs best when the cost of failure is zero. As a rookie, you have a high mistake forgiveness contingent that acts as a mental safety net. Because no one expects a result, your survival instincts don't trigger the paralyzing ego-shielding that kills an expert's progress.

This lack of consequence allows for experimental flow. You're not riding to protect a reputation; you're riding to build one.

Weight of Expectation

It creates a new internal floor for performance, leading to the reality drop. You stop seeing the ride as a playground and start seeing it as a courtroom where you're constantly on trial. This shift from external curiosity to internal pressure spikes cortisol and narrows your vision. You're not faster; you're just more desperate. This desperation is the primary driver of the mid-career crash.

The rookie has a freedom to fail because they're irrelevant. The master has a right to fail because their process is proven. If you can't forgive your own technical errors as a veteran, you will stop growing and start defending a dying skill set.

If you're a seasoned rider… you might find a way to mentally take on the rookie role if necessary.

When Your Skill Bubble Pops

I know my statement isn't based on a scientific study. It's not even measurable, because that would require total honesty from every crashed rider, or at least from an authority who actually knows better. Both are illusions. So let me give it a wild but educated shot here.

Based on my years as a pro racer, street rider, and coach after watching, teaching, and debriefing thousands of riders, I brutally predict this: About 70% of all crashes, on track or on the street, could have been prevented if the rider simply knew their shit better.

Yeah, I said it. Sure, the texting soccer mom in the SUV was the trigger, but was the point of no return on your brake really reached? Was there maybe an escape gap you never even saw because you were busy target-fixating on that right-of-way-stealing car? Or maybe you did see that gap, but your "I-saw-this-in-a-YouTube-video counter-steering technique" wasn't enough to get you there? What about that lane-hopper that made you overreact, when in reality there was plenty of space, but your brain went full reptile mode and locked up your focus?

Cornering crashes alone could fill an entire book. The triggers are out there, but riders are simply not mastering them. Would it be arrogant to claim we could master them all? Yeah, it would. There's always a point of no return, even for the best riders on this planet. That's our 30%. But the rest—the 70%—is pure human error in slow motion.

Skill Score

Let's say every rider has a skill score. A newbie starts at 1. A seasoned rider—or even a racer—could score near 100. Realistically, nobody reaches 100, because there's always more to learn. But let's keep it simple.

Your score depends on where and how you've learned: self-taught, YouTube, books, track days, or maybe uncle Joe who "used to race back in the day." That's what defines your score across the whole riding alphabet; throttle control, shifting, trail braking, line choice, you name it.

But here's the catch. What are those points worth when panic takes over? That's when your "skill score" pops like a soap bubble. Because the real quality of your score depends on something else, something I call mind coolness.

True Skill Multiplier

Mind coolness sets you free. It's that mental armor that lets an out-of-nowhere car just bounce off you mentally, like a rock hitting a wall.

Imagine that. Instead of freaking out, you stay functional. You think. You act. You see options. With mind coolness, you can actually recall your physical skills while being under fire. Mind coolness buys you time. Time creates space. That little space might be the difference between a save and a hospital bed.

It's not something you learn doing slow-speed cone drills in a parking lot. You learn it when the stakes are high. When your focus is locked, when you're cornering at the edge of your comfort zone, when you and the bike move as one.

Mind coolness isn't about fearlessness; it's about function under pressure. It's the moment your brain stays calm while the world spins in chaos. That's when your skill score stops being a fragile bubble… and turns into something solid.

Reaction vs. Panic

Two-thirds of multi-vehicle motorcycle crashes show riders saw the hazard, but failed to react effectively. That's the gap between theory and survival. That's where mind coolness lives.

So this "mind coolness" thing isn't just some fuzzy Zen expression. It's actually the biggest, most transformative skill a rider can ever develop. It's not about being fearless. It's about achieving a functional calmness under extreme input, where chaos turns into clarity and motion turns into thought.

When I say mind coolness, I'm talking about the ability to stay cognitively operational when most people mentally flatline. It's the exact moment when the amygdala (your brain's built-in panic button) wants to

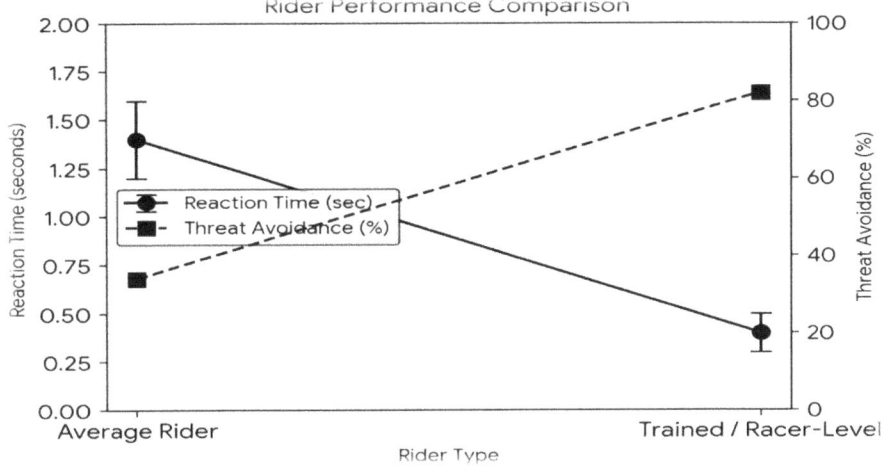

Source: Adapted from NHTSA & Hurt Report data analyses on motorcycle crash causation

hijack the system, but your trained awareness overrides it. That's not natural; it's learned. It's the product of deliberate exposure, precise feedback, and the right kind of stress repetition that rewires how your brain handles threat and motion.

Most training systems completely miss that part. They chase the physical layer; balance, shifting, clutch control, corner entry speeds, but skip the part where it all falls apart under pressure. That's why I say good luck finding a place that teaches this. Because you can't get Mind Coolness by repeating cone patterns in a parking lot. You can't simulate the emotional pressure of a real corner at the limit in a "safe space."

Mind coolness comes from riding at the edge of perception, not just at the edge of traction. It's born when your mind and body synchronize so tightly that focus becomes instinct. That kind of depth demands cornering practice, real-world decision making, and exposure to sensory overload in a controlled environment. That's something only a skilled coach can create. The right trainer sees more than your throttle hand or lean angle. They read your breathing, your hesitation, your emotional spikes. They understand your personality and how you process risk. Then they say the one sentence that cracks through your internal noise and resets how you think on the bike.

At that moment, your focus unchains itself. It stops fighting distractions and starts using them. Your attention becomes elastic. You're no longer trapped by what's in front of your wheel, but aware of the whole picture. That's what real mastery feels like. It's not a trick. It's not a reflex. It's a mental operating system upgrade.

Psychological Takeaway

Riders often operate under the delusion that their "skill score" is a static asset. It isn't. It's a fragile bubble that exists only in low-stress environments. Most training occurs in a vacuum where the ego is safe, but the moment a crisis hits, biology triggers a Limbic Hijack. The brain's survival center seizes control, instantly bankrupting your technical knowledge. You don't "rise to the occasion"; you sink to the level of your stressed-out hardware.

Under fire, your vision narrows to a pinhole. This is the reptile mode, a state where the amygdala floods the system with panic, leading to fatal errors like target fixation. You steer toward the threat 'cuz your brain has lost the ability to process anything else. This is where "preventable" crashes happen. It isn't a failure of physics; it's a total collapse of the mental operating system.

The only counter-measure is mind coolness. This is the hard-won capacity for cognitive override, keeping the prefrontal cortex—the logical pilot—online while the alarms are screaming. This provides the ultimate survival currency: processing time. By staying operational under pressure, your attention becomes elastic. You gain the clarity to see escape gaps that others literally can't perceive because their brains have flatlined.

Reliable skill isn't built through repetition of motion, but through stress inoculation. You have to train at the edge of perception to rewire the physiological response to threat. If your training has no emotional stakes, it has no survival value. Mastery is the process of desensitizing the panic response until chaos becomes clarity. Without this mental armor, your technical skill is just a theory waiting to be debunked by the first SUV that cuts you off.

Excuses

We all know the sound of it. Excuses for pretty much everything. Motorsports and riding bikes provide an astronomical amount of space to find them, polish them, and use them. I could write entire books filled with the excuses I've heard from students, competitors, and—if I'm being honest—from myself.

But we need to define what's actually happening when we behave this way. There's a fundamental human drive at work here: the need to protect your self-esteem and maintain a positive self-image. In psychology, this is called self-handicapping. It's a defense mechanism used to shield yourself from perceived failure or external criticism.

Protecting Your Self-Worth

The primary reason you reach for an excuse is to create a gap between the actual outcome of a race and your own perceived competence. If you try your absolute hardest and still fail, that failure is attributed internally; it's a direct reflection of your lack of ability. That hurts. It damages your self-worth. But if you fail because of an external factor; cold tires, bad traffic, or feeling under the weather. The failure is shifted outside of yourself. It acts as a shield, protecting your core belief that you are, in fact, competent. Excuses are also about social survival. In a competitive environment where reputation is everything, we use them to control what others think of us, desperately trying to reduce the risk of public embarrassment.

"Pre-Set" Safety Net

My favorite category is the "ahead of time" excuse. This is where a rider prepares a reason for failure before the wheels even turn. The psychological logic is simple: if you succeed despite the "problem," you look like a genius who beat the odds. If you fail, you have a prepared, bulletproof reason why. By shifting the blame to the bike's technical condition or some other external hurdle, you aren't just talking; you're identifying exactly where your ego is setting its safety net.

Devastating Long-Term Cost

While excuses offer a quick shot of short-term comfort, the long-term damage they inflict on your growth and your relationships is massive.

Destruction of Integrity Capital

When you lean on unreasonable excuses repeatedly, you destroy your "integrity capital" with others. Eventually, the people around you stop listening to the situational excuse and start judging your character. They conclude that you lack integrity or that you prioritize your ego over your commitments. This breeds resentment. People start to see you as deceptive or self-absorbed, and eventually, they simply stop expecting success from you. This is the death of competitive respect. You might protect your ego in the moment, but you're systematically destroying your reputation.

Zeroing Out the Feedback Loop

This is the most damaging cost to your personal growth. Learning any physical skill depends on a tight feedback loop. Excuses act as a "cognitive shield" that tells your brain: lesson dismissed. If the outcome isn't your fault, your brain sees no reason to analyze your riding. You tell yourself you don't need to change your technique because the problem was the tire pressure. By doing this, you deny yourself the opportunity to pinpoint and correct the subtle mistakes that actually caused the poor performance. You end up hitting a performance ceiling because you're intentionally preventing your senses from receiving the painful, honest feedback necessary for growth. You never fix the problem; you just rename it.

Psychological Takeaway

The drive to make excuses is a survival mechanism called self-handicapping. It's a desperate attempt to protect self-worth by creating a wall between your actual performance and your perceived competence. For the street rider, this looks like blaming a "close call" on a driver's incompetence rather than your own lack of scanning. If you admit you missed a hazard while giving 100 percent focus, that failure is a direct indictment of your survival skills. That's a wound the ego can't stomach. By blaming gravel, sun glare, or "caging" drivers, you shift the failure outside of yourself. You're not protecting your safety. You're shielding the lie that you're already a master of the road.

The most toxic move is the ahead of time safety net. This is when a rider starts whining about a sore back, a "feeling" about the tires, or cold pavement before the group ride even starts. It's a win-win for the ego. If you keep up with the fast group, you look like a god who beat the odds. If you fall behind, you have a bulletproof reason why. This psychological insurance policy is a white flag. It proves you have already prioritized your social reputation over the actual mission of riding the bike safely and effectively.

The real price of an excuse is arrested development. Mastery demands a ruthless and tight feedback loop. When you reach for an excuse on the street, you tell your brain that the lesson is dismissed. If the near-miss was the driver's fault, your brain sees no reason to analyze your own lane positioning or braking readiness. You deny yourself the painful and honest feedback required to survive a real-world crisis. You don't fix the holes in your skill set. You just rename them as "bad luck."

Integrity Capital

Beyond the bike, repeated excuses bankrupt your integrity capital. Eventually, your riding buddies and your own subconscious stop listening to the situational noise and start judging your character. They see a lack of accountability and an ego that's too fragile for the truth. This is the death of credibility.

In all honesty... I was just like that in the beginning of my riding career. Who can even say not to have, or to still live in excuses. But I turned this over to brutal honesty, even if it hurts.

Does this make you vulnerable to others? Oh hell it can, especially to those who are searching for things to hurt. You gotta be ready for that, 'cuz this is the way they polish their egos with. See it this way... this can be a solid 'good' or 'bad' friend detector as well.

Being Unlucky

Myth of the Victim

Believe it or not, but I've been an 18-year-old idiot myself back then. We already discussed this. I've paid big price tags for that, in terms of damage and pain. Well, a good outcome seems to be that this makes me able to share knowledge.

Before I started making a career in racing, I was riding motorcycles on the street every day back in Europe. Pretty much out of control and no limits. Long hospital stays and surgeries were an annual thing for me, and my family suffered along the way.

It hasn't ever been one of those drops, where you just go down and your suit gets a little scuffed up. Oh no. It's always been those crashes where I could have been dead. Gone! Now, what I so much hated hearing while my blood was still not dry yet: "You've been lucky."

Not something I just don't like hearing, but it was also against logical thinking when hearing this while I was looking at that spline coming out of my leg, ending with a weight beyond the hospital bed, and going... "Well, do you really think so???!"

Sure, I do understand totally that the 'final destination' is what I got spared off, and that people give exactly that the 'luck stamp'. Certainly, I didn't feel lucky right there. If I'd have been just a little tiny bit luckier... I wouldn't be in the need for the next morphine shot in the first place. Rather, I was considering myself unlucky.

The Self-Inflicted Loop

This 'slogan,' more or less, got me thinking though. Wasn't it in fact I, who brought it upon myself actually? Yea, the car driver took my right of way, and when I pushed into it literally halfway, I was the unlucky one? The one who went into that intersection way beyond the speed limit?! Was I lucky not to die, when I was actually able to slow down so much that I didn't have to die from the impact?! What kind of loop is this???

Please understand. I don't want to reject religion nor to make you consider your beliefs, but maybe not relying on a guardian angel who covers you with pixie dust when riding, could help you not to cover all wrong doing with the word 'unlucky', and to hide behind it. We are all the creators of the situations we're going in, or coming out.

Therefore, I decided for me personally that there's no such thing as luck or bad luck. Lucky, was just that lottery win you claimed. Unlucky, was when you had only one number wrong.

We all know that this is just an example of many things in life where you can run this slogan as an excuse up ahead, like "…not gonna end up good. You guys know my luck."

Psychological Damage of the 'Unlucky Guy'

What are actually the effects on your psyche when you consider yourself to be the 'unlucky guy', which to me is almost like living in a constant loop and in some kind of 'victim role'? I believe that living under these conditions is weakening mental strength which is counterproductive and demotivating.

Self-Sabotage

The "unlucky" rider preemptively sets themselves up for failure. This isn't just about feeling bad; it's about delivering an excuse for a possible failure before you even make the effort.

Let's say you plan a ride out and say, "With my luck… it's gonna rain anyway." The same thinking applies to championship outcomes: "With my luck… I won't make it." Not only have you just put up a huge blockade to prepare correctly, but you've created a ready-made narrative that protects your ego from the pain of effort without reward.

Mental Weight of Past Failure

When you label a serious crash or failure as "bad luck," you eliminate the lesson, but you keep the emotional baggage. That crash was just a random event that happened to you.

The consequence is that the feeling of being "unlucky" is your brain telling you, "I have no control over this outcome." This perceived lack of control and anxiety is a heavy weight you carry into every future event. Your mind ensures that failure repeats itself by already putting a failure on the next outcome, making you hesitate, ride stiffly, and guarantee the negative result.

External Locus of Control

The "unlucky" mindset shifts responsibility away from your actions and onto fate.

Why practice braking points if bad luck is going to make you fail anyway? This lack of control is demotivating and breeds passivity. Mental strength is built on the belief that effort and preparation create results. By claiming to be unlucky, you surrender your power to change your reality.

Rejection of Learning

A truly disciplined mind sees a crash as 'a breakdown in risk management' or 'a catastrophic failure in preparation.' They take ownership of the variables they could control. When you call it 'bad luck,' you throw away the lesson and guarantee you will pay the price again.

Luck Ratio

You think you're unlucky when you crash? Let's be real. When the bike slides out, you had 100% control over three things just one second before:

(Speed) Your throttle input and when you rolled off.

(Angle) Your lean angle and steering input.

(Brake Pressure) How much force you put on the lever.

The 2% of "bad luck"—the tiny pebble, the cold patch of asphalt, the random gust of wind—only matters when the other 98% (your inputs) were already at or beyond the limit. Bad luck is just the final 2% reason the inevitable 98% failure manifested.

Anti-Luck Manifesto

There is no luck on the bike. There's only risk management and execution. If you're constantly facing disaster, you aren't unlucky. You're simply running a high-risk program. Change the program, change the outcome. Stop looking for pixie dust, and start looking at what the real issues are. Stop playing the victim card!

Psychological Takeaway

Labeling a crash or a near-miss as "bad luck" is a specialized form of self-sabotage. It cements an external locus of control, where you believe your fate is decided by outside forces like gravel, drivers, or the weather. This mindset is a mental parasite. It keeps you in a victim role, which is inherently weak and passive.

When you declare yourself unlucky, you're telling your brain that your effort does not matter. This destroys mental strength and ensures that instead of getting better, you just wait for the next "random" disaster to strike.

The unlucky rider focuses entirely on the final 2 percent—the patch of sand or the car that pulled out. They ignore the 98 percent that was under their direct control seconds before the impact: speed, lean Angle, and brake pressure. Bad luck is almost always just the final trigger for a failure that was already 98 percent complete. If you're running a high-risk program, you're not unlucky when you crash. You're simply a mathematician who finally ran out of numbers.

Using luck as an excuse is a pre-set narrative designed to protect your ego from the pain of effort without reward. By saying "With my luck, I'll probably wash out," you're building a safety net. If you fail, it was not your lack of skill; it was your curse. This prevents you from doing the brutal work of preparation because your mind thinks the outcome is already decided by fate. It's a lazy man's shield that results in arrested development.

Taking Control

A disciplined mind views a crash not as a tragedy, but as a breakdown in risk management. When you delete the word luck from your vocabulary, you reclaim your power. You stop relying on pixie dust or guardian angels and start relying on your own inputs.

If you want a different outcome, you don't need better luck; you need a better program. Stop playing the victim card and take ownership of the variables you actually control.

Seeing yourself being unlucky in general is like being cursed for life. Do you hear how this sounds like and what this can do to your excitement level and having fun?

Well, if you're always unlucky… it would make all your successes just 'lucky'. How does that sound?

❀ Mind Note – Coach's take

"I am not saying go fearlessly faster. You stay in your comfort zone, but stop living in the 'what if'. You can't influence coincidence, so trust what you've learned and that you'll have the tools when the time comes."

— *Can Akkaya*

What's Really Wrong

We've all been there. You're minding your own business, enjoying the flow, and some idiot in a minivan decides your lane is their lane. No blinker. No look. Just a two-ton steel box moving toward your front tire. It feels like a war out there sometimes, doesn't it? "Us versus Them."

The internet is flooded with this stuff. There are thousands of "Biker vs. Cage" videos with millions of views, and every time we watch one, we feel that familiar surge of adrenaline and anger.

But before we get into the technical training in this book, I want to make sure we're seeing the same road. I want to see if your "survival instincts" are as sharp as you think they are.

Observation Exercise

I need you to do me a favor. Scan the code below and watch the video titled "Crazy People VS Bikers." Don't overthink it. Just watch it once, all the way through, and pay attention to the incidents. Ask yourself: How many of these drivers should even have a license? Go ahead and watch, and hold scores. I'll wait right here.

The Audit

Now that you've seen it, let's talk about the score.

If you're like most riders, you probably saw a 12:0 shut-out against the "crazy" drivers. You saw victims in helmets and villains in cars. But if we strip away the "bikerhood" lens and look at the actual physics and the timing of the inputs, the scoreboard changes.

When I watch that video, I don't see twelve victims. I see a group of riders manufacturing their own emergencies. Let's analyze this by clips, because what I see is a 2:10 score against 'us':

Incident. That rider was passing the blue car and went on throttle to also pass the gray car... on the right side. **0:1**

Incident. The car could have given more space, but since nothing happened, is it really worth scaring a teen and especially hitting her car?! We are passing cars like that with every lane split, right? **0:2**

Incident. The rider passes on the right which is technically illegal. Not 100% sure but his speed is well beyond 45 mph. The long rig, he's blaming deep out of his heart, is merging to the right before the rider is even visible. Also, when you pay attention, If it really would have been that "close", why does he come off the brakes halfway and keep rolling next to the truck? 'Cuz he wants to rant and dramatize. **0:3**

Incident. Sure, the car should not have changed lanes, but was it really that close? The rider was definitely in the blind spot, and the car merged extremely slowly so that the rider could have just rolled a little to the left. This has some "I own the road" character, and he should not bring himself nor others in danger by zigzagging, then almost come to a stop on a freeway to discuss through an open window. **0:4**

Incident. Yep, that car passed another car over double yellow. Now those un-helmeted rock stars start playing Sheriff and actually pass cars on the shoulder to chase him down. So that's 'ok' huh?! Seems that the blue car behind one of those guys gets a little angry because they're blocking the street now. Sure, the guy is impatient but he only tells them to go, while the rider is flipping him off. **0:5**

Incident. Yep, the car merged a little early to the right but it wasn't close at all. In fact, the rider stayed super stubborn on his route. Not an inch to the right lane which seemed to be all clear to go around. He even had so much time to rev his ego out. **0:6**

Incident. We've found the first 'crazy one'. It's **1:6** right now.

Incident. This is actually a jerk move. The rider saw the signal, went on the throttle just as much to block the van from merging. F'n dirty move, and the finger tops it off. **1:7**

Incident. Yep, not really clean, but the car had the blinker on and the biker actually slowed down so that the driver probably had to think 'they let me in'. In fact, nothing happened, but the rider dramatizes the incident and to calm his ego. **1:8**

Incident. Another dick move. The rider actually didn't pay attention to the front. The car merges and he could have gone easily on the right lane. Instead, stubborn on the path and honks the driver away. He is looking for trouble with his helmet cam, that's all. **1:9** I'd say. He's also playing the good Samaritan at the end of the clip. What an angel.

Incident. I have no clue what the car driver possibly did wrong. The rider is acting up for nothing. At this point I believe he's only looking for trouble and to play Sheriff. **1:10** for sure.

Incident. The rider is totally in the blind spot of the car. In fact, it never was that close. He didn't have to brake or swerve hard—actually had plenty of time to honk the horn. Nothing happened and isn't worth flipping the bird, 'cuz that happened to all of us once. Can't tell if the driver checked his left shoulder, so I call this **2:10**.

Incident. I seriously have no clue wtf is going on in the last clip, but that lady seems to have issues. There was no incident to see per se.

However, when you look back at what I'm pointing out and 'see' what's really wrong, then that lady is maybe just sick and tired of motorcycle riders in general. This is the picture of what the "crazy people" actually have of most of us: being loud, rude, ego driven, owning the road, and so on.

Trap Of False Loyalty

If you sided with these riders on your first watch, don't feel bad. I'm not judging you, because we all have 'this' in us. I believe it's a kind of protection for what you love. It's like a mother's love for her child; she will defend it before others even when she knows the child did wrong.

This is what I call false loyalty, and when this can get dangerous.

Community's Blind Spot

How does all this come to us, the motorcycle community? Well, here it is. Groups, like the motorcycle community, herd up. We are brothers and sisters who have something in common and we defend what we have no matter what. However, that kind of loyalty blinds us quite a bit and often we're not able to see who's really wrong.

Like, blindly following some leader no matter what comes out of his mouth or whatever he does means you can't see the truth. Maybe favoring a brand makes you ignore its flaws. Or that rock star you've loved to death, even when he was a crack head and alcoholic and beat up his wife. That friend you admire so much, and who seems to be so cool when riding recklessly.

False loyalty makes you overlook or even not see reality very often actually. Sometimes even if you do, you'd fight for it to death or find arguments to achieve peace of mind for something which is actually wrong. If you take an honest look into yourself, then I bet you'll find out that also you have 'this' in you. For most people it comes out subconsciously.

Being in favor of someone/something can be very dangerous, yet can have huge herd effects. That's something the Nazis took advantage of. You, as the individual, feel absolutely OK with it, but you're actually equally responsible for the shit going down, right?! It seems that if 'your hero' looks bad, that also throws a bad light on you, because there's this kinda connection. Bad decision making and not knowing (most of the time) that you're standing on the wrong side is the outcome.

When you watch a video called "Crazy People vs. Bikers," the title has already 'told you how to think'. It has influenced your decision-making before you even saw the evidence.

Look at the lady at the end of the clip (06:45), the one screaming. You might think she has "issues," but look at it through her eyes: she is likely sick and tired of riders being loud, rude, and ego-driven. To the rest of the world, we are the crazy ones. As long as we stay blinded by False

Loyalty, we will keep standing on the wrong side of reality. "That's what's wrong."

Psychological Takeaway

The "us versus them" mentality is a textbook case of Identity Protection. When you identify as a rider, your brain views the entire motorcycling community as your "in-group." Psychology tells us that to maintain a positive self-image, you must view your group as superior and righteous. When a rider in a video acts erratically, your brain registers it as a direct threat to your own identity.

To solve this discomfort, you deploy denial and rationalization. You invent faults in the "cagers" to keep the "tribe" pure, ensuring your ego stays shielded from the truth that your group—and by extension, you—might be flawed.

Defending a reckless rider out of a misguided sense of brotherhood is suicidal loyalty. It's an emotional, tribal reaction that completely overrides the logical, self-disciplined mind. When you justify a rider "rev-bombing" a minivan or manufacturing an emergency for YouTube views, you're essentially endorsing the behavior that gets motorcycles banned, restricted, and hated.

You are surrendering your standards to the lowest common denominator.

This herd mentality turns you into a compliant sheep, sacrificing the community's reputation and your own safety to protect a stranger's fragile ego.

You were manipulated before the video even started. Titles like "Crazy People VS Bikers" are a form of cognitive priming. They tell your brain exactly how to interpret the data before you even see the evidence. By labeling one side as "crazy" and the other as "bikers," the uploader triggers your tribal defense mechanisms instantly.

A disciplined mind must recognize this bias and strip away the labels to see the physics. If you can't call out a dick move because the person making it is wearing a helmet, you have lost your objectivity and your edge.

Gentleman Rider Reset

True loyalty isn't to a brand, a style, or a tribe; but high standards and principles. The minute you stop defending the idiots in your group, you elevate yourself above them.

You stop being a victim of the "us versus them" war and start becoming a gentleman rider—someone whose skill is so refined and whose ego is so checked that they don't need to manufacture drama to feel important. Don't be a sheep for the tribe and start being a role model for the sport.

❋ Mind Note – Coach's take

"It seems that everyone expects loyalty from me. Pointing out things with complete honesty isn't always welcome. You know... truth is a sharp knife, but it cuts best. I mean, what's to learn from someone's mistake if I coat the truth with layers of sugar instead? I'd only show false loyalty, and so to be likable for everyone—that, I can't do."

- Can Akkaya

Don't Be a Fool

Collision of Expectation and Reality

This might sound controversial, but I get to witness a strange phenomenon every single week. Not only with riders I don't know, but also with my own students. It obviously doesn't apply to everyone, but it sure as hell applies to a big percentage of you.

So here's "Joe." Joe just signed up for his first-ever track day. He's done some schooling, has a decent amount of experience, and has watched enough YouTube to feel ready. His visions, wishful thinking, and especially his expectations of how he's going to look out there have reached astronomical levels.

I've seen it a hundred times. Not just with first-timers, but even with riders who have already been through real, hands-on training. They've done the cornering programs, the knee-down classes, and even private one-on-one's. Yet their expectations of how that first track day will go are still sky-high.

The problem? Those expectations are about to collide with reality.

When that happens, many riders go straight into confusion and frustration. They start questioning everything they've learned, thinking maybe the training didn't work or wasn't "realistic." Some will push harder to prove something or crash. Some won't come back to finish what they started.

You might think I'm worried about "losing a customer." No. I'm worried about losing a rider to foolishness. Not more, not less.

Sensory Ambush

I know what they learned works. I've seen it over and over again. But when you're dropped into your first big track experience, you're stepping into a completely different world. It's like getting thrown into a boxing ring before you've ever taken a punch. There's passing happening all around you. The pace is higher than you've ever gone. The track feels wide and unfamiliar.

You're overwhelmed. Your brain is overloaded. You can't process fast enough, and because of that, you can't apply what you already know. And that's when your mind starts lying to you, telling you that what you learned doesn't work. That's the fooling part.

I remember one kid, full of energy and drive. On day 1 of his cornering class, he made massive progress. A real leap forward. Between those days, he bought a new bike and went straight to a track day. Naturally, he was one of the slower riders there, surrounded by faster, more experienced people. He likely got passed a lot, lost his lines, and—not surprisingly—he crashed.

By the time he came back for day 2, he was different. Distant. Disconnected. I could see the frustration all over him. Within the First few laps, he was already over-pushing and trying to "prove" he still had it. And sure enough, he went down again.

Afterward, we talked a lot. It was like talking to a completely different person. Someone who had lost faith in himself and in everything he had learned. He was angrier than confused. And then he even started asking other riders for advice. How could they possibly help? They didn't understand what his actual problem was, nor would they know how to fix it. Still, he listened to them 'cuz it was easier to blame the system than to face the truth.

That's the moment when foolishness wins.

Overload Curve

So, to the rest of you who are about to step into your first real track day: Understand that there's something wrong with what you've learned. It's about NOT BEING mentally ready for the sensory overload that's coming your way at your first track day!

You will feel overwhelmed. Your vision will narrow. You'll be distracted by faster riders passing you, by speed, by fear, by everything happening at once. And if you're not mentally grounded, you'll start chasing it, instead of learning from it.

If you still believe that track riding is just about "having balls," you're setting yourself up to fail. All I try to tell you isn't to be that guy. Don't be a fool.

Psychological Takeaway

A track environment triggers a sensory ambush. The explosion of high-speed data—closing rates and engine screams—consumes your mental RAM. You don't "forget" your training; your brain simply loses the capacity to access those files. Under this load, technical skill is replaced by primal, ineffective survival instincts.

The expectation-reality collision occurs when your vision of being "fast" hits the reality of being the slowest rider on track. This triggers ego collapse. To protect your self-worth, your mind lies, blaming the training or the bike. If you believe the lie, you start "over-pushing" to prove your competence, which is the most common precursor to a high-speed crash.

Acclimatization over Performance

Mastery is a product of processing capacity. Stop trying to be fast and start trying to be smart. Your goal is to lower your cognitive load until your vision stays wide and the chaos feels slow. Once the brain is acclimatized, your technical skills will naturally come back online. Don't be a fool by testing your luck; train your brain to handle the speed.

▓▓ **Mind Note – Coach's take**

"Honesty is the fastest way to prevent a mistake from turning into a failure."

- Can Akkaya

The $28 Suicide

When you pick up a book like this, you might not expect a hard-hitting critique of driver education policy. But I believe this discussion is essential. Let's find out why.

I consider the standard general motorcycle rider education—at least here in California—nothing short of a liability. My extensive knowledge on this subject doesn't come from a desk; it comes from teaching thousands of students on the track and on the street. What I've seen and heard reveals a dangerous crisis in basic competency. Let me give you a glimpse into the alarming lack of rigor that passes for certification, and the psychological fallout that follows.

Misinformation Contagion

I once had a 17-year-old new rider in my 'Cornering School Day' who claimed he was taught by "the certified institution" what 'Trail Braking' is: "...it's applying the rear brake by being on the throttle while entering a turn."

This isn't just incorrect; it's an invented theory. For an institution that supposedly certifies competence, this level of misinformation is an intellectual failure that directly translates into physical danger. I have three theories to explain this profound educational malfunction:

The certified institution genuinely lacks fundamental knowledge of advanced riding techniques like Trail Braking and simply manufactured an explanation to fill a hole in the curriculum.

They understand why the best riders on the planet utilize this technique, but lack the practical expertise, the controlled environment, and qualified instructors to teach it safely and correctly.

(My Favorite) They recognize that the genuine trail braking process involves using the front brake while gradually increasing lean angle. This fundamentally conflicts with their outdated core safety curriculum: "Never use the brakes while leaning." To leverage a popular keyword and "sell" the idea that they teach advanced skills, they invented a version that avoids the front brake entirely. The result isn't education; it's pure, cynical keyword marketing.

Failure of Care and the Cost of Crowds

Another student was a 65-year-old woman who, upon retirement, finally bought a new motorcycle to pursue a lifelong dream. She called me, needing to learn from absolute scratch. I advised her to attend "that" certified institute for the basic course. She flatly refused.

Her story: "I went there, but after an instructor saw me dealing with the bike, they took me out and told me to 'go home and practice.'"

That was a $300 piece of advice: *"Go home and figure it out."*

Practice with whom? The whole purpose of a certified institution is to be the critical, authoritative element in a new rider's life! When I've asked instructors attending my advanced seminars about stories like this, their common defense is: "You know... we are teaching crowds."

That excuse doesn't just "stink," it represents a complete moral and educational failure. It's the easy, expedient path of taking the money and dismissing the person who needs the most attention. This failure to devote time to the individual is irresponsible. This attitude, this educational arrogance, is directly contributing to preventable accidents and deaths.

It took me 30 minutes with that woman to re-establish trust and confidence. This illustrates a profound psychological principle: Confidence is built through mastery, not through dismissal.

Randomly Doomed

Sending people home? Randomly passes? Misinformation? Let's better not call these 'license giving institutions' schools, as this should only go to those that actually teach.

My wife, Marion, followed this path as well: a $270 weekend course. Would she have been ready for the street without me continuing her personalized training? Absolutely not. But she successfully passed the test. This reveals the core problem: Their objective isn't to create a safe, skilled rider; the objective is merely to be "good enough" to pass a minimal test.

Another Phenomenon

The most shocking example, and the true trigger for this essay, is Anne-M. P.. She came to me looking to book my Basic Rider 1-on-1 course, despite having successfully obtained her M1 license. My confusion was immense: How can a rider need to learn from scratch when she has already mastered the licensing process?

Anne was terrified. Her story of the 'certified school' is a testament to the systematic creation of fear and incompetence:

> *"I signed up... I came out of this two-day class as scared as I can ever be! And get this…. I passed!!! I lost count of how many times I dropped the bike... I got a road rash. But they passed me?! I came out more confused than ever. All I could remember is they TRIED to have us memorize acronyms; that was a failure! Going through all of that, and I was given a M1 license?! In no way was I near ready to take a bike to the streets, let alone a parking lot!"*

So… 'schools' pass on a license to a person who fell off the bike and is scared to death? That's like sending her actively right into suicide and statistics. This is a clinical disaster.

Suicide Permission by Law

Now, let's look at the California process I went through as an immigrant. The ability to obtain a full motorcycle license for only $28 was initially bewildering, compared with the odyssey in Europe. Anyone beyond 21 years of age can just go to the DMV—pass a written exam—and will walk out with a temporary driver's license for 12 months. Just like that, and nobody even asks if I actually can ride a motorcycle.

I am an ex-racing professional. Yes, I can ride. But the system didn't know that. It issued me a "suicide permission" or a "license to kill" others on the road without ever validating my ability. They just hand out keys to 200 horsepower motorcycles to 21-years-old decision makers who are released to public roads. What does this sound like?!

Another Loophole

No need to mention that there are a lot of riders who never do the required final riding test at the DMV and to actually get their permanent M1 license. They just keep riding illegally, so no insurance will cover their f'ups. But hey, right?!

Statistics and Its Data

When considering what we just discussed, are you surprised about how statistics look for us? I'm not. Statistics are based on data. Data are facts we can learn from. But are we actually learning from this? I'm not sure about that.

According to the National Highway Traffic Safety Administration (NHTSA), there were 6,335 motorcyclists killed in the U.S. in 2023. That's 15% of all traffic fatalities, while motorcycles make up only about 3% of registered vehicles. Think about that imbalance for a second. California alone counted 583 motorcycle fatalities in 2023. So the question becomes: Why do so many riders end up here?

Most Common Causes of Motorcycle Accidents (2023 Data)

Cause	% of Fatal Crashes	Notes
Speeding	36	The leading factor in U.S. motorcycle deaths.
Alcohol or drug impairment	26	One out of four riders killed had a BAC of 0.08% or higher.
Distracted driving	10–12	Often tied to smartphone use—by either rider or driver.
Reckless or aggressive riding	15	Includes stunt behavior, following too close, and unsafe passing.

Consider This

Now, here's the honesty you might not want to hear: No statistic lists "lack of rider education" as a cause of death. It should though, right?!

And yet, if you look between the lines, it's hiding right there. You can call speeding, poor braking, bad decision-making, or "losing control" what you want... but all of them root back to one thing: lack of proper training. The system and its so-called "well-organized" licensing process don't want to take the blame. I will. Because the truth is, a parking-lot course with painted lines and cones doesn't prepare you for California Highway 1, or for the car pulling out of a side street while you're mid-corner at 50 mph.

Here's that car driver who takes your right of way. Sure, he's at fault. But here's the real question: Have you been trained well enough to handle it? Can you perform an asphalt-pushing, full-force emergency brake? Were you ever even shown how hard you can stop before the front tire gives up?

If you weren't, then how could you possibly know whether you can make it on the brakes or not? That uncertainty—the lack of knowing what's possible—is what kills. When you don't know your limits, you can't make life-saving decisions fast enough. That's where mental coolness comes in. It's not luck, it's trained composure under fire. Skill + mindset = time. And time = survival.

The European Odyssey

These anecdotes—and I have countless others—highlight a systemic flaw. Contrast this with the European model, which mandates a gradual, staged, and deeply invested process, creating a foundation of both skill and risk maturity.

Graduated Path

Age 14. Begin with a 50cc moped, legally restricted to 28 mph. This initial phase, which lasts two years, costs about 50 Euros but involves six classes and a riding hour.

Age 16. Ramp up to 80cc lightweight bikes. The education cost jumps to about 1,500 Euros, requiring 11 riding hours and 24 hours of classroom instruction.

Age 18. Having completed a four-year riding odyssey, the rider faces another 400 Euros for a license restricted to a maximum of 48 horsepower (A2 license). Any traffic violations or crashes during this period extend the two-year restriction.

Age 20. Finally, the rider makes the A-license commitment: another 1,700 Euros, 2 hours of classroom, 11 hours of riding, and a rigorous test. Only then are they qualified to ride a non-restricted motorcycle.

At the time I got my license, the entire European motorcycle industry agreed to a voluntary restriction, capping the horsepower of ALL models at 100 hp maximum. The system prioritized the rider's safe developmental path over the industry's need for instant gratification sales.

Cost of the Minimalist System

My critique of the "$28 Suicide" is overwhelmingly supported by international data comparing fatality rates. The central thesis here is that the US's simplified, non-tiered, and short-term licensing process leads to significantly worse safety outcomes compared to the EU's extensive, graduated system.

Region/Country	Fatality Rate (per 100,000 Registered Motorcycles)	Source Year
United States	58.33	2019
European Union	11	2018

The data is damning. A rate of 58.33 fatalities per 100,000 riders in the U.S. versus an average of 11 in the EU is the final, quantifiable proof that the "quick license" system is a systemic failure of policy and psychological due diligence.

Little Extra Outcome

Furthermore, riders emerging from these 'parking lot schools' carry a burnt-in psychological picture of what "training" looks like: confusing, high-pressure, and unhelpful. This negative conditioning is often enough to convince them never to seek further, proper training, thus locking them into a lifelong state of unconscious incompetence.

The system must change. Now. We can't rely on the pre-frontal cortex development of youth to make wise decisions; the system must provide the essential guardrails. This isn't just about riding skills; it's about the psychology of survival. And right now, the system is failing its riders on both counts.

Psychological Takeaway

The licensing procedure is a product of institutional gaslighting. When a school passes a terrified, unskilled student, they provide false validation. This creates a lethal competency paradox where the rider has legal proof of skill but lacks the actual muscle memory to survive.

The system also ignores the maturation of risk. It bypasses the time needed for the pre-frontal cortex (impulse control) to catch up with the limbic system (thrill-seeking). When a license is this easy to get, it sends a psychological signal that the task is easy to do. That lie is what drives the statistics.

❋ Racer's Mind Note – Coach take

"You know... sometimes it's better to go down on the attempt to save it, instead of going down entirely senselessly just because you gave up."

- *Can Akkaya*

Listening to "Experts"

Let's put this one here into the brain-fart category. Some of you won't be happy with this (you might want to look deep into yourself).

Yes, I know you're all excited about riding, and you might be searching for ways to get better, hopefully in "no time." But taking the shortcut of searching the internet for answers will most of the time just lead you into confusion rather than a valuable solution.

How do I know? I talk to my students—thousands—and this is the consistent problem I encounter.

The Problem with Unverified Information

You are flooding your brain with data, but you have no quality filter:

Not everything on the internet is true or right. How do you know the stuff you're reading is information of quality?

You don't know that "motorcycle forum expert" behind the keyboard. Are his or her credentials sufficient? Is that person just saying something they believe is right?

And here is more, because even if the information *does* have quality: Did you REALLY understand what it tells you to do? How do you judge if you're doing it right after all?

No, 'cuz this isn't math! Math is logic which leads to a single solution if you follow a strict path, but what we're doing is trying to control the chaos that comes with tons of unknown variables. Variables that EVERY individual deals with differently!

The Math of Counter-Steering

Let me illustrate the failure of this learning method:

Each time I ask my class "Who knows what counter-steer is?" and all hands go up. Impressive, right?! But now ask me how many I see in my drill who are truly doing it correctly before I start working with them: I'VE SEEN ONLY THREE STUDENTS IN THOSE YEARS OF TEACHING who could demonstrate it correctly.

Yes, most of them have their license, miles, sometimes four decades of riding under their belts. They've read the crap out of books and forums, watched all the videos, and even taken other riding schools. Why are they still not getting it?

Failure of Imagination

Would you agree that "reading" a book about climbing the Alps is different from actually "really climbing" the Alps? Agreed?! Well let's keep this in mind and move on here.

Motorcycle riding isn't a static thing. This is loaded with emotions, variables, and "feelings." It's not just black and white; it's lots of gray zones. A book can't make you feel these things, and its content finds a place in your mind based entirely on the imagination of the reader.

In other words, what if you read a book on how to ride a motorcycle, but your imagination gives you a different understanding about it? The result is that you take out your bike to try those things, and you'll do them wrong. Yes, reading is power, but in fact, you don't learn from it that much. It helps you think about it, but there's no guarantee and no control if you fully understand comprehensive subjects.

Tyranny of the Forum Expert

Motorcycle forums are packed with "experts" who are lending out their half-knowledge under the soft blanket of anonymity and are covering new riders with "good tips" about braking, steering, and the all-time favorite: body positioning.

Consider the new rider who posts a question about "body positioning on a sport bike." It doesn't take long for tons of experts to offer their versions, which are all different. The confused newbie has to listen to the loudest, rudest, and most aggressive corresponding "expert," because that obviously must be right.

The outcome is that the "expert" recommends doing Hanging Off like Rossi does, because the "perfect" body position is, to be so far off the bike that you can see yourself in the mirror. Really?! Yes, that's *technically* correct for a professional racer, but it's highly dangerous to suggest to a rookie street rider who obviously has to learn essentials like even shifting the gears.

The new rider listens to it because they don't know what's wrong and what's right, and their hope for getting free help makes them skip over reality sometimes.

I can't make these ego-driven people shut up, because I don't want to give them what they're actually looking for, attention and neither should you.

Please stop listening—or even asking—on forums. If you don't know if your starter or the relay is the reason your bike doesn't fire up, then ask a forum. But not about things that can have a bad influence on your health, for maybe the rest of your life!

I actually believe that when you drop questions like this, you have no idea about the quality of answers, and you don't even care. You're actually only looking for communication, friends, and showing a picture of your bike. Have all my blessings to do just that.

Gap-Filler Phenomenon

There is another phenomenon I've observed, and that's about your brain.

I recently saw a post where a rider asked "experts" for the procedure of trail braking. Stunningly, there was only one comment right out of ten. Anyway, the interesting thing was to see that even a simple procedure seemed not to be understandable enough for the rider, based on the counter-question he replied with.

His counter-question was: "...so does that mean that I'll have to open the throttle while I'm still on the brakes?"

And here is the thing: there was no suggestion of doing that in the correct procedure list! Not even close.

I believe that some things (over-excitement, fear, anxiety) can offset logical thinking, which could downgrade a brain temporarily. The brain is trying to put puzzle pieces together when confusion (or missing intellect) leaves a gap, even if the puzzle piece doesn't fit. It makes the brain search for things you've heard, felt, experienced, and builds a puzzle piece that very likely includes substances of whatever you believe is right. Funny enough, in some cases, I believe that this non-fitting puzzle piece is built with a substance of your wish-thinking of what's *hopefully* right.

Triple Cost of Bad Advice

Following the advice of a false "expert" who is merely seeking attention or confirming their own half-knowledge is far more damaging than just a wrong line on a forum. It imposes a triple cost on your riding development:

Muscle Memory Damage

The most insidious damage is the neurological cost. When you attempt to execute faulty techniques. Like exaggerated body positioning or "opening the throttle while on the brakes" based on misunderstood forum tips and your body is building incorrect muscle memory.

The time you spend practicing a bad technique isn't just wasted; it actively creates a new obstacle. When you finally receive proper instruction, you must spend twice the time and mental effort to first unlearn the bad habit before you can even begin to learn the correct one. You're effectively paying for the mistake twice.

"Proof" of Failure

The forum expert's advice promises a shortcut to speed or skill. When you follow their advice and inevitably fail (or crash), your brain registers this failure as proof of your own incompetence.

The false expert never sees the outcome, but the rider is left with a damaged confidence core. Instead of concluding, "the advice was wrong," the rider concludes, "I am incapable of doing this." This psychological damage reinforces the very self-doubt you're trying to overcome.

Cost of Misdirected Trust

Your progress in motorcycling depends entirely on finding an instructor, a mentor, or a system you can trust (the one holding your rope on the Eiger North Wall).

By following the loudest, most aggressive, or most convenient source of information, you cheapen your internal meter for evaluating authority. You train yourself to accept low-quality counsel, making it harder for you to recognize and submit to the discipline of a *true* expert when you finally encounter one. Your most valuable asset, your trust, has been devalued by free, anonymous counsel.

Wish-Thinking Trap

The problem with anonymous "experts" isn't just their bad advice, but their ability to exploit a fundamental psychological weakness: the desire to hear what we want to hear.

This is the substance that often builds the faulty puzzle piece in your mind. The truth about riding mastery is that it requires slow, methodical practice, controlling fear, and accepting the Mastery Loop of failure. This is hard, disciplined work.

When a rider is confused, anxious, or impatient, their brain doesn't just look for *any* answer; it looks for the easiest or most flattering answer:

A newbie might be secretly afraid of leaning the bike over. The aggressive forum expert who says, "Just hang off like Rossi and you'll be fast!" appeals directly to the rider's desire to bypass the hard work of learning chassis dynamics. It's an easy, visible action that *feels* like the solution, satisfying the wish-thinking that speed is just a matter of manly aggression, not subtle technique.

When you hear something that confirms your *existing* bad habit—like an expert claiming, "The most important thing is to be easy on the front brake"—you latch onto it, ignoring three other experts who told you the opposite. You use the false expert to validate your comfort zone and shut down the uncomfortable truth.

You are seeking validation, friendship, and a vision of effortless speed. The forum expert is happy to provide a false positive that scratches that emotional itch, leaving you satisfied but dangerously misinformed. Remember: The advice that makes you truly better is usually the one that makes you feel the most uncomfortable.

What? Am I too straight up right now? Well, go think about it. Also, if you see yourself in this role as an "expert" here. Let's try to lean back and understand something here by not feeling offended with the messenger.

Look, all I'm saying is that you need to see the Alps yourself. If you need a guide to show you the best and safest way to climb up that Eiger North Wall, then you've got to be sure what that guy is capable of, because he's the one who's holding your rope!

If you're a smart kid, you might be able to learn algebra just from a book. Math doesn't make you bleed though. Math doesn't kill you.

Psychological Takeaway

Reading about riding is abstract theory. Executing it is dynamic chaos. When you learn from a screen, your brain builds a mental model based on Imagination, not reality. This creates a deadly illusion of competence. You believe you understand the physics, but your body can't perform the action. You "know" the theory while your front tire is washing out.

Your brain hates the vacuum of confusion. It fills gaps with Wish-Thinking, the easiest, most flattering answer available. Forum "experts" exploit this by offering ego-boosting shortcuts. If you're afraid of leaning, you'll latch onto "hanging off" tips because they feel like a solution that bypasses the scary work of chassis dynamics. You aren't seeking truth; you're seeking confirmation bias to stay comfortable.

Cheap advice isn't free. You pay for it in muscle memory damage. You're effectively practicing how to fail. When you finally get real instruction, you have to spend double the effort to unlearn the garbage. Worse, when the bad advice leads to a scare, you don't blame the anonymous expert, you blame your own talent. You conclude "I'm just not good at this," which is a lie manufactured by poor sources.

Discomfort Metric

If advice makes you feel "cool" without requiring brutal discipline, it's trash. Real growth is uncomfortable. A forum expert doesn't care if you bleed. A real mentor is holding your rope on a cliffside. Math doesn't kill people, but following a keyboard warrior into a decreasing-radius turn could.

※ **Mind Note – The Way**

"The impediment to action advances action. What stands in the way becomes the way."

— Marcus Aurelius (Stoic Philosopher)

Dragging Knee Makes Faster

Of course not. How could it?! I mean, just because the knee puck is on the ground doesn't mean you're faster. How disappointing, huh?! There is, I believe, a lot of wish-thinking and some mental stuff going on with this. That's why I want to display an actual physical skill in this lecture.

There is something to it, I totally agree. When I saw King Kenny Roberts dragging knee on TV back then—oh boy, I wanted it badly. And yes, just to have this as a goal and the urge to get it finally down made me faster. So, yea, once you get that knee dragging you gonna feel like Superman. It's a huge confidence boost and you're in contact with the enemy. This means that will also make you faster. This however, is more of a mental boost rather than an actual physical skill that makes you faster.

Illusion of Speed and the Cost of Bad Habits

This actually can cause you to be way slower by fooling you into believing you're fast at the same time. That's what most sportbike riders don't even see. Subconsciously they're riding either on lines which give them an unreasonable lean angle so that they finally get that knee down, or they overly stick their knee so far out that there isn't much lean going on. No lean means no corner speed, and vice versa.

Most of the time this is a guarantee for creating habits which extend the time of realization and correction, unless they work with someone who really knows. Good luck with that.

An Example

I just remember a great example. There was a so-called "instructor" who was "working" with a kid on a Supermoto track. I took a cigar and a coffee to observe from a distance. That boy was frickin' fast on his mini bike. His body language, lines, and braking attitude were just about to be there. Then he got "advised" to get that elbow down, which was pretty much the only instruction he received. So, the next three laps I could tell the kid was mentally so busy with this, and it made him slow down already.

Then his advisor walked up on the track and led him on such a messed-up late apex that I could see dirt coming up on his rear tire. So, at least subconsciously, the guy knew that this would cause a leaner angle. Yep, after five more laps, the kid got that elbow down, but that was literally not the same kid that I saw initially. He was hanging off so extreme that he actually couldn't operate the throttle properly. His line on that particular turn was so bad that it broke all the momentum towards the apex. It was SEEMINGLY slower than before. Then he stopped the boy once more and advised him to do the same on all the other turns and walked proudly away. Guess what the kid looked like on a full lap?!

So, this demonstrates very well that you can break things easily, right?! Dragging a knee or an elbow doesn't mean much, actually, right?!

Stiff Knee and the Learning Delay

Another effect could kick in, and that's that a knee is stiff and pointy and that it turns into a "side stand" which is in the way of leaning more. Ergo, the rider runs way wide all the time and can't get any faster.

Rule of thumb: the faster you go; the more lean you have to compensate for it with. That's something dangerous, though. With this, you could go out and keep pushing it while your eyes and brain are not ready yet. Additionally, your body positioning is in the way of allowing that extra speed/lean. All of this is the struggle which you don't understand, or don't know how to fix.

So, you waste lots of time watching video after video. You might have spent five grand on an overrated racing school and do lots of track days, but still! You might not even "see" all of this and you believe you're good, just because you assume it can't go any faster because that knee is down.

In all the years of figuring this all out—in high-level pro racing and especially during decades of teaching riders—I've truly seen a lot of bad stuff. It actually includes myself, when I wanted it so bad back then. It messed me up for so long. Yes, it felt good and fast, but I wasn't really. I extended my own learning curve by making this a priority. I began to understand that I had to learn things in the right order, time, and doses.

Psychological Takeaway

Dragging a knee provides a hit of external validation that tricks your brain into equating "noise" with "skill." When the puck scrapes, your ego declares victory and shuts down the learning process. This creates a false illusion of mastery. You assume you have reached the limit of the bike because you have reached the limit of your comfort zone. In reality, you're just satisfying a mental itch while your technical development flatlines.

Chasing the scrape is outcome-based learning, which is the enemy of discipline. You start manufacturing dangerous situations—messed-up lines and awkward body positioning—just to get the f'n reward. This creates a mental block where the knee acts like a physical and psychological kickstand. Instead of flowing with the machine, you're stiffening up to reach the ground, preventing the very lean angle you think you're achieving.

Focusing on the "show" is a form of self-sabotage. By chasing a knee or elbow drag before you have mastered the essentials, you bake in catastrophic habits. You're posing, not riding. This sensory distraction consumes the cognitive bandwidth you need for throttle control and line selection. You're wasting mental energy on a photo op while the actual physics of the corner are falling apart beneath you.

Invisible Mastery

True skill is often invisible. The best riders don't hunt for plastic-on-asphalt contact; they focus on process and execution. If you want to be better, you have to kill the desire to look better. Stop chasing the scrape and start chasing the discipline of the correct line. The knee will find the ground when your technique demands it, not when your ego begs for it.

I know you want this because I've been there too. It's a hurdle one wants to take. I get it, but I've seen real bad stuff based on this kind of eagerness in all those years.

Nuts n' Bolts

Demolishing the Golden Calf

There is an undeniable boundary between the rider and the bike. Most of the time, I'd say, there's far too much boundary. Let me explain...

Here she is. You finally made the dream come true and got yourself the motorcycle of your dreams. It was hellishly expensive, but you worked hard for it, and you deserve it. A machine that comes with all the electronic goodies modern technology has to offer, a machine designed to devour corners.

Yet, you're not too worried about those two-inch "chicken strips" (the unused edge of your tire), because you don't want the bike to get hurt at all. Instead of noticing the huge blockade you've set up, you invest another into fancy rear sets and additional bling. Each time you clean and polish it, you fall in love with it over and over, until you're afraid to even go for a ride.

Are you mad at me now? Don't be, because I only want to open your eyes and help you take the first step toward becoming the rider you're envisioning yourself to be, the rider this cornering beast deserves. I'm not saying you should stop maintaining or cleaning it, but you're likely overdoing this to the point where it has become a problem. Admiration has overridden logic.

Mechanic Mentality

Believe it or not, high-level racing ain't much about "motorcycles." They're only delivering their best to enable the rider to perform at and over the limit. They're simply tools, like the shoes for Michael Jordan.

You are making this piece of equipment a "Golden Calf," a god-like sculpture you admire for its beauty. I'm not blaming you; I love my bikes and always take care of them. But the moment I swing my leg over that seat; this goes through my head: Nuts n' Bolts!

Consider a mechanic. He also has an attachment to his tools, but imagine if he would only touch them with white gloves and instantly search for scratches after usage. Imagine if he used that phillips head screwdriver and instantly regretted it. What if he refused to turn on his electrical tools so they wouldn't wear out? You have eventually become that mechanic.

Anxiety-Grip Cycle

A motorcycle is, at its core, a collection of parts held together with nuts and bolts. All of that stuff is replaceable and repairable. You bought yourself into it, and if it breaks, you fix it (It's a great opportunity for common-sense upgrades, by the way.)

Relax, because the intense anxiety you feel about crashing is exactly what makes going down *more* likely than you hope. This anxiety manifests as stiff movements, leading you to:

Fail to use the bike at its full potential.

Fail to lean the bike into the corner as much as it could actually swirl out.

Your emotional attachment dictates a "protective reaction" that keeps you far from the bike's mechanical capabilities, leaving that two-inch chicken strip as a testament to your fear.

Don't be mad at me. I'm just the messenger. Just ask me how I know, because I get to see this crippling fear every single day.

The only way to truly honor your dream bike is to use it as the high-performance tool it was designed to be.

Capping Your Potential

The consequence of admiring the motorcycle too much goes far beyond a scratch on the paint; it becomes a self-imposed cap on your own potential. When you elevate the machine to a "Golden Calf" status, you're psychologically making the bike more important than the rider. Your subconscious mind accepts that its primary mission is no longer progression, but preservation of the asset.

This leads to two destructive outcomes:

You stop seeing the motorcycle as a variable tool you can influence, and start seeing it as a fragile artifact that must be protected. This prevents you from making the necessary aggressive inputs required for mastery. You subconsciously believe, "The bike is perfect; my inputs might break it."

By refusing to allow the bike to lean, you deny yourself the opportunity to find the actual mechanical functions of it. The result is that when you *do* crash, the failure is interpreted as a catastrophic, random event rather than a fixable error in technique. This prevents the honest self-assessment required by the Yin & Yang chapter.

Your admiration for the beauty and cost of the machine is actually a powerful form of performance anxiety that's entirely self-manufactured. It ensures that the bike's capability will always remain greater than your willingness to explore it. Only when you internalize the Nuts n' Bolts philosophy can you free your mind to push beyond the mental limit.

Irreplaceable vs. The Repairable

Ultimately, we are all dealing with basically two primal fears: to get hurt/die, and to break something. By exponentially reducing your admiration for the damn thing. So it turns into what it actually is… an object: the wrench for the mechanic, the hammer for the roofer, and you address the second fear. It is, and will be one day anyway, replaceable. It's repairable. You're kind of not.

This "thing" isn't perfect, anyway. Nothing is. This philosophy goes in pretty much all directions in life, doesn't it? The more you love something or someone, the more your protective instincts are triggered. Love can make you blind, and so you might make wrong, overly conservative decisions. Only when you internalize the Nuts n' Bolts philosophy can you free your mind to push beyond the mental limit and prioritize the one thing that truly matters: your own development as a rider.

Psychological Takeaway

When you worship the machine, your brain switches from growth mode to defense mode. You've turned the bike into an extension of your ego. Now, every corner isn't a chance to learn; it's a threat to your "perfect" object. This creates a subconscious "hard cap" on your performance. You physically can't lean or brake at the limit because your brain treats a scratch like a personal injury. Your "chicken strips" are just visible symptoms of an invisible mental cage.

Fear of damage creates physical rigidity. This isn't just "being nervous". It's a neurological feedback loop. The brain perceives the bike as "fragile," so it commands the muscles to be "careful." Careful on a bike means stiff, and stiff means slow and dangerous. You end up in a death grip because you're trying to "hold" the bike together rather than letting the damn chassis do its job.

A "Nuts n' Bolts" philosophy shift is a cognitive reframe. By mentally stripping the bike of its "dream" status and viewing it as a bucket of hardware, you kill the anxiety of loss. You have to treat the bike with the same cold utility as a roofer treats a hammer. If the hammer breaks, you fix it. Once you stop caring about the tool, you can finally start caring about the work.

Value Displacement

The core issue is that you've placed the Value in the wrong object. You're protecting the repairable (the bike) and sacrificing the irreplaceable (your development and safety).

Until you prioritize your own evolution over the bike's resale value, you aren't a pilot. You're just a high-speed janitor polishing a trophy.

(You know… I always have to smile when getting this philosophy across to my students. I actually love to customize the crap out of my bikes :-)

Rethinking the Learning Curve

You step onto the track, fueled by a ferocious need for speed and a stack of instructional knowledge. You expect a steep, exponential ascent: a constant, dramatic drop-in lap times with every session. I know you do. But here's the harsh, honest truth you need to internalize right now: learning isn't a steep exponential curve.

While that rapid-fire growth isn't impossible, it's a rarity. For most of us, the path to mastery is less a rocket launch and more a tide cycle, moving in waves with only a gradual, upward trend. This is where the wisdom of the old school comes in. It's what my grandmother used to say: "Sometimes you have to take a step backwards to finally make two steps forward."

But for the majority of track riders and racers, that tide will inevitably recede and reveal a long, flat stretch of sand. They will hit the plateau, and if they don't grasp the crucial psychological lesson embedded within it, they will get stuck there for a long time.

When Knowledge Fails

So, you're stuck. Confused. You don't understand why the speed has dried up. You've put in the work, haven't you? You've studied every damn book, you've scoured the videos, maybe you even invested in top-tier rider schooling. Your mind is loaded with *correct* information. Yet, you're not getting faster.

The inner dialogue turns venomous. You start questioning the very knowledge you've acquired. Nothing feels right anymore. Worse, the harder you try to break through, the slower, messier, or more dangerous the riding becomes. That deep, corrosive frustration sets in, and the first insidious thought of quitting pops up. You eventually keep going, but only by conjuring up lame excuses.

What?! Do you feel offended by this honesty? Good. Why don't you ask me how I know this shit?

The simple reality is that knowledge acquisition is only the first step. The creation of your personal learning curve requires time and trial-and-error, and you have virtually no influence over the timing or intensity of its waves. Those fluctuations depend on variables far beyond a textbook: your character, your psychological state, external life situations, and the cost of crashing.

Knowledge vs. Exploration

Crashing is the ultimate, costly trial-and-error. It forces a significant backward step because you learn the painful, bad outcomes. To illustrate the difference between knowing and doing, let's look at my old home track: the Nürburgring Nordschleife in Germany.

Imagine that section above. I could teach you precisely how to fly through it at 147 mph on the absolute ideal line. I could tell you the exact inch of asphalt for the latest possible braking marker. That teaching is 100% right on the money.

But can you possibly pull that off on your first try? *No.* You would more likely injure yourself. The Nordschleife is 12 miles long with 154 often-blind turns. I could lead you for ten perfect laps, showing you every brake point and apex. Your lap times would rise and fall, but with an overall upward trend, which is a good thing. Why? Because even if you had the physical abilities and mental fortitude to instantly attack at the maximum possible speed, you'd still die. You can't possibly memorize 154 unique corners well enough in ten laps to execute them flawlessly at the limit.

The lesson is this: I can hand you the map, but YOU are the one who has to explore your potential on the terrain. That burden is on you.

Resource Exploration Lag

Let's try a more tangible example. Say you were struggling on mediocre street tires, but we now mount a set of the finest MotoGP race slicks on your machine. You go out and make a little progress. But it's extremely unlikely you're capable of riding them at their fullest possible potential.

These tires deliver a new resource—a new grip ceiling—and you must take the time to explore that ceiling on your own terms. The MotoGP engineer can tell you how they must be ridden; their information is 100% correct. But the exploration, the utilization, and the confidence still depend entirely on you to explore their full capabilities.

The real danger comes when you hit that plateau without understanding this resource lag. Frustration takes the wheel. You start questioning everything you've learned, and if you have a strong competitive nature, you will get hurt. Mentally, and eventually, physically.

The Path Through the Plateau

If you allow impatience and corrosive frustration to infiltrate your process, you will only extend your time in the plateau trap. To accelerate back onto the steep learning curve, you must adopt a deliberate, psychological approach:

Be honest and look at your riding and your ego without flinching. Accept the limits of your current capability.

Have faith and trust the knowledge you've acquired and the process of adaptation. The information is correct; your integration is simply lagging.

Be smart and don't force speed. Focus on isolating one small concept per session, not lap time.

Relax and rest, because a tired mind and tense body can't process and integrate new resources. Sometimes, the fastest way to get faster is to take a day off.

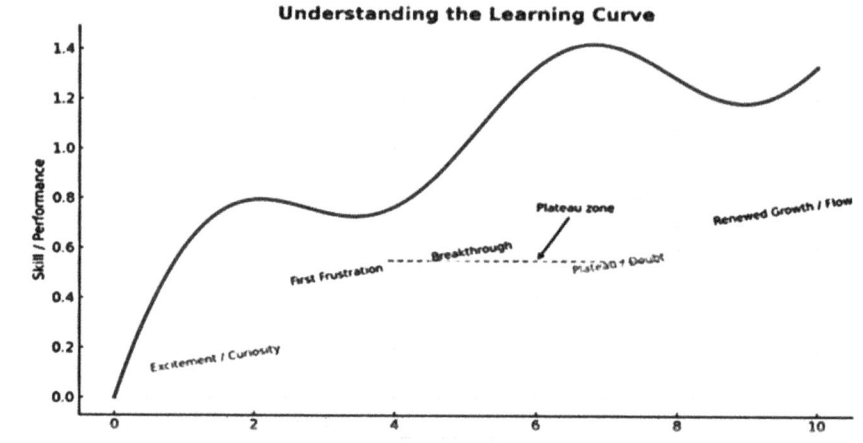

Breaking the Plateau Mentality

The plateau isn't a failure; it's a necessary incubation period. It's the gap required for a complex skill to move from the conscious, analytical part of your brain to the subconscious, instinctive part. Pushing through this requires a fundamental shift in your mental strategy, transforming struggle into structured growth.

Power of Process Focus

The first, most critical move is to stop chasing the lap time. Your fixation on the outcome and the unmet expectation, is what's fueling the frustration. Instead, you must redirect your powerful focus to the process. Stop trying to go fast and start trying to execute one specific, correct technique perfectly. Don't worry about the full lap. Worry about hitting that apex, or maintaining that specific brake pressure on a single corner. This replaces stressful external pressure with a manageable internal control system.

Accepting the Resource Lag

You must acknowledge the psychological delay—the resource lag. When you're given new, correct information, your knowledge is instantaneous, but your capability is not. Your system isn't yet capable of utilizing that resource. Trust the information, but accept that you're still in the verification stage. This understanding fosters patience and drastically reduces the urgency and frustration that fuels the negative spiral.

Trust of Exploration

Your intellectual trust in the information—your reading, your schooling—must be forged into experiential trust. You need to test the limits of the new technique repeatedly, in a structured way. This transforms the abstract knowledge into unshakeable confidence, because *you* have personally confirmed that the line works, the brake point holds, and the tire grips. This isn't blind faith; this is exploratory trust earned through deliberate, focused repetition.

Strategic Relaxation and Honesty

Speed isn't brute force; it's precision under pressure. If you're tense, fatigued, or angry, your body can't integrate new, complex movements. You must become somatically honest and recognize that frustration or physical exhaustion is your true current limiter, not the quality of the instruction. Sometimes, the fastest way to get faster is to take a strategic step back. Relax, rest, and allow your brain to synthesize the complex data while you're off the bike. A quiet mind is an integrating mind.

Look. The learning curve isn't a straight line up. It's just like life itself: sometimes you have to get hurt to truly understand. It takes guts to admit, and not to get lost in excuses or questioning. However, sometimes when I felt I had hit a plateau, I was brave enough to tell my team. They showed solidarity and we skipped chasing lap times immediately: "Why aren't you just go out and do some wheelies for the fans!?"

Psychological Takeaway

Your brain has two speeds: the analytical mind (fast at learning theory) and the basal ganglia (slow at automating movement). A plateau happens when the analytical mind is full, but the basal ganglia hasn't finished "writing the code" for your muscles. Most riders mistake this "processing time" for a dead end. They try to force progress with conscious effort, but you can't "think" your way into a motor skill. You have to wait for your biology to catch up.

When the clock stops dropping, the ego feels threatened. To avoid the pain of "being slow," your brain triggers a doubt cascade. You start blaming the tires, the track, or the coaching. This isn't just a bad mood; it's ego defensiveness creating a physical "lock-up." Tension is the physical manifestation of a mind that's trying to negotiate with the limit instead of f'n exploring it.

There is a massive gap between knowing a tire will grip and feeling it. This is the resource lag. Even with 100% correct data, your nervous system remains in "verification mode." You can't bypass this phase. If you try to jump from "I read about it" to "I'm doing it at 140mph," your survival instinct will trigger a panic response that overrides your technique. You have to "earn" the trust through low-stakes repetition.

Power of Strategic Regression

The "step backward to take two forward" is a cognitive load hack. By ignoring lap times and focusing on one tiny detail, or even just "doing wheelies", you drop the performance pressure. This lowers the cortisol in your system, relaxes your muscles, and finally allows the brain to move the new skill from "working memory" into "permanent storage."

You aren't quitting; you're clearing the cache so the processor can run faster.

That Thing About Progress

Pivot Point

If you engage in any activity, you progress. If you like what you're doing, you progress faster. If you like it and have the conscious goal to progress, you'll progress faster and more efficiently. It's as simple as that.

Why does it take so long with motorcycle riding, and especially racing? Because of the possibilities of breaking things, getting hurt, or even dying. The natural risk introduces a powerful psychological handbrake that must be overcome.

First, we need to agree that making progress isn't endless. Sorry to say, but your clock is ticking. Just like the progress of physical growth, your body and mind will eventually come to a pivot point where the rate of improvement slows down.

There is an upside to this, though. Just like your body, your progress as a rider goes further when you're physically and mentally in shape. Don't feel discouraged if you're not in peak condition or are on the older side. Just accept the fact that progress has its limits, and that limit depends on many factors. There's a reason why racers retire, right?

Ladder into the Sky Metaphor

Let's use a metaphor for progress: climbing a high ladder, all the way up into the blue sky. That ladder is so high that you can't see its end. That's cool, because you don't actually know how far you'll come. So, get your ass up there!

The ladder is the progress.

The sky is the unknown, ultimate potential of your height.

Stages of the Climb

All the way down low, when mastering those first rungs, a lot of people could help you (instructors, friends, basic classes). You rush up that ladder real fast.

You realize that most of those people can't reach you anymore to hold you or guide you. The general advice is no longer effective. Luckily, some brought specialized ropes (advanced skills), but even they only go *that* high up. The higher you climb; the less accessible help becomes.

The fun you're having doesn't scare you, but you realize you're getting slower. The air is thinner up there, and your body gets tired. You're not getting younger, and the competition gets stronger. You start having thoughts about losing grip and you look down, but the helpers below are small and their voices can't be heard. The higher you climb, the more mental it gets.

You keep going, but suddenly, some rungs are missing. You're stuck because you don't have the specialized tools to fix them on your own. But there are professionals who have them on hand, but they have no issue with the height you're at. They're waiting for you to call.

Lap Time Timeline

Let's be more realistic and look at lap times, and there's nothing more immediate and brutal than the clock, man. Let's use the progression at a track like Laguna Seca:

Imagine your first time on a motorcycle at Laguna Seca Raceway.

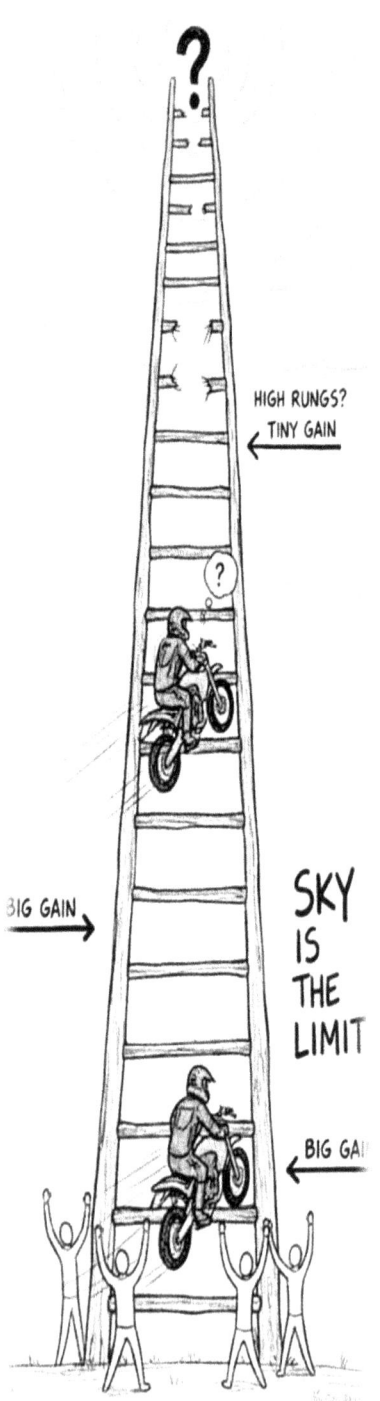

Your lap time could probably be measured by a calendar. You dedicate two years, and you return to the track: you're minutes faster per lap now! A year later, you've mastered the basics and are running at a pace good for C Group. You progress quickly to B Group times, and all is right with the world.

Then, the pivot point hits:

It suddenly takes two full years of effort and better equipment just to make A Group lap times. You finally get to racing, and while you're backfield in the amateur leagues, you're still progressing by seconds per lap.

But as the competition gets serious, the returns diminish sharply:

It takes another two years to become a champion in that amateur league. Your lap times are now progressing by only half-seconds, even though you and your equipment are significantly better and more costly.

Another year or two go by, and you're a semi-pro competing on the national stage. Your times progress by only tenths of a second. This required an exponential increase in physical conditioning, mental discipline, and financial commitment.

You reach the world stage and become a professional. Now, it takes another one or two years to become the guy to beat. Your final progress is measured in mere hundredths of a second, the difference between pole position and the second row.

You are faster than ever before, but the gain is infinitesimally small. The cost, the commitment, and the risk required to earn that final hundredth are orders of magnitude greater than the effort it took to shave off those first few seconds.

Consequently

You need to understand and accept this reality. The pursuit of progress is always worthwhile, even when the gains become infinitesimally small. That's just like the reality for MotoGP factory teams, who have a crew of up to mechanics and engineers working throughout a season and putting multi-million dollars into it just to find another hundredth of a damn second. The air is damn thin up there!

You can't expect from yourself—nor from those who help you—to keep making big steps up that ladder all the time. Your way up there is filled with hurt, pain, plateaus, and costs. Not just that... your body and soul also will reach peak performance one day. If you put yourself under that kind of progress pressure, you'll lose this fight!

Psychological Takeaway

The Inverse law of progress dictates that as you approach mastery, the emotional and material cost for each gain increases exponentially, challenging your internal belief system.

When you start, rapid gains deliver dopamine hits, creating the unrealistic expectation of continuous, steep improvement, the "rocket launch" Illusion. This sets a damn dangerous psychological precedent. As you climb, the effort (physical, mental, financial) for smaller and smaller gains increases exponentially. This directly challenges your internal belief system.

You must acknowledge your pivot point with somatic honesty. This is the biological and psychological reality that improvement will eventually slow and meet natural limits. Accepting this prevents later frustration, anger, and learned helplessness when demands outstrip your capacity.

Navigating the Plateau of Refinement

The middle and high rungs are an emotional grind. Your brain gets fewer dopamine rewards for massive effort, leading to doubt and questioning the value of your work. The expertise gap demands the humility to seek highly tailored, external coaching, breaking your ego's self-sufficiency, as nuances become too specialized to identify alone.

Chasing "hundredths of a second" isn't just physical; it's an exponential increase in mental discipline and emotional resilience. This psychological pressure demands exceptional mind coolness and ego management.

Embrace the Inverse Law for Sustainable Growth

Understanding the inverse law frees you from self-defeating "progress pressure." You must shift your internal valuation. Psychological reward must come from the process of refinement, the mastery of control, and the deep satisfaction of flawless execution – not just dramatic leaps in performance. This is your counter-ego discipline: finding technical victories over "the old you" in every subtle aspect of riding.

Mastery is a lifelong journey of diminishing returns. Accept the inverse law, manage your damn expectations, and find profound satisfaction in the continuous, incremental refinement of your craft.

Be aware of reality: progress is a timeline with acceleration to a pivot point where it slows and narrows to its end.

※ Mind Note – Coach's take

"Someone gave their blood and bones to become what they became. They make it look easy, which might come through as talent. Don't take their credit away!"

- *Can Akkaya*

PART II: Understanding

That Rear Brake Thang

The Myth

With all these years of teaching—especially street riders—I do know how much they love their rear brakes. This is more psyche than anything else, though, and most of it comes from what and how they have been taught. The rear brake becomes a mental comfort blanket, a 'safe' alternative to the terrifying front lever, a habit reinforced by instructors who don't know the physics or the survival stakes. I've even witnessed a license instructor tell a new rider that a locking rear wheel "is what it is," even when the rider raised concerns about it.

I know that this will be extremely controversial, but I want to clear this logically up a little for you. Let's say, something to think about.

Phony Formula

Let me begin by pointing out that most riders have been taught to use the front brake at 70%, and the rear brake at 30%. If this sounds plausible to you, then I don't even understand why. Don't feel offended. Just bear with me here and let's have a deeper look into this.

When I heard this brake ratio, I started asking those who are teaching it to tell me what the exact substance for this formula is. Nobody could answer me. Now how messed up is that in the first place?! I kind of believe that these numbers must be based on something, so I have a theory.

When looking at an average sport motorcycle and its brake system, you'll find two big brake rotors on the front. Two big brake calipers and a braking master cylinder anywhere from 16 to 20mm. Now, if you compare these numbers with what's in the rear—a way smaller rotor, a caliper with a single piston, and a small rear brake master cylinder—you'll see a math ratio of about 70/30. That's where I believe this "let's just teach that" thing is coming from. I'm glad that there's at least some kind of substance behind this, but let's see where this actually goes.

Straight up. If I were a beginner rider and some instructor (messenger of disinformation) would tell me to use the front brake at 70%—then I'd have some deep questions for him/her:

How do I know what a 70% on the front brake is, when I don't know what a 100% is like?!

What's the 'formula' to quickly do the math while I'm panicking right into the car who just took my right of way?!

Why don't you teach me to use my front brake at 100%?!

Then I'd question a curriculum which obviously keeps 30% of my survival chance away by not learning all of its potential!

Do you see the conflict I'm having with this? Do you share these thoughts with me so far? It actually gets even more interesting making some thoughts in regard to the rear brake now, so let's see.

Where the Rear Brake Disappears

I know about five professionals from back then who actually used the rear brake. There are more today in MotoGP, though, but let me come back to this later. Why? That's because these guys know how to use the front brake at 100%, and 100% of front tire capabilities. Once that front brake force is established, the rear end is going to lift off the asphalt. Ergo: ZERO% rear brake available! Yes, I compared you with pros, but understand that I have 70% of our cornering school students doing stoppies within only an hour.

Let's have a look at a more math-based example. A motorcycle with good front brakes can decelerate with a force of about 1G. Now let's say you're that kind of riding specialist who can actually operate that front brake just as much so that the rear tire doesn't leave the asphalt, and so the rear brake is actually usable. Now how much extra G's will this generate?!!! Like what?... 0.00001G's?

That's about the energy it takes to fart through your jeans! Now consider how much mental resources you've spent to push that little fart out without making a mess!!!

This points out difficulties:

You gotta be a darn specialist on the front brake in order to 'just' have that rear end on the ground and so to give that rear brake a valuable existence!

Just that should ring the bell of how much mental resource you have to give away to make both at same time work at their limits.

Cognitive Load Trap

Another one? About how difficult it actually is to master front and rear at its best? Sure, let's do that. Let's say you're braking out of higher speed at 50% of the front brake resource, and at the same time 50% of the rear brake resource. That would be moderate deceleration. Now let's say while you moderately brake, you'd add more braking to the front. More and more. At one point, what will you have to do with the rear brake in order not to lock it up, even when you never changed the '50% rear lever pressure'?!

This points out more difficulties:

What you can get out of the rear brake is depending on your front brake abilities!

The rear will lock, the more weight moves to the front and down, based on your front brake usage.

In order not to lock the rear, you'll have to ease off the lever pressure while you add more front brake.

Now I'm asking you, from the deepest logical thinking: which new rider can even control that, especially during the 3 seconds you have before you die in the damn car?! Yea, it's not even just all this. It's also what it does to your brain. A locked rear wheel will also lock your brain. In certain situations, you might even come off the front brake because it can swing and slide the bike from one side to the other. This will extend your braking travel and probably narrows your sight even more. The rear brake, in the wrong hands, can turn into a death trap.

Focus on ONE Survival Tool

How about we forget this thing instead? How about releasing ourselves from these chains and learning to ease into the front brakes at their 100% capabilities? The relief of having to operate both in an extreme situation can be the difference between life and death, because your brain is very likely capable of mastering ONE only, and that should be the one which not just has most of the braking force to offer, but also the one where all the physics goes! To the front and down. I'd say, rear brake is unnecessary with all bikes which are able to do a stoppie. Just to give it a rule of thumb. You'll need to learn how to max out all of the potential your front brake has to offer.

Exceptions to the Rule

Are all bikes the same? No. There are categories of bikes which actually have a use for the rear brake. Cruisers, for example. They have a low ass and high up front, so the geometry is different. Their suspensions, tires, and brakes aren't as good as you find them on more sporty bikes. Higher weights play into this as well. About the same goes for Adventure bikes.

What you need to learn here is, how to max out the front brake first. Then how much to add rear brake the moment the front is maxed out, means, how never to slam both at the brakes at same time. A rear brake lever is also difficult to feel. You wear different boots, foot position vague, uphill/downhill, all this while weight moves forward. This makes cornering for some riders difficult and inconsistent as well. Also here, the focus on the front brake only could be a massive relief for you.

Again, I know that this (more than an opinion) is splitting the room, and I agree with you that the exact dose of using the front and rear brake is more brake! However, for the majority of riders and where they're at level-wise, they're not able to pull this off while they're panicking right into the car!

Sure, the rear brake might not be bad in some situations of street riding: an up-hill launch, or some real slow maneuvers where the front brake could rock you off balance. Emergency braking... that rear brake is levered out in no time when done right.

Psychological Takeaway

In a three-second survival window, your brain doesn't do math. The "70/30" rule is a death sentence because it demands a complex calculation during a state of total panic. This triggers decision paralysis. While you're trying to balance two different pressure curves with two different limbs, you're bleeding away the reaction time you need to live. By the time your brain processes the "ratio," you've already hit the car. You have to simplify the decision to a single, 100% action: Front Brake.

The rear brake is often a psychological crutch. Riders are terrified of the front brake's power, so they retreat to the rear pedal because it feels "safer." This is a lie. This survival instinct actually robs you of your best chance to stop. Using the rear brake gives you an illusion of control while you're actually ignoring the only tool—the front lever—that can generate the 1G of force needed to save your life. You're trading effective physics for a darn false sense of security.

A locked rear wheel doesn't just skid the bike; it locks the brain. The moment the rear slides, your focus shifts from "stopping" to "managing the slide." This attention hijack consumes 100% of your remaining mental bandwidth. You stop looking for an exit and start staring at the fishtailing rear end. A tool that was supposed to help you has now become a sensory distraction that guarantees a collision.

Simplify your emergency braking. Eliminate decision paralysis by focusing solely on maximizing front brake pressure. Understand that the rear brake is an unreliable tool for low experienced riders.

Practice the living dead out of this, or find a school that knows what they're doing. This can be done in a parking lot, which is pretty much all they are good for.

Being Able to Brake at All Times

Betrayal of "Safety"

You've been taught lies in the name of safety. From your very first license course, institutions have instilled a fundamental, crippling fear: "Stay away from the front brake when turning/leaning!" This isn't just misinformation; it's a psychological crime. It disarms you of your primary survival tool—your front brake—and replaces it with crippling mental blocks and dangerous habits. This chapter exposes the betrayal of "official" training and unleashes you to master the most critical skill for survival and control: the ability to brake, intelligently and aggressively, at all times.

Yes, this is more or less a physical skill, but there's quite a bit of mental material, so please bear with me.

Straight up: 'BRAKING' IS THE PRIOR SKILL TO STAY ALIVE. Agreed?! Well, I'm hearing it every day. I see 99.9% of my students braking, and their performance on the brakes is actually shockingly bad. Furthermore, I ask them who taught them and what was their message. Their answers are even more shocking.

In fact, ANY curriculum of motorcycle driver's license-giving institutions is telling new riders to "Stay away from the front brake when turning/leaning!" I believe that this is already a CRIME to say, because I believe that you gotta be able to make use of your brakes AT ALL FREAKING TIMES! Don't you think?!

Mental Blockade of Fear

There is much more coming with what they teach. Mental blockades which I, as a coach who is teaching the total opposite, have to remove. Manifested habits and empowered anxieties before they're actually able to learn how it's done right.

So, their message is either liability-based or simply from not knowing how and what to teach. Things like 'you will roll front over' and 'you'll go down on a turn' is what they say. Yep, that could be true if you haven't been trained to do this properly! In fact, this kind of information, and its mental effect, automatically triggers a certain reluctance towards using the front brake, which is actually our primary weapon for scary situations. The blockade is so deep in their heads, that most of the riders are not even using 50% of their actual front brake potential, which is another guarantee to get hurt, or even to die.

During their 'training', they actually emphasize overusing the rear brake and locking the rear wheel, saying that this is the way to go.

Lethal Responsibility of Bad Information

My point right now is, that if you as an instructor, knowingly or not, contribute to a rider's reluctance for front brake usage, you're equally responsible for his/her death.

Because trail-braking is an essential skill to learn to be able to slow down even out of a full lean angle. Trail braking isn't just for racers. It can triple a street rider's chance to not get hurt when taught properly. Besides this, the wrong information also leads riders to an over-usage of rear brake which causes even more confusion and extends their learning curve additionally.

Not just that. These institutions come up with irrational, made-up stuff of what trail braking is, very likely only for the reason that they have a 'findable keyword' on their website.

"Add Throttle While Braking" Madness

I am sure that there are advanced track schools who are teaching Trail Braking, and not just us. Are they doing it right? I don't know. Our program does for sure. Recently, I just became aware of what one of the certified license-giving schools had interpreted wrongly from an ex-MotoGP World Champion. I can't even get my head into what they came up with there, and that's to add throttle while you brake!!!?

That doesn't make ANY sense, unless you want to negligently hurt riders! Adding throttle into the brakes will extend your braking travel, and with that, Trail Braking lost its status as a survival skill. Furthermore, isn't this against what they're saying in the first place, to stay away from brakes while leaning?! However, I can't even imagine what that does, and even that MotoGP star came out with a video on YouTube that this BS is truly not from him. Just picture what this is really all about!!

I only became aware of this when a few students told me about it. Now here is 'the good part' of this. In all those years teaching American riders, I've never seen any student actually doing this total bullshit. Now what does this tell you about their teaching quality and efficiency?

Why You Need Trail Braking

You think a street rider doesn't need trail braking? You're dead wrong! You need this, but it's gonna be hard for you to find the right school to teach you, because you don't know what's wrong and what's right. I know we are doing this right. Just know that this goes beyond reading about it. To understand trail braking at its fullest and operate it safely, you need to remove BS habits and to master many drills until you get it.

I do know that this might sound like a rant to you, but it needs to be said and acknowledged. Otherwise, this will never change for the good.

Psychological Takeaway

Licensing institutions instill a direct, visceral fear response tied to the front brake lever, a negative conditioning that compromises safety and skill development. By drilling "never touch the front brake in a turn," they program a f'n visceral panic response into your nervous system. This is a psychological crime.

Trail braking is the ultimate psychological tool. Being able to brake while leaning shifts your locus of control from external (the road) to internal (you). When your brain realizes it can control speed and geometry at any lean angle, the panic disappears. You move from being a passenger hoping for the best to a pilot in total command. It replaces the anxiety-driven freeze with proactive, deliberate action.

Learning to trail brake isn't something you do on your own. This comes with tons of knowledge and requirements that are based on your current skill level.

That ABS Thang

You know what high-level motorcycle racing is? That's like emergency braking for an hour. The G-forces make your sweat leave your face forward. When you come out of that fairing at 340km/h, you barely feel wind impact due to the high volume of G-force. All this occurs without ABS.

I know this is extremely controversial, because most of you feel safe having ABS, and it was probably a purchase decision. There's a reason why ABS isn't in motorcycle racing, and that's literally the indicator for why you're not 'that' safe. Don't worry, because ABS also has its positives for where you're at right now, but I'll come back to this later. So why is this more or less technical subject in a book like this? It's because this is also a thing which can make you live in a fantasy world.

False Hope

Do you know those comparison videos? There's a non-ABS bike which has helper-bars/wheels installed so that the demonstrator can't crash, versus an ABS bike on slippery ground. When watching this, you might conclude that ABS is the way to go, while what I see is quite some BS.

My first argument is a little thin but it has value. In the picture below, the amount of cat litter they've been rolling on is unrealistically high. That's maybe a one in a million chance to happen, but it could. A more realistic comparison would be on dry asphalt, which is what you're rolling on, 99% of the time.

However, while you see the ABS bike do its job perfectly, you see the non-ABS bike lose control and slide on those helper bars in no time. Is that an objective comparison though? I'd say no, because the rider on the non-ABS bike is just flipping the damn switch. He's not even trying not to end up on the helper bar! Now you put Rossi on that bike. He might have ABS look bad, because he'd very likely be able to brake at a more consistent rate, instead of on/off/on/off.

Physics of Travel Extension

Now we're looking at the way ABS is designed. Let's keep it simple here though. A sensor at the wheel/s tells the control module that it deals with a locked wheel and releases brake power to a certain amount, and then back to full brake power. Back in the days when ABS came out, it was literally fully releasing all braking power and then back to full brake power, which was a wild horseback ride. Yes, that's been dramatically smoothed out over time, but it still comes with that one downside, and that's the fact that ABS actually extends your braking travel, just because of the way it's designed:

The line should be a consistent peak force, but ABS creates a sawtooth pattern of ON/OFF/ON/OFF.

This is why ABS isn't in motorcycle racing, because the guys would have to brake earlier! The ABS opens and closes the brake/s in a certain frequency, so in other words, from one extreme (full lock) to another extreme (full release). That's the brake travel extension right there.

Concluding, a rider can learn to brake 'just that much on the tire limit, well dosed to not to lock the wheel,' to have a more consistent braking travel/absorption. Yes, you will need to get there, but once you are, you will agree with me that at a certain rider level, ABS is in the way of being able to stop sooner, and that could be the difference of being alive or dead. At this point, I actually believe that no software/computer should take away available braking power from my survival chance. I know that's harsh, but think about it please.

The Sportscar Experiment

Look, I encountered its real value when I finally had a sports car which came with ABS. You might know that ABS is designed to keep a car steerable under braking. So here I was in an icy parking lot to explore what it can do for me. I slammed the brakes as they said I could and the ABS gave me brake on/off impulses. Now while this was happening, I started to steer to the right as they said I could. What happened was way different though, because when ABS gave brake ON, the car kept pushing forward even when you steer right and when the ABS gave brakes OFF, the car was pushing straight forward on the ice. Yea! All it was, was like a robotic motion to the right, kinda with the pulse of the ABS. That isn't how you make an escaping gap!

I did the experiment again, but this time I slammed the brake and when ABS came on, I faded out on brake pedal pressure till ABS was off, and all of a sudden, the car was making a right turn while I was slowing down.

The Crutch

So, if you have ABS, you could turn it off. I won't ask you to do that because it ain't all bad. That's of course depending on where your level is at right now. ABS will cover your 'panic grab,' which will be there when you're low on skill yet and you don't have the mental coolness to not overact. It also gives you another 'sensor' for the tire limit, and that might make you able to judge if you can make it on the brakes, or to have to hit that escaping gap. Well, your level of mental coolness will show by then. So yea, it ain't all bad.

Though, if you want to keep living with it, I suggest practicing emergency braking till ABS kicks in, so that YOU KNOW how that feels like. If you don't know, and that thing kicks in, you're very likely going to come off the brake because that sensation is new to your brain, and so to give up on braking travel.

Linked System Theft

You may have a linked braking system with ABS, where a controller sends 70% of available braking power to the front and 30% to the rear automatically? If so, I just hope you can turn it off, because you've been robbed of pure braking power. That controller takes away 30% of braking force and so, in turn, 30 damn percent of survival chance. If you can shut it off, then make experiences with it. You probably entirely disagree, but the moment you shut the linked system off—that will be the moment you agree with me because you're going to feel that extra braking force immediately.

Seeing is Believing

Lucky you, if you have a bike with adjustable ABS, it's possible to adjust its sensitivity. Then I suggest you do a big experiment. Do it and you'll agree with me if you still have doubts about my arguments here.

Go to a parking lot and have chalk with you.

Put ABS in the highest possible sensitivity.

Put out a rock to mark the place where you start braking.

Come in 2nd gear at 30mp/h and brake from the rock DOWN INTO ABS at full braking power. This and your speed need to be very accurate throughout the experiment.

Mark the spot where you came to a full stop and name the ABS level to it.

Now you lower the ABS level and do exactly the same drill again, until you're down to level one of ABS sensitivity.

There you'll see that the more you lower the ABS level, the shorter your braking travel has become. Now imagine what a well-trained rider could do without ABS. This will be an eye-opener, so do it!

Well, if you still struggle with all that practical logic, there will be the day when you find out yourself. And again… relax. It ain't all bad. As I described it in another chapter already, electronics make riders feel too safe and they skip on practicing. You CAN NOT rely on it. You NEED to practice emergency braking. This is your survival plan A!

Out-braking ABS

If, for whatever your reason is, you don't believe what I'm saying, there's a heck of a good video to watch:

ABS systems have been developing dramatically, and there will be the day when it overcomes human feel. That'll be the day when I can stop warning riders.

Psychological Takeaway

The brain naturally favors shortcuts. ABS provides cognitive ease, tempting you to stop developing the high-level feel required for threshold braking. This creates a mental check-out; when you delegate braking to a computer, you stop learning where the actual limit of grip lives. Relying on the "safety net" doesn't make you safer—it makes you less skilled.

There is a distinction between perceived safety and actual physics. ABS feels safe because it prevents skidding, but it functions by repeatedly releasing brake pressure. This "on-off" cycle often extends your total stopping distance. If you believe the technology is a magic shield, you may subconsciously increase your speed or decrease your following distance, unaware that you've traded a shorter stop for a more stable one.

If you've never triggered ABS, the violent pulsing through the lever during an emergency can cause a total attention hijack. The sensation is so alien that many riders instinctively let go of the brakes out of shock. You must familiarize yourself with this feedback in a controlled environment so that in a crisis, the pulsing is handled as a data point rather than a distraction.

Self-Efficacy vs. Automation

True survival depends on self-efficacy, the trust in your own ability to modulate pressure at the limit. Electronics should be your backup, not your primary plan.

I know you're most likely skeptical of what I'm saying here. If you are, go use the parking lot experiment to see the difference in stopping distances across different ABS settings. It'll be an eye-opener. Once you prove that a trained hand can out-stop the computer, you move from being a passenger to a pilot.

Hurt, Pain, and Dying

Even if it doesn't appear this way, racers are not on a suicide mission. It's just that they need the rush to feel alive, but that doesn't mean they like to get hurt.

The shocking truth is this: racers are less afraid of injury, pain, or even death, less as they're to not be able to race anymore.

That sounds messed up, doesn't it? In fact, top professional racers go down an average of twice a weekend during a typical season. At this level, crashing has simply become part of the game. It's so normalized that often, nobody on the team even asks why you've crashed, unless they see an opportunity in that crash to make the bike even better.

These racers are highly motivated aggressive machines. They're ego-driven, they're not team players, and they take no prisoners. But where the hell is the connection to you, the regular street rider or amateur racer?! Let's see.

Universal Instinct vs. The Contract

Mother Nature gave us a solid survival instinct, unless something is fundamentally wrong with you. EVERYONE has this, even Marc Márquez, just like all the other elite racers. You're not alone with this fear. Nobody wants to die. That single fact should provide you with a measure of relaxation already.

But elite racers are different because they're on a "bigger than life" mission. They signed a contract with themselves: to live with the possibility of getting hurt or even dying.

Crashing in MotoGP happens once or twice on average per race weekend. Their bodies are covered with scars and titanium plates. Blood, bandages, and the smell of some kind of pain-easing lotion on those bruises is your new aftershave cloud. Mick Doohan almost lost his leg; he re-joined the championship in the same year. Impressive, isn't it?

Or the legend of Jorge Lorenzo at Assen TT Circuit, Netherlands. He went down while qualifying and broke his collarbone in multiple pieces. That's hellishly painful. His arm hung down like the pointer of a broken watch. His lap times were promising a victory on Sunday afternoon. Lorenzo flew home to Barcelona, got immediate surgery, and flew back to the Netherlands, where he was on the podium the next day.

Don't you dare mention money as the motivator. If you think this way, you have never truly understood what commitment means. No, this is the same fundamental drive that makes a firefighter run into a burning house to save a kitten, while the average person says, "Forget that kitten."

I remember I crashed so hard at Bruno Circuit in Czechoslovakia in qualifying once. One of the highest high-siders I've ever had, landing on my hip bone. This is like dropping out of a 2nd floor window right onto the hip and adding about 90 miles an hour to it. It turned out it wasn't broken, but the bruises and pain made me walk like Quasimodo for four weeks. On the way home I called my team for tests at Nürburgring, where they had to lift me onto the bike. Guess what... I'd do it all again. Kinda f*cked up, isn't it?

So, what is this powerful, life-altering commitment?

Overriding Force

This commitment is something that's also stored inside you, and it needs to be discovered by yourself. Because everyone is different, the trigger is personal.

What is stronger than the fear of getting hurt, and at times can defeat the top level of all fears, the fear of dying? That's passion and love!

The pro racer's fear of not racing is greater than the fear of crashing because the loss of the passion is perceived as a greater death than the injury itself. The crash is a temporary setback; the loss of the ability to engage the passion is permanent emotional paralysis.

Signing Your Own Contract

I know you might not see yourself in this picture as a street rider, but you are! You don't have to sign such an intense commitment contract, but a fraction of that attitude is all you need to dramatically improve your riding. You must go and sign that contract of 'possibility to get hurt' with yourself.

By this, I'm not saying just go be fearless and purposely ride over your abilities. I'm saying to peacefully live with the possibility, and it will relax you. That's a way to stop living and riding in the "what if…" anxiety zone.

When you accept the possibility of the worst-case scenario, the power of that fear dissolves. You replace the energy of constant internal self-preservation with the powerful, calming energy of conscious commitment. Your primary fear will no longer be the crash, but the failure to execute your defined pattern, and that's a fear you can control.

Eliminating 'What If' with the Process Block

The final layer of fear reduction involves actively dismantling the mental habit of 'what if' thinking. This is the nervous noise—the stream of scenarios your brain generates when it lacks a constructive, immediate task: What if I miss the apex? What if the rear tire slides? What if I get hurt?

This type of thinking is the enemy of presence and precision because it forces your mind to live in a negative future rather than focusing on the present pattern.

Re-frame the Scenario

The pro racer has already signed the "contract of commitment," meaning the possibility of injury has been accepted as a prerequisite. Therefore, the "what if" thought is already answered.

When a 'what if' occurs: Instead of letting the thought spiral into fear, immediately and consciously provide the committed, accepted answer.

Amateur Thought	Master Counter-Thought
"What if I crash here?"	"So what? If I crash, the bike is 'Nuts n' Bolts,' and I've accepted the risk. My focus is the next pattern."
"I made a mistake, now I'm scared."	"I'm going to fix it and do better next lap/turn"

By instantly answering the negative hypothetical with a statement of acceptance and commitment, you rob the 'what if' of its paralyzing power. You stop wasting precious cognitive bandwidth on things you can't control.

Process Block

As detailed in the Chaos Control chapter, your mind must be engaged in an active, precise task. The "what if" is the mental space that opens up when your mind is idle.

The moment you feel anxiety creeping in, instantly force your attention back to the smallest, most immediate physical pattern you need to execute:

Lock onto the next pattern. Throttle roll-on. Eyes to the next way point. Breathe.

You are essentially mental gardening: pulling out the weed of the "what if" thought and immediately planting the seed of a defined action. This practice of mindfulness through physical action is the only way to ensure the energy of your commitment is channeled into performance, not wasted on anxiety.

Accept the fact that you could get hurt, and that will lead to relaxation. Relaxation leads to inner peace. Inner peace helps you make fewer mistakes.

Hammer and Nail

Up for an experiment?

Go make a self-experiment (under your own responsibility of course). Go hammer a nail into a wall by constantly worrying about those fingers of yours. You'll start shaking and sweating. Your hand which leads the hammer towards the nail tenses, and you're very likely about to be in pain.

Now reset. Before you hit, you take a second to breathe out and look at that nail, just as if you'd have done this a thousand times before. Your shoulders are dropping in relaxation, and now you're telling yourself "I might hit my fingers, but that's okay." I'm not saying hit harder or faster. You do this in your comfort zone.

I wonder what the difference is going to be, because there's still a fair chance of missing that damn nail. But replacing the pressure of '... I better hit that nail man,' with a relaxed body and soul, your chance of hitting that nail on its head is quite a bit bigger. Hey, even if you really miss and hit your finger. I bet that you even deal with the consequential pain easier, with less anger. Don't you think?

Inner peace, baby!

Psychological Takeaway

You're paralyzing yourself with 'What If' scenarios. That anxiety is the handbrake on your performance.

The "commitment contract" is the conscious decision to accept worst-case scenarios (injury or death) as a prerequisite for performance, transforming fear into conscious commitment and securing inner peace.

Fear of Loss vs. Contract of Acceptance

For master riders, the fear of not being able to engage their passion (a "greater death") is stronger than the fear of injury or pain. For you, signing a "commitment contract" means moving from the anxious "what if" zone to peaceful acceptance of the worst-case scenario. This controlled act of fear dissolution robs that fear of its paralyzing power, liberating immense mental energy. This liberation is the key to focus.

The Power of Reframing

The "what if" stream of thought is the nervous noise of an idle, fearful brain, the enemy of presence and precision. The solution is a cognitive restructuring technique: immediately confront and defeat the "what if" with a statement of acceptance and commitment. For example, the anxious thought, "What if I crash here?" is instantly countered with: "So what? If I crash, the bike is 'Nuts n' Bolts,' and I've accepted the risk. My focus is the next pattern." This stops the anxiety spiral and reclaims cognitive bandwidth.

Channel Commitment into Action for Inner Peace

The "process block" is your practical tool. Since "what if" anxiety thrives when your mind is idle, the moment it creeps in, you must instantly force attention back to the smallest, most immediate physical pattern. The ultimate psychological reward of acceptance is relaxation (like the hammer-and-nail experiment). Relaxation leads to inner peace, which in turn leads to fewer mistakes and greater precision. Your commitment ensures your energy is channeled into controlled performance rather than wasted on paralyzing internal self-preservation.

Stop fighting the inevitable. Sign your commitment contract, embrace acceptance, and transform paralyzing anxiety into precise, peaceful action.

▓ Mind Note – Tradeoff

"The only thing we have to fear is fear itself—nameless, unreasoning, unjustified terror which paralyzes needed efforts to convert retreat into advance."

- Franklin D. Roosevelt

About Commitment

A Fraction of it is All You Need

Anyway, I can see why you might not see the benefit for yourself as a street rider in this book. But let me tell you that there's value for you here as well. Like what? Let's call it 'commitment.'

Think of it. Marc Márquez crashed 108 times, and that's only during the time in premier class, not even including the years since he threw a leg over a bike the first time. The total number of crashes and injuries must be astronomical. The pinnacle of crashing was in 2023, where he went down 5 times at the German Grand Prix.

But not like simple drops. Some real bad shit, man. Additionally, fan cult and press made him the villain of the sport. Something you also gotta deal with on the mental side. That however, is something he turned over to an unleashed will. This shit can either break you, or it powers you up.

Despite all this, he made the impossible possible, only with two 'weapons'... competitiveness and commitment! After an actual career-ending crash and many surgeries later, that 8-time world champion became an under-dog.

Then he signed a contract, way under his value—with a hell of a smart success bonus clause—to become a factory rider again. He broke one record after another in absolute dominance and became world champion. The biggest comeback in all of sports history!

Triggers: competitiveness, commitment, fear of failure, AND everything else you can read in this book.

And you're still not seeing yourself in any of these pictures, when you drop your bike in a parking lot? When your suit and bike got a scratch and you have a little rash on your wrist. When your ego gets hurt the most and you feel embarrassed, and your brain is in a constant loop of "what if that had happened on a fast turn," and "I should stop riding now."

Wake up! Accept things the way they are. You fight with a sword; you'll get a cut! You play with fire; you'll get a burn. Live with this philosophy and you'll start learning from all of it, including the dark side of riding motorcycles. For you, a fraction of this kind of spirit and power of will is all it takes sometimes.

Psychological Takeaway

A parking lot drop is a "mental crash" for street riders. You have to stop treating a mistake as a reason to quit and start treating it as the entry fee for mastery.

Elite commitment is the transmutation of negatives. When Márquez crashed 108 times, he wasn't failing; he was paying for data. Most street riders let a single scare drain their confidence, but the "pro spirit" uses that scare as fuel.

I am not saying go crash, but a fraction of that kind of spirit will do the f'n job for you. Commitment is the decision to accept the inherent risk upfront so you can finally learn how to handle the machine. It's the equalizer that allows you to stop being a victim of your own nerves.

Embrace commitment as your psychological equalizer. Transform negatives into fuel, accept the inherent risks, and cultivate even a fraction of that unbreakable will to push beyond setbacks and unlock your full potential.

※ Mind Note – Coach's take

"I have you doing things in this class you never heard of. Stuff you'll think is physically impossible to do. It'll change everything you believe to know!"

— *Can Akkaya*

Reestablishment of the Hurt

There is a saying in the motorcycle community: "The question isn't if you're going down. It's when are you going down!" Pretty dumb, but this is what it really is, no matter what level or category of rider you are. That goes for racers, track riders, and all street riders. For racers, though, it's easier for them to deal with it. We're not even talking about it when coming back to the pit crew, unless there was a technical problem. For the regular rider, it's a big deal.

Why Crash Acceptance Comes Easier for Pros

Adaptation. You can get used to crashing. It's part of the job.

Mission focus. They're on a mission with clear goals. Their focus immediately snaps back to the objective.

Acceptance. They knew and accepted the inherent risk when they signed up.

Physicality. They're athletes who know how to take a hit, and they know 'how to crash.'

But mainly, it's because the professional does the opposite of what the amateur does. The regular street rider can't stop looking down on the broken bike he loved so much. The rider can't stop thinking about it, and what might have got him there. They're overly analyzing the shit out of the scenario, which the brain replays in a constant loop.

Search for an Excuse

Most of the time, this loop is just a 'search for an excuse.' And you need that excuse not just for others, in order not to look too bad, but mainly for yourself. A good excuse or a smooth reason why you went down makes it easier for you to open that wallet and come back to riding.

The problem: most riders actually don't know why they crashed, unless someone else is truly at fault. They say they don't know, but maybe this is just another ego protection, or the hope for an easy resolution for a comeback? They might also have a hard time admitting that they are at fault, which is a fact at 100% since there was nobody else involved. I've seen riders under the power of denial driving back out to the place where they laid it down, just to understand it. At that point, all you're doing is running what you know about it in that loop again and again and it gets even more frightening. Your brain tries to construct something that releases you from reliability as good as possible, but subconsciously you actually know that you f'd it up. That's the stone-cold truth.

Denial Loop

We had a student crash during our cornering class at Little 99 Raceway. He swore to God that he wouldn't know why he went down on exiting T4. At this point you need to know that Turn 4 is the easiest turn on our track and almost a straight line when done right.

Knowing this, we gave this crash a 99.99% cause due to stupidity or a tech issue, so he blamed the track for being slippery. We countered with logic, bringing to attention that none of the other 29 students were falling. Then. he blamed the tires instead.

This is truly exhausting, because we saw him being aggressive, inconsistent, and rough. He insisted on going to T4 to analyze, and all that was to see there were scratch marks on the asphalt, which indicated that he must have been on an extreme, irrational line. He refused to believe that, but it turned out that another student caught the scene on camera. The truth was that he had to go behind a slower rider and, to entertain himself, he was doing huge zig-zags. He made them so big that he ended up being almost off the track on dirt. Now here is what he said: "I don't remember that."

I really don't want to bore you with this story, but even later after class he said things like "…still, I'm not sure." Needless to say, we replied with a good-bye. However, this is how hard you can make it on yourself and others. Hammering this untruth into your own head until you believe it yourself.

Simple Response

There are many ways to make the whole situation easier on yourself.

The racer ignores it and shows how f'n bad ass he can be.
The track rider just says 'seems I've tried too hard.'
The street riders say 'well, I guess I f'd up.'

No overanalyzing, no brain research for an absolution. If you do just that, you actually allow your brain to sort it out: I target fixated, I tensed up and disallowed the bike to lean, and ran off the road. This is the learning effect you'll be missing out on otherwise.

Reestablishing Your Will

Whether you get hurt or not, your soul will be hurt. So… Now what?!

No Injury. Let's pretend you didn't get hurt. You could look down to the scuffs on your riding gear and try to squeeze a smile out while saying "seems I got away with a black eye here." If you do that, you will be very likely also taking the damage to your bike easier. Trust me, that smile is hard to push out, but I had to smile once just from trying so hard to smile. And boom, it was all easier from there!

Injury. Now let's say you actually got injured. Yea, that hospital stay could buy you a lot of time to analyze the crap out of it. But what if you're not and don't ask your friend to bring a pic of your broken bike, and just ask if it's worth repairing. Instead, you could ask them to bring the marketplace motorcycle section and demonstrate how bad ass you can be!

When your relatives ask what happened, you either say "oh well, I f'd up", or you might say the truth and that you target fixated, and both ways could end up with a "but hey, you know how much I love riding!", and smile! From there, everything will go easier. For you, and for them!

There is just that mental scar you'll have on your soul for the rest of your days. See it like a reminder of what not to do. You might find some real good 'scar lotion' in terms of education, and you might forget the sting.

Psychological Takeaway

Your brain uses denial to create false absolution, sacrificing critical learning for the sake of ego protection. This triggers the denial mechanism, and your brain's attempt to minimize personal fault. The over-analysis loop is often a search for an external scapegoat to "absolve" you.

When you construct an external excuse, Loss of Learning is the critical cost: your brain fails to update its risk assessment, guaranteeing a repeat performance. This reinforces fear. By not owning the mistake, the cause remains external, breeding helplessness, the mindset of the victim rider. The internal fight against truth is mentally draining.

Trauma Integration & Resilience

Ownership as empowerment is key: saying "I f'd up" shifts the locus of control back to the internal. You own the solution. Emotional regulation signals acceptance, reducing the emotional scar. The "scar lotion" (education) transforms the "mental scar" from paralyzing fear into a learning cue. Education provides the specific tools to avoid repeating the mistake, processing the event as a costly lesson.

Take responsibility. Embrace ownership, and apply the "scar lotion" of education. This is the only path for a crash to become a powerful catalyst for growth.

❀ Mind Note – Coach's take

"All you're looking for is to get pulled on a fast lap, and hope you can establish without knowing the exact how's and why's. Well, good luck then."

— *Can Akkaya*

Growing Balls

We've already discussed the actual meaning of 'confidence,' but there's something else riders are hiding behind that word. What they're *actually* saying is, "I need to have bigger balls." Besides the deep-seated expectation that exactly *this* is going to happen within the next hour, they also shut down when it doesn't. At that point, they stop even trying to see the problem. They fall into a stubborn statement like, "That was a waste of time." They won't even ask for advice or what to try next, because subconsciously they know what's coming: probably something they won't 'like hearing.'

This is Martial Arts. Not a Video Game.

Look, if you want to learn to play the piano at its best, your natural expectation is to first master the deep fundamentals, to repeat constant loops until they're ingrained, to get through challenging passages over and over. That attitude toward the process often doesn't exist for some when it comes to riding motorcycles. For them, it seems to be all about "balls."

Now, let's add the possibility of death and costly repair bills to the game. In addition to that, there's the crushing weight of embarrassment challenging such a rider's manhood. While listening organs are overwritten, brain functions are down by 50%. That rider, in desperation, asks for the final straw... "Can't you just pull me on a fast lap?" Needless to say, this isn't just happening with some track riders. This is happening in any category of riding. Sometimes, they even ask to go and demonstrate—"How fast can you go?"—hoping a visual demonstration will magically imbue them with skill. In the end, they're just looking for a shortcut so they don't actually have to talk and learn about it. My response to nonsense like this is simple and covers a lot: "Son, I'm not a circus clown. I'm trying to make you become a Samurai, who is willing to flex the bow for three years before he actually uses an arrow to shoot. This is martial arts. Not a video game. If you let me, I'llbe able to polish your balls, pet them, keep 'em warm, and yeah, they might grow a little throughout... but for now, I'll have to work with your existing size of balls!"

This is quite a wake-up call, isn't it?! What frustrates me is that there's only a 50:50 chance of an actual wake-up happening. Well, let's discover what the reasons for this might be.

Psychological Takeaway

The "bigger balls" mindset fundamentally conflates bravery with competence. True confidence is the result of mastery, precise inputs, and risk management, not a prerequisite for reckless speed. This error is rooted in an ego-driven performance identity: riding is linked to self-worth, and admitting fear or lack of skill is seen as a blow to your ego. This makes you resistant to the slow, methodical process of learning that requires humility. The demand for "being fast" is an attempt to absorb skill through osmosis, avoiding the painful work of practice.

Psychological Barriers to Mastery

Your demand for instant gratification is repulsed by delayed mastery. When the expected breakthrough isn't delivered, you shut down and resist instruction because it clashes with your desire for shortcuts. Subconsciously, you harbor a fear of "unlikable truths," anticipating that genuine improvement involves confronting your weaknesses and slowing down. Things that are counter-intuitive and ego-bruising. This "bigger balls" mentality often implies an external locus of control, that speed is an attribute one can "acquire" from a coach, rather than an internal capacity painstakingly built through effort and repetition.

❈ Mind Note – Coach's take

"Confidence isn't about having bigger 'balls.' It's about knowing your limits and pushing them with precision, not bravado."

— *Can Akkaya*

Fear Tradeoff

We all know fears, and we exposed a ton of them already. They come in many variations, even turning into anxieties, like the fear of *being* fearful. As a young kid starting to get really good at it, I literally rejected having fears. I lived and rode in total denial. I acted the part of the fearless guy, but I always knew I faked it. Kinda funny when you think of it, isn't it?!

In the middle of my amateur racing career, I was closely following MotoGP. That was at a time when these guys dealt with 500cc two-stroke rockets that had no electronic aids at all. All I did was try to pick something up from everyone: Wayne Rainey's analytical style, Mick Doohan's mental strength, and Kevin Schwantz's aggressive riding style. All of them seemed extremely impressive while making no signs of being fearful.

One day, Kevin announced his retirement, and I believe he said something like, "...I don't have to be scared to death anymore." Now, how impressive is that? A rider of that caliber tells the world on a hot microphone that he was scared. I was shocked. Deeply. Now who the hell am I, denying to be fearful?!

But how in the world did they do this? Casey Stoner said something similar, but while he was on the track, the man looked like a completely different person. Fear often exposes itself through body language. There was never anything like that. There must have been something in them that allows them to shut it all off while being a relentless warrior, but after the fact, it comes down on them like black rain.

At that point, I began to believe that this control is possible by working with fears as a tradeoff. To use fears and to identify weak points in order to become even better. I began to understand the fact that the higher the level is, the less it's about physical riding skill, and the more it's about who is defeating and controlling fears best.

A pinpoint example is Casey Stoner. His approach on Turn 3 at Phillip Island in Australia was quite spectacular. Besides his elegance, he was power-sliding there *because* he was afraid to lose the front tire on that turn. He was about a second faster, based on fears. "...it was the safest way for me," he stated. Now, how badass is that?!

Needless to say, I discovered a lot for myself and the rest of my racing career. I'm certain that this Fear Tradeoff can reflect on any category of motorcycle rider, just on a different level and for a different purpose: Safety and Precision.

Fear Tradeoff for the Street Rider

The street rider doesn't need to power-slide to be safe, but the core psychological mechanism—using fear to enforce a safer, better technique—is exactly the same. The fear tradeoff means acknowledging a specific fear and deliberately *channeling* that anxiety into a concrete, safer input.

How to Use Your Fear as an Advantage

The fear tradeoff means recognizing that fear isn't a weakness; It's your subconscious mind flagging a point of failure in your risk management program. The amateur rider freezes, or denies the fear. The master rider uses that signal to identify the precise technical input required to perform better.

Your fear is your most honest coach. Listen to it, understand what it's pointing at, and then use your mental aggression to commit to the safer, more disciplined action. You don't eliminate the fear; you simply channel its energy into perfection.

Psychological Takeaway

You are likely living in total denial, acting the part of the fearless ride. This is a psychological dead-end. When you deny your fear, you're overriding genuine risk signals with your ego. Realize that the highest level of riding isn't all about physical skill; it's about who defeats and controls their fear best. If you stop trying to be the "fearless guy," you can finally start using that emotional energy.

Your data stop treating fear as a weakness and start treating it as data, flagging a specific point of failure in your risk management. You don't need more courage; you need a fear tradeoff. You must trade the energy of your panic for the power of precision.

Trading panic for precision true mastery is the transformation of fear. You don't eliminate the signal; you repurpose it.

Fear flags the gap in your skill. Your job is to use that emotional urgency to trigger a disciplined, automated response. Acknowledge the signal, listen to what it's pointing at, and channel that energy into perfect execution.

You can't eliminate fear. Acknowledge it, listen to its signal, and channel its energy directly into disciplined, corrective technique. Trade the energy of panic for the power of precision.

❊ Mind Note – Coach's take

"Don't get me wrong. I love my bikes, and I love modifying the crap out of them. But the moment I put my ass on that seat- I'm the captain on the ship, and I ask it to function as expected. Nut's n' bolts baby!"

— *Can Akkaya*

Protective Reactions

The Demon's Deadly Command

Everyone has a demon sitting on their shoulder, a primal voice waiting to hijack control. Nobody is free of this guy. We are not robots, and every human decision, even on a motorcycle, is colored by momentary fear or anxiety. Pro racers are also not immune; they too possess a fundamental survival instinct. The only difference is that their mental "panic bar" is set exponentially higher than yours. The key question is: What, and how, do we deal with that demon once that bar is reached?

I guarantee you've experienced this countless times. It's that split-second on a turn when a flicker of insecurity flashes—*is this going to end well?* That's the moment the demon pops up, and his first command is to trigger a 'protective reaction'.

That term sounds positive, doesn't it? As if your body is saving you. But in the context of high-performance riding, this reaction is the very mechanism that gets riders hurt.

Panic Cascade

The instant you feel 'too fast' on a corner, a cascade of disastrous events begins—all triggered by the demon:

The "Oh Shit" tense-up. Your subconscious floods the system with adrenaline. You stop breathing, and every muscle tenses. This stiffens your entire chassis and immediately sends stress through the handlebars, making the bike twitchy.

Vision collapse (target fixation). Your eyes go down, narrowing your field of view onto the asphalt directly in front of the bike. The demon tells you to look at the very thing you fear: the patch of dirt, the guardrail, or the tree where you're supposed to die. The further down you look, the faster and more terrifying the scenery rushes by.

The panic inputs. Following the demon's lead, you either chop the throttle (a massive weight shift forward, which could cause the rear to slide) or, worse, grab the brakes simultaneously (could cause a lost front wheel).

Standing the bike up. You instinctively yank the bike upright, which is the safest-feeling position for the human body, and immediately lose your ability to steer, sending you hurtling off the road.

All of this happens within 1 to 2 seconds, but the intense focus makes it feel like an eternity.

Failure of Bandwidth

This is the deadly trap of the protective reaction. It sounds positive, but it's the shit riders really get hurt from. Your bar was reached, and panic took you over. The demon made you narrow your sight and overreact. While you *feel* faster than ever before, you've probably been never slower than that exact moment.

This leads to false judgment and disastrous decision-making. You weren't at the mechanical limit; you were at the mental limit and beyond.

I have seen this too many times: riders recall these protective reactions, run off the track, remain hard on the brakes on the dirt, and immediately tuck the front wheel. Collarbone broken, pretty much for no good reason because they were still miles away from the bike's technical limit. They report, "I was going too fast."

No. Technically, you weren't too fast. You just followed that voice in your head, and that demon lied to you.

The master's speed is managed by instinctive precision (unconscious competence). The crashing rider's speed is ruined by primitive self-preservation (protective reaction). True safety lies not in being slow, but in raising that mental bar until the demon's voice is just a whisper you choose to ignore.

Too Good to Be True

Now, what's the help here? The solution might sound deceptively simple, but it has worked for me and for hundreds of students who have gone through our programs. I don't claim it works on everyone, but it's the essential starting point for regaining control.

Red Flag Response Sequence

Your body is the first warning sign; it throws up a series of Red Flags long before the crash happens. You need to train yourself to listen and see them coming:

Tension? RED FLAG.

Target Fixation? RED FLAG.

Holding Your Breath? RED FLAG.

Your body is the beginning of the panic sequence. The demon starts talking, and your mind begins the process of surrender. Responding to that red flag is key to cutting the connection.

The Counter-Command

The solution is to physically talk it away, loudly and clearly into your helmet.

This strategy works because it forces your brain to execute a conscious command instead of defaulting to the primal, 'I give up' process. You're immediately making your brain busy with a corrective action rather than allowing it to be hijacked by panic.

For example:

The demon. "Oh, you're too fast! Look at that tree where you're going to die!"

Your counter-command. "EYES UP! LOOK THROUGH! BREATHE!"

You must deliver this command to yourself clearly and with conviction.

Conviction is the Core

You must instantly convince yourself that you can handle this, and that you're technically not too fast.

Don't follow that voice. Fight it with every cell in your body. When the demon tells you to chop the throttle, your voice must command, "Hold the line!" When the demon tells you to tense up, your voice must command, "Loose hands! Breathe!" This aggressive act of self-talk is the only way to re-establish conscious control over the protective instincts that are trying to kill you.

Psychological Takeaway

Your primitive survival instinct is a damn liar. When you hit your "panic bar," your brain triggers a protective reaction. The "oh shit" tense-up, vision collapse, and panic inputs. While these feel like your body is trying to save you, they are actually a cognitive bandwidth collapse. You aren't reaching the bike's mechanical limit; you're hitting a mental wall where fear overloads your ability to process speed.

The demon on your shoulder tells you to stare at the guardrail and chop the throttle, effectively guaranteeing the crash you're trying to avoid.

Safety requires you to recognize red flags before they turn into a funeral. Holding your breath or white-knuckling the f'n bars are early-warning signals that you're about to surrender control to the demon. If you don't intercept these physiological cues immediately, the panic sequence becomes an automated script. You have to train yourself to see tension as a signal that your judgment is failing long before the tires actually lose grip.

The Counter-Command

Physically shouting "EYES UP! LOOK THROUGH!" into your helmet, is a cognitive circuit breaker. It forces your brain to execute a conscious, functional instruction instead of defaulting to a primal "I give up" response. By barking these orders with conviction, you re-engage your brain's pilot and silence the panic. You must substitute the destructive instinct of self-preservation, and prevent letting the demon steer; take the bars back.

Anxieties

The Fun Killer

While we define 'fears' as that momentary panic grab, I think 'anxieties' are actually worse. They're potential fun killers, aren't they?! Anxieties are the thoughts, visions, and feelings which can make you have sleepless nights, or even bad dreams.

I think we don't actually have to go deeper and agree what anxieties are leading up to than this: physical anxiety symptoms are bodily reactions to perceived threats, including a racing heart, sweating, trembling, and shortness of breath. These can also include muscle tension, headaches, stomachaches, and feeling dizzy or weak. That goes into creating hold backs, constant mental and physical tensions, killing fun, numbs motivation, leads to frustrations, panic attacks, or even into real mental sickness.

When I was a young amateur racer, I discovered that I could deal with momentary fears easier. Using them as a trainer for my reflexes and to trigger physical riding skills. That doesn't work with anxieties, so my goal was to work on just that.

I don't want to bore you with these lists, but I think it's a necessity to see the spectrum of anxieties. However, I was aware that anxieties are part of the game and that these are part of human nature. In other words, I won't be really successful defeating them. Finding ways to 'reduce the pain' was what I was aiming for.

Well, let me start with a funny one:

Spectrum of a Rider's Mind-F*ck

Anxieties of having anxieties

Anxieties of getting into fears

Anxieties of getting into trouble

Anxieties of getting hurt/injuries/dying

Anxieties of failure/performing

Anxieties of losing/winning

Anxieties of causing hurt to someone else

Anxieties of running into debris/deer's/cars

Anxieties of darkness/rain/heat

Anxieties of your tires (trust)

Anxieties of riding around blind turns

Anxieties of left turns/right tuns

Anxieties of uphill/downhill roads

Anxieties of lane splitting

Anxieties of your suspensions (trust)

Anxieties of speed/brakes

Anxieties of technical issues

Anxieties of breaking something/damage

Anxieties of embarrassment

Anxieties of the unknown and coincidences

Anxieties of running out of gas (which makes you go see a gas station as double as much)

Etc. etc. etc. (you go complete your list!)

Needless to say, this list is way extendable. But let's be done with that and go right into a phenomenon I just can't get a grasp of:

Because you're sitting there all night—fully aware of your anxieties or not—and watching another motorcycle crash compilation video on YouTube!!!??? What's that for? Trying to make everything harder on you, or are you subconsciously looking for an argument why you shouldn't ride anymore? These would be the only two logical arguments for this, well, unless you have a fetish for seeing someone's femur/bones sticking out of the flesh. Tell me, because I don't understand it.

Some riders I asked say that they're trying to learn something from it. Really? What might that be? Learning how to smash someone's mirror off the car? How to flip the bird? Learning that probably at a time, that the rider got himself into all those situations? Well, that would be a good one!

Dealing With This

Why am I telling you all this? Well, you and your surroundings are the designers of your anxieties. You need to learn to identify and to remove the potential for more anxieties you're possibly putting up onto yourselves.

Easy to Deal With

Just like watching all those senseless videos—self-imposed pressure and whatnot. I'm sure you know that there are comparable things around you to work on. Those are the easy ones actually, so how about just skipping on this crap for once!

Medium to Deal With

I think these here are mostly based on trust issues. Mostly about riding or around the bike itself, let's say about not trusting your tires. There are a few options here. One would be to just buy new/different tire sets. The other one is to find ways to start actually believing in them, like logically saying to yourselves: "...man, these tires are made for millions of riders around the world, and they're tested by people who are making millions of dollars per year. They should be fine for where I'm at!" Kinda like a logical self-convincing thing.

Or when you feel anxieties taking you away, you could start singing, or talk yourself into the riding process: "here is my entry, let's read the line to the apex..." Use breathing techniques and command your muscles to relax. Lean back mentally, as if you're sitting on a sofa and watching a movie. I'm sure when you now look into yourself, you'll find something useful here.

Hardcore to Deal With

This anxieties category won't ever go away, unless you're forced to, just like racers, who are dropped off like Marines right into enemy territory every day. Anxiety of getting badly injured or to die is in this category. Everything you could die for/with in life, will always come with that bad taste. However, I loved to race so much that I'd have died for it, just like a Marine who swore to protect and to die for it. Kinda a pride goes along with it and your badassness can shine to the outside of your body, if this is making sense.

But there are less dramatic forms of anxieties and solutions. Let's take 'Fear of failure' as an example. This one can be actually useful. The fear of failure can unleash extreme strengths when well balanced. Yes, you could also apply to convince yourself, to sing—even lie to yourself: "...I love who I'm and what I do right now. I love this bike. I love these tires" ... even if you maybe don't actually. It can be whatever helps to get you through the moment.

Help Yourself

By now, you've read a lot in this book, and I'm very sure you'll see things of use. Yin & Yang, equalizing negative vs. positive, nuts n' bolts, or chaos control, just to name a few. As I said in other chapters. There's no healing for the hardcore stuff, but a way of reduction to an acceptable level. How much? That depends on your nature, of who you are, your mental and physical strength, and mainly on how old you are. I'm not sorry to say that, because go ask me how I know!

Rearview Mirror Effect

And how can I tell if a rider is full of it?! Besides only seeing a person's eyes or body language, the way the rider operates the bike is very telling. Or while riding, their head and eyes are all over the place—right, left, up n' down. They're extremely busy checking their rear-view mirrors... constantly. Not just a peek, no—for a significant amount of time.

What's lost is their actual path. You know, the way they would have more likely had an influence for prevention.

What are you looking for there, in those credit card-sized mirrors?! A semi-truck hitting you? How big is that chance if YOU did your job right so far?! Maybe a car out of control, slinging into your back? Sure that's a thing, but I doubt that you'd be somewhat in control from there, because from there, it'll be all about coincidences which you don't have an influence on.

Look... I'm not saying not to peek into your mirrors again. I don't! But there's too much. So much that also leads to anxieties. This is like being in a rock concert. You won't see a whole lot of that show when you're constantly looking back into the darkness, waiting for the beer to strike the back of your head. That's what that's like.

The "beer cans" are flying, if you like it or not. The chance is relatively small getting one to the back of your head. Trust, you have the tools in your skill box if there's a slight chance to prevent them. If you don't have those skill tools and you don't search for them... what does that make you?!

Psychological Takeaway

You're vibrating with chronic mental tension because you're living in a future that hasn't happened yet.

Anxiety is a profound "f'n fun killer" because it prevents the flow state, requiring active mental techniques to minimize and repurpose it.

It is critical to distinguish momentary fears (immediate, panic grabs) which train reflexes, from anxieties (chronic thoughts, visions) which are debilitating because they're future-oriented and non-specific. This consumed mental landscape wastes cognitive energy. The self-sabotage cycle is exemplified by watching crash compilation videos, and you actively feed your own fear.

The rearview mirror effect is a metaphor for anxiety-driven distraction: Your mind fixates on a past or uncontrollable future threat, sacrificing focus on your actual path. Worrying about what might happen behind you causes failure to focus on what is happening in front of you.

Reduction and Repurposing of Anxiety

The goal is reduction to an acceptable level through active mental techniques. Easy to deal with (self-control) requires removing self-imposed anxiety sources like senseless videos. Medium to deal with (logical convincing) involves using self-convincing ("These tires are made for millions of riders") and mental redirection (singing, commanding relaxation) to break the anxiety loop.

Hardcore to deal with (acceptance and reframing) dictates that anxieties related to death or injury can only be managed through acceptance and repurposing. "fear of failure" can be flipped into a useful motivator that "can unleash extreme strengths when well balanced." This includes self-convincing if it helps you through the moment.

Anchor your focus firmly in the controllable present. Repurpose your anxieties, reclaim your mental energy, and master the present moment.

❀ Mind Note – Coach's take

"It's not so much about how you went down. It's mostly about how you get back up!"

— *Can Akkaya*

Self-Imposed Pressure

Learning to Win

Have you ever noticed that moment when you realize you actually can win this thing—or you can hit that perfect lap time—but everything immediately turns into a mess?

Remember that ping-pong game against your competitive brother? The moment you get the advantage, the pressure causes your wrist to tense up and you miss the shot.

The poker game with the extreme pot: you bluff, but that extra bit of nervousness makes your hand tremble and gives away the tell.

The desperate married couple trying to conceive: they stop having fun, but after years of trying, they finally give up and relax about it… and suddenly, she's pregnant.

The common denominator is self-imposed pressure. The moment the goal shifts from process to outcome (from "playing" to "winning"), the primal brain activates, introducing chaos where there was calm.

Pole Position Panic

The more you're in this winning state, the less it pressures you. I know it sounds funny, but you literally have to mentally 'learn to win.'

I remember my very first pole position as an amateur racer. It looked extremely promising to win my first race. Man, the excitement kept me on high voltage all night. Or was it the pressure not to fail?

Standing there on pole position, I was scared to death to make a jump start. I literally froze up and was constantly overthinking the clutch lever. My focus was destroyed, my muscles tensed, and I even stopped breathing. My heart was racing. I didn't make a jump start—I came off the grid dead last!

But then, something kicked in which I didn't know about myself: a killer instinct with an unstoppable will to win, no matter what just happened. I felt instantly relieved from that pressure because the goal was no longer "don't screw up the start" but "hunt and survive."

I was a cornered tiger making it from last to fifth position in five laps, fighting without considering consequences—like a mama bear protecting her cubs. I could see the top four in front of me, and then, inevitably, I crashed.

Jekyll and Hyde Switch

Something essential happened to me there. It was the realization that there's a switch inside me that needed to be triggered. Put me in a 'nothing to lose' scenario, and you'll have a massive problem.

I figured that the mere search for that switch was making a difference already. I found out what literally turns me from a nervous Dr. Jekyll to an unstoppable Mr. Hyde without losing control.

I won't tell you what that trigger is. This is something personal which I don't want to share, and for the simple reason that everyone is different. You must find your own personal, constructive trigger to create your competitor persona. This impulse to search is fair enough to start your journey.

Consequences on the Street

Are you not seeing yourself as a street rider in this? You absolutely should, because you too, have a competitive nature—either against the clock, against a riding partner, or against yourself. The connection is undeniable.

We can use competitiveness as a motor to accelerate progress, but it's also one of the unhealthiest things you can do to your riding. You need to keep this energy in check because the consequences are painful, costly, and can lead into dark rooms of frustration.

The goal is to harness the 'killer instinct' without the 'consequences.' It's about performing as though you're in a 'nothing to lose' situation *before* the pressure of 'winning' locks up your wrist.

The Balance

The feeling of "self-imposed pressure" comes from focusing entirely on the outcome—the win, the fast lap, or the perfect pass. When the pressure mounts, your mental effort goes into *trying not to fail,* which is the precise moment you introduce chaos.

To achieve the necessary balance and neutralize this performance anxiety, you must shift your entire focus back to the process. This is how professionals "learn to win."

Winning Countermeasure

In the prior chapter, we discussed Chaos Control through establishing patterns. That lesson becomes your ultimate weapon against self-imposed pressure.

When the anxiety hits—when the starting light is about to drop, or when you feel the pressure of the guy behind you—your mind must instantly pivot away from the outcome and lock onto the next pattern.

By consciously forcing your mind to execute the very next physical step in your established pattern, you bypass the emotional, panicked brain and activate the part of your brain that handles automated, controlled action.

This isn't about ignoring the pressure; it's about repurposing the pressure. You take the nervous energy that would make you freeze and channel it into an aggressive, precise commitment to the immediate task. By nailing that one small pattern, you give yourself the confidence to nail the next one, which leads to the eventual, consequence-free win. This is the ultimate balance.

Psychological Takeaway

The moment you start obsessing over the win, you trigger a primal brain hijack. You lose your fine motor skills because you're thinking about the trophy instead of the turn. The moment you focus on "winning" or perfection, self-imposed pressure activates a fear-of-failure state, introducing chaos and sabotaging fine motor skills.

When "Winning" Causes Losing

The desire for a specific outcome triggers a shift from calm, "playing" behavior to a primal, fear-of-failure state. This primal brain hijack floods your system with anxiety, disrupting focus and breathing, and paralleling the destructive protective reaction cascade. The "nothing to lose" trigger demonstrates this. Peak performance often occurs when the pressure of winning is removed, freeing you from the constricting fear of failure. Unchecked competitiveness, while a motivator, is a double edge, creating pressure that leads to darn poor decision-making and chaos, especially on the street.

Counter Pressure with Pattern and Process

The core solution is a fundamental cognitive shift: from "I need to win this race" to immediate, patterned action: "Throttle at X, clutch out to friction point, eyes on first apex." This redirection actively disengages the anxiety-laden primal brain. The "winning countermeasure" is to leverage harmonized patterning (from "Chaos Control") as your ultimate weapon. Consciously pivot away from the outcome and lock onto the very next physical pattern. This skips the emotional brain and activates the part of your brain responsible for automated, controlled action.

Don't sabotage yourself with outcome-driven anxiety. Welcome the process, trust your patterns, and transform pressure into precision.

※ **Mind Note – Coach's take**

"Everything in life has an expiration date!"

— *Can Akkaya*

Pressure

Needless to say, that nothing is ever good by being under pressure. To learn to deal and to regulate how much it influences you—that's the trick. We already discovered a lot of types of pressure as they come from external and internal sources:

Self-imposed pressures

Based on fears pressure

Success pressure

Embarrassment pressure

Competitor pressure

Pressures are more or less situational, and how much you can absorb is also depending on your daily form, so what kind of shape you're in that day, mentally and physically. Pressure isn't constant; it increases or decreases based on the external context of the event. Sample key situational factors include:

Stakes of the outcome. A race for a World Championship title carries objectively more pressure than a mid-season test session.

Audience size. The presence of fans, cameras, investors, and rival teams directly increases the perceived pressure.

Familiarity. Competing at a new track or on new equipment is naturally more stressful than riding a familiar circuit on a familiar bike.

Your daily form determines your mental and physical resources for absorption. In short, the pressure is the weight of the expectations, and your daily form is the strength of the shoulders carrying that weight. Both determine your performance.

Pressure is a result of the external stakes multiplied by internal stress level. The ultimate freedom comes when you can trick your mind into thinking the stakes are low. You have to manufacture a "good day" feeling to keep up physically.

The Hornet Strategy

I personally could deal with pressure best when I analyzed 'the situation I'm in.' Most of the time the conclusion was that I had 'nothing to lose.' In that mental state, I was functioning at my best. However, there were situations when I could have lost it all. Finding a way to snap into it ain't that easy. Can you always be successful and end up doing what you wanted and needed to achieve? No, of course not, because this is also depending on how your opponent's use the pressure leverage on you. Wanna know what that kind of strategy would look like?

Let's say it's the final race of the season, and you're leading the championship points table that much, that coming in 3rd is enough for you to claim the champion title. Now that gives you some reason to relax and to make sure that you don't get hurt in all timing sessions, while I'd make sure that 'I'll be around you,' like an angry flock of hornets. So even I could get away from you during the race—I'd rather not leave you alone to create pressure on your soul.

Getting you into dog fights, breaking your focus, making you count points. Our little fights would give other opponents the opportunity to keep up, so that there's no way for you to drop off. You'd constantly hear and feel my presence. It'll be the longest race of your life!

See, knowing exactly what situation you need to master means knowing what kind of pressure will be coming at ya. If I were in 'your situation' there, I'd see what you're up to, based on 'your situation'. Just that, could keep pressure on me more regulated and would make my mind going into it more confident.

The Street Connection

Yea, I know you're not seeing this as valuable for your street riding. It's in there though. Your pressures and levels are just on a different scale. Mostly self-imposed or created by fears.

Like, buying a $35k bike gives you pressure to look good as a rider. Like, if you care too much what others think about your chicken strips. These kinds of pressures are more or less easy to strive off with a smile on the face and a "dude… I really don't care. Let's just enjoy this new bike."

Or, there's that rider passing you on the canyon road and higher stake pressures kicking in—failure, embarrassment (just to name a few). Then, when your ego kicks in—that's when it's getting hard to say "Nah, let it go man."

You might set yourself a goal and limits before you head out to your favorite canyon road. Knowing that these situations are a possibility, you say… "and I will let it go!" Hope you can see the connection now.

Also, YOU are a slave of success pressure. The more you want in your life as a rider, the more pressures there will be. You go do track days too early in your riding career and just based on this, I can tell ya that you're going to make a ton load of mistakes, based on these kinds of pressures. You'll deny seeing it, and so you keep going, wondering why you still have those chicken strips.

Psychological Takeaway

When you're red-lining your stress levels, your brain actually stops processing clearly. This is high alert leading straight to cognitive disruption.

When pressure spikes, your system transitions from fast, effective muscle memory to slow, destructive overthinking, resulting in a performance choke.

When High Alert Goes Wrong

When pressure spikes, your smart, fast, muscle-memory brain checks out. It hands control over to the slow, overthinking part of your mind. You stop riding and start thinking about riding ("Am I leaning enough?" "I shouldn't crash this $35k bike."). This overthinking stiffens your body, slows your reactions, and kills your feel for the limit, which is why mistakes happen when you push too hard.

The Trap

The second psychological killer is the collapse of your attention. High pressure shrinks your focus down to the single thing that's stressing you out. You stop seeing the corner exit and only see the opponent's front tire, or you lose tire feedback and only hear the voice counting points.

This is attentional tunneling: you lose the full picture and the peripheral awareness that keeps you safe and fast. Your brain becomes stuck fixating on the threat, not on the process of riding.

Don't let high alert become a choke. Learn to recognize the signs of overthinking and shrinking focus. Trust your training, expand your awareness, and remain focused on the process, not the threat, to enter the zone and perform at your peak.

※ Mind Note – Truth

"Most men would rather deny a hard truth than face it."

— *George R.R. Martin*

Being Desperate

I'm sure you also have some stories to tell about something you wanted so badly that it hurts. Boy, have I been in this kind of desperation many times. Desperation is generally a bad state to be in, but just like with some other mental cracks, this sword has two sides. Most of the time though, the desperation sword will cut your flesh with its rusty side, leaving ugly scars.

I like to define them as long-term desperation and short-term desperation. While, for me at least, long-term desperations seem to be more controllable. Like, at the beginning of the riding season, you set a desperate goal to achieve at the end. There are many 'distractions' down that long road that can pull you away from that intense, singular focus of desperation.

Short-term desperation though... oh boy. That's like when that street rider hits the road and sees another rider 'to chase,' overriding any self-awareness about whether they're even capable of keeping up. Or that desperation of trying to pull off a new personal best lap time, which completely overwrites the reality of the worn-out tire set you headed out with. Man, when I think of all the mental screw-ups that come together here, this is almost 'the hub' of some real bad shit going down. If you're not ending up in a hospital, you're setting yourself up for some deep mental wounds.

Here's how short-term desperation manifests and sabotages your ride:

Getting into aggressive mode. Not controlled aggression, but a frantic, ill-timed surge that throws off your rhythm.

Ego-driven decision-making. Prioritizing looking fast or winning over safety and proper technique.

Irrational thinking. Dismissing warning signs, ignoring limits, or believing you're invincible.

Target fixation. Locking onto the obstacle or the rider you're chasing, rather than looking through the turn.

Rushing inputs. Braking too hard, accelerating too early, or initiating steering too abruptly, leading to instability.

Loss of peripheral vision. Your tunnel vision narrows, making you miss critical environmental cues or escape routes.

Tightening up on the controls. A death grip on the handlebars, stiff arms, and locked knees, which prevents the bike from flexing and moving naturally beneath you.

Ignoring fundamental techniques. Abandoning your training and relying on brute force or luck instead of precise execution.

Poor body positioning. Becoming passive on the bike or actively fighting it, instead of flowing with its movements.

Compounding errors. Making one mistake and immediately trying to overcorrect with another desperate, ill-judged action.

Loss of enjoyment. The ride becomes a stressful ordeal, driven by internal pressure rather than the joy of motorcycling.

Identifying the Desperate Rider

You don't need a degree in psychology to spot desperation. It's often glaringly obvious in both the rider's actions and their results. For a coach, it's one of the first things I look for. For a rider, learning to recognize these signs in yourself is the crucial first step to breaking the cycle.

On the Track/Road

Choppy, jerky inputs. Their braking, steering, and throttle application lack smoothness. There are sudden, harsh movements rather than a fluid progression.

Late & harsh braking. Often braking too late for the corner, forcing aggressive lever pressure and making the bike unsettled.

Rushed corner entry. Trying to 'throw' the bike into the turn rather than smoothly initiating lean, often resulting in running wide or losing the front.

Early & aggressive throttle. Cracking the throttle open too soon or too violently, especially when the bike is still heavily leaned over, leading to rear-tire slides or loss of traction.

Erratic line choices. Inconsistent lines through corners, frequently adjusting mid-turn because they didn't set themselves up properly.

Overtaking aggression. Making risky, ill-advised passes simply to stay ahead or "prove a point," often with insufficient space or planning.

Stiff body language. Visibly rigid on the bike, not flowing with its movements. Head often pointed down or fixed on the ground in front of them, not looking far ahead.

Consistent near-misses. Frequently getting into situations where they almost crash or almost run off the road, but escape by luck rather than skill.

Off the Bike

Obsession with speed/lap times. Their conversation is dominated by numbers, comparing themselves constantly to others, rather than discussing technique or flow.

Excuses, not analysis. After a less-than-ideal session or ride, they blame external factors (the bike, the tires, the track, other riders) instead of analyzing their own inputs or mental state.

Frustration & anger. Easily agitated or visibly angry with themselves or others, especially after perceived failures.

Impatience. A general restlessness or unwillingness to slow down, practice fundamentals, or accept incremental progress.

False confidence/braggadocio. Overstating their abilities or dismissing dangers, often a cover for underlying insecurity or the desperate need to impress.

Reluctance to take advice. Dismissing coaching or feedback, believing they already know best, even when struggling.

Shutting Down Desperation

Identifying desperation is half the battle; the other half is having a plan to regain control. When you feel that familiar surge of impatience or the urge to force it, execute a deliberate mental reset. This isn't about giving up; it's about choosing wisdom over recklessness, and process over panic. Here's your action plan to shut down desperation:

Immediate Retreat

Drastically slow down. Reduce speed by 10-20%.

Relax Body & Grip. Loosen handlebars, drop elbows, relax shoulders, breathe deep.

Mental Check-In

Acknowledge it. "I'm desperate. Not helping."

Identify triggers. What caused this feeling?

Shift focus. Stop thinking about speed. Focus on one technique (e.g., braking, throttle).

Intentional Reset

Reaffirm fundamentals. Mentally rehearse one correct technique.

Visualize success. Briefly close eyes, see yourself doing it perfectly.

Small goal. "Perfect X for the next 3 corners."

Ride for YOU. Remember the joy, not comparison.

"One More Time" Rule

If reset fails. Stop for the day. No more pushing. Go home. There will be another day.

Shutting down desperation is self-discipline. It's choosing long-term growth and safety over short-term ego. The fastest way to get faster is often to slow down, reset, and rebuild with a clear, calm mind.

My Personal Perspective Shift

How I get out of desperation is by telling myself that there's something else much more important than this right now. Simple things like life itself, tomorrow, there will be another lap, another championship. That always took the immediate importance out of what I just wanted so desperately. It made me calm down and gave me elbow space, and wiggle room for the mind.

Psychological Takeaway

Desperation is a self-inflicted mental trap that paradoxically *reduces* performance by hijacking the rider's cognitive and physical control. It stems from an ego-driven, outcome-focused mindset that overrides learned processes, leading to rushed inputs, compounded errors, and increased risk. The ability to identify its signs—both in observable behavior and internal states—is crucial.

Counteracting desperation demands a deliberate mental reset protocol, prioritizing conscious physical relaxation, a shift from outcome to process-focus, and a vital perspective shift that re-prioritizes long-term well-being over immediate, frantic desires.

True mastery is achieved through patience, discipline, and a calm, controlled mind, not by f'n forcing the issue.

❀ Mind Note – Coach's take

"When you're in deep desperation, there's nothing else to do but to hold on and to see where it goes."

- Can Akkaya

Chaos Control

Patterning Your Way to Mental Coolness

I've already discussed how the influences of the mind can recall inappropriate physical skills under panic. Now, let's reverse the equation and see how you can use physical skills to create more of that missing 'mind coolness.'

Please understand that your current physical skill level is secondary at this point. The true relevance is how you mentally put all those physical actions into harmonized, consistent action.

To demonstrate where we're heading, let's look at two extremes: the total beginner and the highly paid professional. While it's not a fair comparison, it points out the one thing you HAVE to work on: consistent patterning.

The Chaos of Joe vs. The Precision of Gusto

Joe

Here is our brand-new rider, 'Joe.' His first inevitable f-up doesn't take long. With harsh, in-and-out movements on the clutch, Joe struggles to find the friction zone. His inconsistent throttle doubles the mistake, and the bike responds violently. This freaks Joe out, closing the time window for an upshift. His bike is screaming at high RPMs, yet he's barely moving. His upshifts are uncoordinated.

Now he's cornering, but his downshifts are so out of line that they destroy his momentum. He ends up pulling the clutch throughout the turn because he doesn't know what gear he's in, and he fears the engine brake will low-side him. The inconsistency of his brake/throttle inputs is the final straw, and his eyes are frantically following every possible distraction.

This lack of "mind coolness" results in uncertainty at best and a crash at worst. Ergo: Chaos.

Gusto

Now, let's look over the shoulder of professional 'Gusto.' He's on his lap of the French Grand Prix in Le Mans. Gusto is currently running a lonely race, which changes his strategy: his tire management modulus is ON to ensure he gets the rubber through the final laps. Gusto isn't pushing the ultimate limit, but he is highly focused and totally dialed in.

While his lap times are seconds slower compared to his best qualifying time, since the beginning of the second lap, he has been executing the exact same lap time consistently—one after another, separated by mere tenths of a second. This isn't about performance speed; this is precision.

His riding is a masterpiece of repeatable patterns:

Braking. He is nailing every braking marker, every initiation point, with the precision of a Swiss watch. His braking pressure decay (the rate at which he releases the brake lever) is identical in every corner.

Shifting. All upshifts and downshifts occur at the exact same places on the track. The engine note is a metronome—the downshift blips and clutch releases are so perfectly timed that the rear tire never judders, regardless of speed.

Attitude. He hits the identical maximum lean angle, throttle position, and apex with the same attitude and body motion on every pass.

Gusto's confidence is rock solid in knowing he will finish the race this way. He has transformed the chaotic demands of racing into a continuous, harmonized sequence of predictable patterns. His speed is a product of his consistency. He controls the machine not with force, but with established, automated rhythm.

Quite a difference in dynamics, huh?

Now, let's look at a third example: You.

Imagine riding an oval, completely within your comfort zone. Imagine you'd shift up twice out of the turn and down twice toward the next. Now, add a reliable line to it and decent throttle-brake transitions.

Picture yourself doing all of this in the same manner, pace, and feel at the same time and in the same place, over and over and over again!

If you did that, you have to admit that absolutely NOTHING could ever go wrong, correct? It's a functioning, consistent pattern from your first lap on.

This is what 'Joe' has to work on. Patterns help to establish muscle memory, and muscle memory leads to automatism. The consistency leads to self-control. This control not only gives you confidence (as defined by "knowing your sh*t"); it's also the most fundamental form of risk management because you know you'll be fine as long as you stay within the established parameters.

In the end, it even helps you to be more focused because you stop over-thinking and instead just take care to perform the very next pattern, then the next, then the next. You remove the chaos by practicing reliable braking, shifting, and throttle patterns.

Shifting Pattern Example

Shifting is a great place to start controlling the chaos:

The upshift pattern. You must establish when to shift. You may have to glance at the tachometer for a while, training yourself to ALWAYS upshift at an exact RPM. The more accurate you are, the sooner it will establish a sensory pattern. Once established, you won't need the tachometer; the pattern will create a feel and sound for it—ergo, your eyes are up where they belong: down the road.

The downshift pattern. Your downshift pattern occurs within the braking travel. You train yourself to let the tachometer needle drop to an exact RPM. The clutch comes out elegantly and smoothly, with no "chunky" feeling, and that needle never goes beyond on every single downshift. This, too, establishes a feel that replaces the glance at the needle—ergo, your eyes are up where they belong: down the road.

Next, you focus on aligning the timing for up and downshifts according to acceleration and deceleration so that the gaps between every shift are identical.

Again, shifting is just one example. Find an on-board video of a couple of laps of a MotoGP rider. Crank up the volume, close your eyes, and just listen to those up and downshifts... PATTERNS!

There is a fun example of Marc Márquez, listening to a recording of himself. With no video playing, he could tell within seconds on which track the sound was taken. The patterns are manifested in flesh and blood.

Now picture you've established patterns for ALL of it—throttle, brake, steering, timing for your knee motion, viewing, lines... everything! You control the chaos by establishing a repeatable pattern for each physical action. This is what your own personal mind coolness looks like.

Safety as a Pattern

I hope you can now clearly see the immense safety gain that comes from riding off of established patterns.

Just like Gusto, who confidently knows he'll finish the race because he stays within his patterns, your consistency becomes your ultimate safety mechanism.

A pattern is a self-calibrated baseline. If a downshift sounds different, if the brake pressure doesn't feel the same way, or if your line is unexpectedly wide, an immediate warning sign comes up. That difference—that break in the pattern—is your internal alarm system telling you that chaos has been introduced and that you're approaching your mental or mechanical limit.

By practicing the pattern, you train your body to recognize the vibration of error. This allows you to correct the small deviation *before* it turns into a "protective reaction" and a crash. Your consistency becomes your safety barrier, turning your focus from frantic reaction to calculated, immediate correction.

Psychological Takeaway

Randomness keeps your brain in a state of high-alert panic because you never know how the bike is going to react. You don't "find" calmness; you build it. By making every input identical, you remove the guesswork. Mind coolness is the byproduct of adhering to a pattern, not a feeling you wait for before you start riding.

Power of Automatization

Every time you have to think about a downshift or look at your tachometer, you're burning valuable cognitive energy. Consistent patterning is the only way to reach automatism. When machine operation becomes reflexive, your cognitive bandwidth gain is massive. You stop obsessing over your hands and feet, which finally frees your eyes to look "down the road where they belong."

The pro doesn't think about shifting; they listen to the metronome of the engine. If you want to stop the mental overload, you have to turn the ride into a series of automated, predictable loops.

Internal Alarm System

Consistency isn't just about being "smooth"—it's your ultimate safety mechanism. Once you establish a baseline for how a turn feels, any break in that pattern becomes an immediate Internal alarm system. If a downshift feels "chunky" or you're six inches off your line, your brain recognizes the "vibration of error" instantly.

This allows you to make a tiny, calculated correction *before* the situation escalates into a panic. By staying within your established parameters, you create an error-free zone where safety is a logical certainty, not a lucky guess.

Equalizing Negative vs. Positive

Converting Anxiety into Time

Sometimes you don't understand why things are the way they are. But when you lean back and think of it logically, and less with a frustrated heart, you might see further into the darkness. You might detect something that makes you even stronger. Instead of feeling numb, you might find something you can turn into an advantage. Let me give you an example.

As a young amateur racer, I did discover that I had a big advantage from the get go. Whatever was new, I was up and ahead with it. A new track nobody dealt with before. A new section. New asphalt conditions. A new team, or a change to other tire manufacturers. A race bike I'd never seen before. Put the entire racing league into a new situation, and I was able to find competitive lap times in literally no time, within a session or less. This get go skill—a good feel for distance, speed, and possible grip level—was an immensely positive feeling for me. Such a confidence boost.

Cracking Confidence Problem

But it also got to me bad when I realized how much this skill worked against me mentally at the same time.

Here's the problem in numbers: Setting the top lap time that soon meant my opponents were creeping up on me in bigger steps—while I was progressing in much smaller steps in terms of lap times.

Now, what would this do to your brain, your ego, and your confidence? Your initial confidence starts cracking, but the confidence of your opponents is gaining. That doesn't feel right. The pressure of maintaining the lead replaces the joy of gaining it.

Consequently, I had to improve on the issue mentally—without taking the original physical advantage away. A compromise? With what? No, I found an equalizer.

Trading Ego for Process

This required some self-convincing in the beginning. I had to stop analyzing the lap times and start analyzing the time I had bought myself. The realization hit: The massive head start—that initial, faster lap time—didn't just stroke my ego; it bought me time.

While my opponents were still struggling to find the basic line and the base grip level, I could already spend my advantage on:

Refining reference markers. Deepening my understanding of every single brake point, turn-in point, and apex marker.

Bike setup and tires. Spending precious minutes dialing in the suspension and finding the right tire compounds, making the bike inherently faster for the long run.

So, mentally, I found a way to compensate for the emotional negative (the fear of being caught) and turned it into a strategic positive (deepening my physical and mechanical control). Of course, they were still creeping up, but seeing the bigger picture found more of my acceptance. I traded a temporary ego boost for a durable, long-term strategic advantage.

Street Rider's Dig

You might think "equalizing" stuff is only for racers fighting the clock, and that this doesn't apply to you as a street rider. You might have to dig deeper to see it, because I think it absolutely does. The street is a thousand times more chaotic than a track. Your negatives aren't lap times, they're threats and anxieties. Your job is to stop letting these negatives consume you and instead use them to buy you mental time.

The Panic

A car cuts you off, or a deer jumps out. Your brain defaults to target fixation, staring at the danger, and you feel the surge of panic and the loss of control. That's the negative.

The equalizer. That immediate, gut-punch of fear is actually a siren that buys you a split second of heightened awareness. You must immediately redirect that awareness from the threat to the solution.

The action. Instead of letting the fear make you freeze, you must use that raw surge of adrenaline to instantly engage your Zen zone training: Relax your hands, look where you need to go, and execute the counter-steer. The fear didn't make you crash; your failure to use the fear as a launch signal did.

The Ego

You've been riding the same canyon route for five years. Nothing ever happens. You stop thinking about your patterns and start letting your mind wander. That comfort is the biggest negative.

The equalizer. You need to proactively generate a strategic negative to break that mental laziness. Force yourself to use that routine route as training time.

The action. Choose one element; braking, corner entry, shifting. Then commit to executing it perfectly for the entire ride. Treat every signal light as a braking drill. Treat every corner entry as a perfect counter-steering exercise. You're turning the 'boring predictability' of the street into a positive time investment, deepening your patterns so they're unbreakable when the real chaos hits. You're using the time advantage to refine your riding, just like the pro racer on a new track.

The Distraction

A driver texts through a light, a car cuts you off again, or someone rides your ass. The anger and frustration consume your mental space. That's a distraction that can kill you.

The equalizer. You must recognize that anger is a wasted resource that pulls you out of the Zen zone. You convert that negative energy into a detached, analytical positive.

The action. When you feel the anger, you instantly flip the script: "This driver is my training aid." Instead of raging, you analyze the *threat* he presents and immediately establish a new safety buffer. You use his mistake as a live scenario to practice your detachment and predictive risk assessment. You accept the chaos, but you refuse to let it control your focus.

Psychological Takeaway

The problem is letting temporary ego/emotion consume strategic focus. The equalizer principle is the conscious decision to trade short-term emotional satisfaction for the durable, long-term strategic asset of mental time and clarity.

Trading Ego for Strategic Time

Your initial get-go skill creates a cracking confidence problem: as opponents close the gap, the pressure of maintaining the lead replaces the joy of gaining it, turning skill into a mental liability. The equalizer strategy is to redefine your head start not as a source of ego, but as a resource that buys time. Intentionally trade the temporary ego boost of holding a massive lead for the durable strategic advantage of investing that time into refining markers and dialing in bike setup. This converts the "fear of being caught" into acceptance and focused, constructive work.

Flip the Script for Durable Skill and Safety

The underlying psychological mandate is to refuse to let a momentary negative feeling (frustration, anger, anxiety from tough roads or idiot drivers) consume your focus. Instead, you must "flip the script," forcing your brain to see that negative as a strategic signal that buys mental time. This mental time must then be immediately reinvested into reinforcing fundamental riding patterns and mental discipline. This ensures that daily struggle is converted into durable, foundational skill. For street riders, this means using frustration to buy yourself time, clarity, and safety.

Don't let ego or emotion dictate your progress. Take up the equalizer principle: consciously trade temporary satisfaction for strategic mental time. Flip the script on negatives, convert them into assets, and build unshakeable, foundational mastery.

Confidence

This is actually funny, more or less. You know that racers are easier to coach? Yeah, they come to me and can define what they're lacking, or they have very specific goals they want to work on. Sure, I have one or two who only say, "I want to drop lap times," but that percentage is very low.

That's a different story with street riders. The percentage is vice versa here. Sure, some say, "I want to become faster and safer," which has the same low depth as saying, "I want to drop lap times." Most of them just round it up to "I need more confidence." Same low depth. Right?

Yes, my job is to find out what exactly it takes to boost a rider's confidence, but what the hell does that word actually mean?! Until then, it's just a fancier term for "I'm peeing in my pants," isn't it?! In fact, nobody has actually even defined the word properly to me yet.

Simply put... *Confidence is to know that you know your shit.*

I think the term 'confidence' is overly abused. What you're actually telling me is that you wished you had bigger balls and that you're looking for a super-quick fix. Isn't that the truth?!!!

My answer to this is as simple as this request: Look, with all the coaching coming your way, maybe those balls grow a tad throughout, but I'll have to work with the existing size of your balls right now!

Three Pillars of Confidence

There are riders who see another rider and think, "Why does he look so confident?" The possibility is very high that the exact rider is thinking the same about you right now.

Your goal should be to at least get to know the exact area that's keeping your confidence low. What exactly is the reason for lacking confidence? That has to be nailed down, even if it requires a deep, honest look into you.

There are three areas to be confident with in motorcycle riding:

1. *Knowledge*
2. *Operational*
3. *Mentality*

Knowledge Gap

Knowledge should be more or less easy to get, but here is the ugly truth:

Most riders don't know what they don't know.

Some reject obtaining knowledge because they think it just comes with time.

Some even deny they lack knowledge.

Right here, brutal honesty with yourself is necessary in order to understand that you're not as knowledgeable as you may believe you are.

The lack of knowledge has a direct influence on operating that motorcycle properly. For example: Just because you believe you KNOW how to shift, doesn't mean that you really know ALL about it. The belief of knowledge might keep you away from better gear choice, better shift timing, and a solid downshift pattern, etc.

Lack of Knowledge = Lack of Operational Ability

Operational Trap

Operationally, you might manifest a lot of bad habits, and like most riders, you depend on yourself to experience the entire spectrum. You might never fully grasp the entire nine yards of counter-steering because of false information, bad advice, or some YouTube rock star. However, the decision of your "point of achievement" is entirely up to you, and that person is still the one who doesn't know their own shit.

A heavier weight is the bridge from the operational side to the mental side. Example: Are you worried about breaking your bike? Are you worried about hurting yourself? Is this based on not trusting the bike itself? Maybe because you don't trust those tires? Maybe it's because the bike is a tad too heavy for you? Too much power to deal with?

I've seen students who literally collapse mentally just because they jumped on a bike they'd never been on. They break out in a sweat and literally forget how to bring it into first gear. So here we go:

Lacking Operational Ability = Lacking Mental Strength

Mental Circle

The heaviest weight that causes being low on confidence is mentality.

Do you trust yourself making the right decisions? Are you overly distrusting of others? Are you constantly considering if this is the right hobby for you while riding? Is the demon on your shoulder constantly talking to you? Are you overly doing the What/If math?

If you can answer only one of those questions with a "yes," then you just found the circle closing on you. If "no," then you might be hitting a plateau, or you're lying to yourself. Don't feel offended. I've been there myself. However, it always seems to come back to this:

Lack of Mental Strength = Lack of Knowledge

Faking It and the Self-Energizing Circle

Can one fake confidence? Heck yes, and sometimes it helps to overcome things. But in the end, it's only something temporary. Trust me, a professional racer will figure out false confidence really quick, and once it's discovered, you'll be thrown to the lions. Faking confidence in the wrong place and getting caught makes you maybe never recover mentally from it. You better deal with constructive honesty instead and know your place until you've really worked up to it.

Given/False Confidence

That's a big one, actually. I call it given confidence—the kind that comes from nowhere and relies on nothing. It can come from yourself or, more often, from your surroundings.

You know the drill: getting a participation ribbon for literally everything. That instructor who keeps telling you how good you look. That best friend who says how great you sing and that you should go on *American Idol*, despite the fact that you're about to crack windows. That's a lie you buy into.

Here is my daughter Jill. I taught her from scratch in a parking lot, and she ran all my scheduled classes and one-on-ones. Her progress in a very short time window? Astronomical. She comes in and says, "I'm done with C group. They're slowing me down too much." I agreed, and she moved up to B group.

That day, B group was generally slow. Now, how did she look? Absolutely great, right?! And so she faces me, totally excited, saying she'll be in A group next month. My alert bells were ringing, and I told her to keep it in check. I saw it coming.

In the next class, B group was generally very fast. And now what did she look like there? Real bad, right?! She came in crying. Her confidence was shredded to pieces by reality, and it took us about three months of rebuilding her trust and motivation. Yeah, no shit!

(By the way, Jill went from starting in a parking lot to dragging knees in only one year. The speed was real.)

But this was a crucial eye-opener for her, and I believe it actually came right on time to put her realistically in her place.

Given Confidence is a liability. It makes you make decisions—like moving to A group—that your actual skill set can't support. It convinces you that the job is finished before the work is even half-done. The emotional crash that follows is brutal, because the failure proves the praise was a lie.

You can't borrow or be given true confidence. It must be forged from the heat of objective, repeated success that you earn when nobody is watching. If the only proof of your skill is what other people tell you, then you've built your confidence on sand.

But when confidence levels match Reality…

... something magical happens...

You're entering a wonderful place where all those layers of worked-up confidence have become a self-energizing circle. It opens even bigger doors to a world of freedom and clarity. A confidence that breaks barriers, holdbacks, and worries.

On a side note... you know that some people actually call a person with that kind of confidence level "arrogant?" Yeah, that's a thing. I actually believe that a more ego-driven personality expresses it this way. Maybe it's a simple way for them to waive someone off who might be "stronger" than them—just a sign of their own insecurity, maybe?

Aura of Confidence

Think of a famous rock star whose confidence level has been brutally worked up. That's a glowing energy that fills the room. Isn't that actually also a reason why you admire this rock star so much? It's not so much about the fortune and the fame; it's more about that glow of confidence which can bend steel and almost makes the guy seem arrogant. It seems that guy can do things others don't.

If you look a world champion in the eyes, you'll get an unspoken "Yeah, you better not mess with me, pumpkin!" message, and he doesn't even have to push that message. That's coming out by itself, out of every cell, scar, and atom. That's just how your aura can look like when you know—that you know your shit very well.

Go to Work!

Psychological Takeaway

Don't use the word "confidence" as a polite mask for the fact that you're terrified. When you ask for more confidence, you're usually looking for a shortcut to "bigger balls" without doing the work. True confidence isn't a feeling you summon; it's the cold, hard realization that you actually know your shit. If you can't define exactly what is holding you back, you aren't lacking confidence, you're lacking a map of your own incompetence.

Your knowledge is likely full of holes because you don't know what you don't know. On the operational side, your bad habits act as anchors. If you can't instinctively counter-steer or trust your tires, your physical inability will eventually crush your mentality. This is the circle-closer: if you don't trust your own decision-making or the demon on your shoulder is doing "what-if" math, you will plateau. Mental weakness is almost always a symptom of a lack of knowledge.

Given confidence is a lethal liability; it's the participation trophy of the motorcycle world. It comes from the instructor who over-praises you or the friend who tells you how fast you look because you're leading a slow group. This is a lie that makes you move to the fast group before your skill set can support it. When reality eventually hits, the emotional crash is brutal because it proves the praise was fake.

Aura of Mastery

When your confidence level finally matches your reality, you enter a self-energizing circle. This isn't arrogance; it's a glow of energy that comes from every cell and scar because you have zero doubt in your ability to handle the machine.

You know… it's actually easy to 'look' like a rock star, and maybe to fake that kinda confidence… But what you can't fake is that you are still not hitting a solid G chord and sending it though those amps down to an audience!

※ Mind Note – Coach's take

"Rome wasn't built in one day! It took even longer to rebuild it!"

- *Can Akkaya*

What Bad Feels Like

Often, I see riders looking to modify the crap out of their bikes, and nothing is wrong with it. You know, I love it too. Some bling here and there to give it that personal touch. This, of course, can also take you away to a 'now I'm scared to break it' place, which you can read about in 'Nuts n' Bolts.' Kinda normal when you spend so much time and money into it. We, or I should say I did, exactly that mistake to my own daughter Jill.

I got her a 400cc bike, and yeah, it was a commuter and looked accordingly. So this is my first 'excuse.' My second excuse is—she wanted the mods so bad that there was no way around it. I have more. I had to do some safety repairs on it anyway. Good one, huh?!

Another one is that I love to do things like that, and the last one is that I have the urge to make her as happy as I possibly can. Besides... What can be better than to do stuff like this together with your kid?!

Since I know about the mental aspects, I saw it coming and called it out, so that she is prepared for it. In her case, it would have been tough for her to either ride a commuter or a rock star bike, since she fell in love with it and it's just her nature. BUT! We purposely limited the mods to bling, looks, weight reductions, and ergonomics. Why? This is what this chapter is about.

Rock Star Effect

I told Jill, when you look like a rock star, but you can't play the guitar that well yet, that this will cause some pressure on many ends, additionally to the fear of breaking this bike.

People have expectations that you hit that G chord perfectly upon stage.

You want to hit that G chord better than ever before.

The embarrassment of a real cricket-played G.

Summed up: It's gonna lead to tension and will slow you down for a while, and of course it did. But it was important to know about the effects, because just smiling it away is better than ending up in frustrations. So, if you're a relatively new rider and can't resist making that bike look like the ride of a rock star... know about it.

'What Bad Feels Like' Effect

The reason why Jill and I didn't go into 'performance upgrades' yet is simple. A new rider actually doesn't have the skill to get the best out of that expensive front fork yet. The knowledge of setting it up right is missing. Sure, you can hire someone, but then you lose a chance to learn by doing it yourself. Also, the knowledge of how it's actually to feel isn't there yet,, so you're not even able to tell the suspension engineer what the damn thing does.

Besides that, such costly investment puts additional performance pressure upon the rider's shoulders. Thinking that these race slick tires, those extremely expensive brake calipers from Italy, or that setup-to-your-weight suspension, are going to make you safer is actually really questionable. How can a high-performance tire help you better when you can't even get it up to operating temperatures yet?!

Plus, you're still making all those weird little mistakes which even the most impressive chassis wouldn't compensate for. The biggest thing you'd take away from your learning curve is that you don't get to know what 'bad' feels like, in order to get to know what 'good' feels like. No physical comparisons created.

'Let's See What It Can Do'

It's not always necessary to not have the best tires on, just to give it an example out of the wide spectrum of performance upgrades. This can have some great effects on a more experienced rider, if it triggers the 'explorer spirit.' Getting into a 'let's see what I can do with it' mode makes you learn to adapt and to just play, but kind of with more fun actually. Explore!

More Effects

I believe this can be an essential tool for the high-level rider, and to step up the game. If you go out on a stock bike and line it up against track-prepped bikes, that can unleash a beast in you to take it to the maximum possible. The fighter spirit is triggered.

Or, because you and everyone around you knows that this is a fight against windmills, and you switch back into the 'explorer mode.' And because there are less expectations of yourself—and from the outside—you are riding now in a pressure-less world.

So, also here, there are things that can work mentally against you, but there are also opportunities to turn them over for the good. Additionally, there's another effect that's often overlooked. Imagine you look like a rock star and your opponents figure out that you're actually not... that would actually elevate their eagerness to get ya real bad. Wouldn't it?

Imposter Trap

The pressure you feel from your tricked-out bike isn't coming from the outside; it's the gap between your external appearance and your internal skill set. You paid for a costume that's too big. The bike is writing checks your skills can't cash, and your brain knows it.

This forces your focus onto avoiding embarrassment instead of actively learning. Your brain is screaming: "Fraud!" and that anxiety is what makes you twitchy. You're trying so hard not to look slow that you forget how to actually ride fast. You paid money to make yourself slower. Think about that for a second.

Calibrating the Senses

Your butt, your hands, and your brain need a memory bank of bad feedback. If you jump straight to the best suspension, your body doesn't know the difference between "great" and "holy-sh*t-my-spine-is-broken."

The hard lessons you get from that sh*tty stock fork—the pain of a harsh reaction, the feeling of the tire slipping way too early—that creates a hard neurological floor.

When the upgrade works, you register the *improvement* as a measurable event. Without knowing the baseline of failure, you're not learning; you're just coasting on credit. You're dumbing down your own feeling machine.

Freedom of No Expectation

This is the power of the stock bike. When you roll up on the commuter, your opponent's brain says, "easy target." Even better, your own brain says, "No pressure, just fun."

Those pricey race calipers or the carbon wheels make your brain work overtime worrying about scratching or breaking them. The stock bike makes your brain shut the f*ck up and just RIDE. You're automatically allowed to fail. You get to rediscover the pure, dumb fun of playing with no cost.

You remove the external barrier and reveal the raw skill—the only thing left to blame is the rider, and when the expectation is low, that's not a threat, it's a hell of a challenge.

Psychological Takeaway

There's a dangerous gap between the bike you're sitting on and the skill you actually have. You've built yourself an imposter trap. Premature upgrades create an imposter trap that inhibits sensory learning and replaces focus with performance anxiety.

Sensory Calibration Loss

The mismatch between your high-performance bike and your skill level forces your mental energy away from learning and directs it toward avoiding embarrassment. The resultant tension and anxiety slow learning and create twitchy, error-prone riding.

The core issue is the inhibition of the feedback loop essential for learning. Without first establishing a sensory baseline of "What Bad Feels Like," a rider is unable to truly calibrate and appreciate "What Good Feels Like."

Premature upgrades cause the rider to "coast on credit" and degrade their internal feeling mechanism. Consequently, the body can't register subsequent mechanical improvements as objectively measurable, learned events.

Underdog Effect

Freedom of No Expectation, is the psychological antidote. Rolling up on a stock, unremarkable bike automatically lowers external and internal expectations, creating a pressure-less world where you can truly focus on learning.

Don't chase a "Rock Star" image. Prioritize building your sensory baseline of "What Bad Feels Like" over expensive upgrades. Enjoy the freedom of the underdog, and truly learn to ride by feeling, not by faking. If you learn everything the right way… you'll be a rock star in no time.

※ Mind Note – Coach's take

"Putting a $2k rear shock into your bike? On your skill level? Isn't this like hiring Einstein as your first-grade math teacher?!"

— *Can Akkaya*

Awareness

There is a fine line between being able to focus and 'awareness.' The urge of being able to be aware of EVERYTHING can ruin the ability of focusing. It seems though, that everyone is ASKING you to be 'aware' of everything, including yourself.

Being aware of something makes your entire system pretty busy: brain functions, eyes, ears, muscles, hell—even smelling sometimes. I'm questioning whether you have the capacity as a new rider to spend all these resources of your body, while you still struggle with the fundamentals of riding the damn bike.

Imagine you're riding through a city, or in heavy traffic on a freeway. Your brain is in high alert mode and operates just that one way. Just that will limit a new rider's ability to ride the bike itself. Your brain makes your ears, eyes, and nose operate at 99% to catch anything that could possibly kill you. That makes your muscles start tweaking and twitching all over the place and that will have an influence on your bike's handling. Quite a dilemma, huh?!

Don't feel like this here is only addressing new riders. For me, many riders fall into this gray zone, and that's from new riders up to A group level track riders. Because I see it almost every day. Here is that C group rider, thinking of himself being good enough to join track days now—figuring that being surrounded by 50 others of that kind, will create the same awareness issues the city ride does to them. Or the B group rider, who lives in denial and her ambitions overwrite her talent, and that brain is actually running hot in high alert mode.

Consequences are… making irrational passing decisions, mistakes being in a constant flow, getting hurt or hurting others! That rider who is about to join A group for the first time. Deep inside he actually knows he isn't ready for this yet. Yea, he might be better about filtering his awareness level, but his ego overwrites everything when he gets passed by pretty much everyone throughout those 20 minutes. He's trying hard to keep up but only runs into mistakes or even crashing.

Hyper-Awareness Kills Automatic Skill

When you ride a motorcycle at speed, 95% of your actions (counter-steering, throttle modulation, braking feel) are handled by the fast, non-conscious part of your brain—muscle memory. Too much awareness is the conscious brain interfering with the automatic system.

External Overload

While one form of hyper-awareness is internal, another is external, resulting from cognitive overload.

Your brain becomes "too aware" of external factors that don't help you go faster. This could be checking your lap timer every corner, worrying about the rider behind you on the street (the "Hornet Swarm"), or constantly calculating championship points.

This irrelevant awareness is "noise" that drowns out the truly critical signals. This forces your commander brain to waste precious energy filtering this noise instead of processing vital data.

What you need is to find ways to keep that brain away from shifting into alert mode, which is mostly triggered by self-imposed, over awareness of everything.

External Focus and Rituals

The way to manage "too much awareness" is to deliberately shift your focus away from the internal self and onto external, controllable targets.

External Cue

Instead of thinking, "I need to turn smoothly," you focus your awareness on an external cue—the target.

"Look at the apex."
"Focus on hitting the brake marker."
"See the exit point."

This shifts your awareness from *how* your body is riding to *where* the bike needs to go, allowing muscle memory to handle the details.

Rhythm and Rituals

Use small, repeatable routines to regulate your mind's hyperactivity.

After a close call or a big mistake (when hyper-awareness spikes), use a ritual to clear the conscious mind. This could be a deep breath on the straight, or a simple mental command like "reset, focus, go." This forces the brain to dump the "noise" and return to the simple riding process.

Ultimately, high performance requires accepting that you can't be perfectly aware of everything.

Attempt to Achieve What's Not Achievable

You have absolutely no influence on coincidences. Waiting for them only creates more anxieties. Looking for something that doesn't even exist yet creates visions of what could possibly be coming your way. The attempt to prevent coincidences isn't just impossible, it only puts your mind and body under massive pressures and constant tensions. Your confidence level stays low, because you can't achieve what's not achievable.

At our school, we are addressing 'over awareness' from day 1, and ongoing. Rituals and patterns are what we're using. Viewing techniques, shift patterns, thinking/sorting processes, filtering priorities. This sounds compact and easy, but is actually a whole lot more in depth, so good luck finding this in some parking lot. There, I said it.

Psychological Takeaway

Hyper-awareness leads to "paralysis by analysis," as the rider switches from the fast pilot (muscle memory) to the slow mechanic.

Too much conscious awareness interferes with fast, non-conscious muscle memory (smooth throttle, quick braking). This makes you second-guess your training—consciously monitoring inputs ("Am I leaning enough?").

This is too slow for traffic, causing hesitation, stiff hands, and delayed reactions. In heavy traffic, your brain goes into "high alert," attempting to process every threat, leading to sensory overload and draining mental resources from fundamental bike handling. This is the "noise" of irrelevant data (obsessively checking mirrors, anticipating every "what if" coincidence) that drowns out truly critical signals.

Street Rider's Solution

The strategy for managing hyper-awareness is to deliberately shift focus to what is controllable and actionable. Instead of internal self-monitoring, focus awareness on external, predictive cues in traffic: "Where will that driver likely pull out?" "What do those brake lights tell me?" "Where is my escape path right now?"

This shifts awareness from how your body is riding to what is most likely to happen next, allowing muscle memory to handle the physical execution. Use rhythm and rituals to regulate mental hyperactivity. After a close call, use a simple mental ritual (a deep breath, a command like "Scan, Plan, Act") to clear the conscious mind. Practice filtering priorities: Focus intensely on the 2% of information that's actually relevant to your immediate safety and path, rather than trying to consume 99% of all sensory data.

Being hyper-aware of everything leads to "paralysis by analysis." Trust your inner "pilot." filter the "noise," focus on external, predictive cues, and use rituals to anchor your attention in the present.

❋ Mind Note – Choke hold

"Take time to deliberate, but when the time for action has arrived, stop thinking and go in."

— *Napoleon Bonaparte*

Why New Riders Don't 'See'

The Lethality of Ego

Congratulations! You bought the machine. You can balance it. You know how to shift up and down. You've mastered the brake and the clutch. You may have even aced the circle test at the DMV and secured your license. All of that proves only one thing: you know how to *operate* a motorcycle. That's literally the bare minimum.

At this crucial juncture, the majority of new riders suffer from a profound visual handicap. They don't see that there's a vast, dangerous world of skill yet to be learned. They're prisoners of the most insidious barrier to mastery: they don't know what they don't know.

Objectively, rolling down a straight road or passing a low-speed skills test is an irrelevant measure of competence. The truth only shows in critical situations. That's when the chaos hits, the margins disappear, and you prove what kind of rider you truly are.

Lethality of Ego and Denial

Let's be honest, we were all there. Picture your 18-year-old self: self-centered, ego-driven, and feeling f***ing invincible. Being 18 is practically a guarantee for 'not seeing' the immense distance between being prepared and being proficient.

But irresponsible youth isn't the only culprit. Ego makes us blind, regardless of our age. That ego drives us to deny the truth and, more dangerously, to wish away the fundamental possibility of death and dismemberment.

Death is an undeniable certainty. We are exposed out there. It doesn't matter how expensive your helmet is or how robust your leathers are, there will always be a 'point of no return.' The less skill you have because you don't see, and the more ego drives you because you deny, the more likely you're to get injured or worse. That's the cold, hard truth of the equation.

The Neighbor's Crash

This isn't just about young hotshots. Consider my 64-year-old neighbor. He got his license, bought a sportbike, and—despite my urging—smiled away my invitations to cornering clinics. His response: "What?! I can shift and I can brake already." Denial.

Later, he was talking about watching YouTube crash videos, claiming to "learn" from them. What exactly is there to learn from watching someone else's mistake? Staying alive? Well, I wasn't surprised when he crashed. Broke his elbow, shattered his fingers. Bike totaled. I looked at him afterward, and he was still smiling it away, manufacturing a litany of excuses. He still couldn't see. The power of denial is a deadly thing. I've been there, and I've learned to 'see.'

Lesser the knowledge, greater the ego.

These new rider stories demonstrate that those who know the least often have the least respect for the motorcycle and the risks of the road. That, fundamentally, is why new riders don't see. Motorcycling is no f***ing video game. Your life is on the line. To move to the better side of Einstein's equation—More knowledge, lesser the ego—we must embrace the pursuit of mastery.

Compare riding to baseball. Just because you can throw a ball doesn't mean you belong in the Major Leagues. Little league teaches discipline. High school teaches positioning. College teaches strategy and peak performance. Even professional coaches have ongoing certifications. It's a culture of continuous, structured improvement throughout an entire career. That's how they learn to "see" the subtle nuances of the game. To become a rider who can truly see, you must adopt this continuous improvement mindset.

Pillars of Vision

Watching YouTube is only the first step. You learn more from doing than from watching. To develop the necessary vision and skill—to achieve the kind of mastery needed when a car cuts you off mid-blind turn—you must focus on these pillars:

As Malcolm Gladwell suggested, achieving mastery often requires 10,000 hours of intensive practice. You need that deliberate exposure to create upper limit references for yourself and your motorcycle. You need to know, without conscious thought, exactly how much leaner angle or brake pressure you have left when a crisis erupts.

To truly "see," you need to ignore the irrelevant. You must consciously filter out the distracting scenery, the unimportant chatter, and the pressure of others. This intense focus allows you to ride with a higher degree of awareness, building the mental coolness required to handle critical situations with precision, not panic.

Psychological Takeaway

The Dunning-Kruger Effect traps riders into believing they're more skilled than they are, leading to lethal blind spots.

"Mount Stupid" Trap

Right after gaining basic proficiency, riders hit the riskiest point: "mount stupid." They have just enough skill but are unaware of the vast knowledge they lack. Ego actively grows inversely with true knowledge, shielding you from admitting the need for more training.

Confront Your Denial

After a near-miss or crash, your brain immediately activates denial by manufacturing excuses ("bad road," "reckless driver"). This denial protects your ego but is lethal, as it prevents accepting responsibility for internal feedback and learning. Wishful thinking about invincibility leads directly to careless actions.

Goodness starts with the courage to admit what you don't know and embrace the necessity of continuous learning.

"Car Driver Awareness" Class

With every class, event, and seminar, I learn something new about the people I coach and the patterns behind why riders crash—or never progress. Gathering intelligence isn't just curiosity for me—it's the foundation of how I build programs. Every story, question, and mistake is a piece of data.

And one realization hits deeper than it might look at first glance: most riders don't even know what they're really looking for when they sign up for a motorcycle class.

When I ask directly, I usually hear: "I want to be more confident." I think I need to fix my body position." I don't know, I just want to feel safer."

These are fine answers, but they're not the truth. Once riders start opening up, the specifics begin to surface: "What do I do when I hit debris in a blind turn?" How do I avoid a deer?" How do I react when a car merges into my lane?"

All good questions—but here's the kicker: they're asking for isolated solutions to random scenarios. They want quick, surgical fixes for moments that are unpredictable, unique, and emotionally charged.

Illusion of a Quick Fix

When I tell them I can't answer that directly, some actually get frustrated. Why? Because they want certainty. But think about it—how could anyone, including me, give a 100% correct answer to a scenario without knowing these facts:

Your exact speed, lean angle, and distance to the object.
Your line, your braking point, your tire grip, your reaction time.
Your sleep, hydration, and focus level that day.
Whether you target-fixated, panicked, or stayed cool.
Whether you even saw an escape route.

Every one of those factors matters. And they're all invisible in a verbal question. So sure—I could say "Just counter steer"—but that's not teaching. That's throwing words at physics.

When I cut short these kinds of seminar questions, some think I'm dodging or trying to upsell cornering classes. But that's not it. The truth is, a real explanation would take drills, live corrections, and hours of practice to make it stick. Otherwise, it's no different from reading about swimming while standing on dry land.

All Roads Lead to Cornering

Let's play this out. You want a realistic class? Then how about this: I send you through a series of blind turns covered in debris, and you go back and forth until you stop panicking. Or you ride down a sun-blinded straight while deer and cars randomly jump into your path. Or an SUV-driving soccer mom on a phone drifting into your lane at 70 mph.

That would be a "Car Driver Awareness" class, right? But no one can offer that, because it would end in ambulances. The survival skills you're asking for don't come from replicating chaos. They come from learning to control yourself inside it.

Here's the Core Truth:

When you hit debris in a blind turn—what's the procedure? You need to corner.
When you avoid a deer—what do you do? You need to corner.
When you dodge a car or hit an escaping gap—what do you do? You need to corner.
When you emergency brake but keep enough awareness to steer away? You need to corner.

That's why a cornering class is the survival class. Everything else—slow-speed maneuvers, parking lot cone drills, "confidence workshops"—is just theater if it's not teaching you how to truly manage your machine under pressure.

Cornering is the Mental Operating System Upgrade

You can't learn that kind of mental coolness from cone drills that every other parking lot school copied from YouTube. You learn it from focused cornering, because cornering demands absolute presence. It connects all systems: braking, throttle, line choice, vision, body position, and brain function.

When you train the art of cornering in the right sequence, something happens:

You stop freezing. You brake like your life depends on it—because sometimes it does.
You spot the escape gap. You counter steer into space instead of fear.

And suddenly, you're not a passenger of panic anymore, you're a pilot of precision. And let's be honest—what's more fun than that? A cone on a f'n parking lot? Please!

So, what's "mind coolness"?

It's that calm, razor-sharp mental state where time seems to slow down and your body does exactly what it's trained to do, without interference from fear or overthinking. It's the space between stimulus and reaction—the millisecond where riders either survive or don't.

It's not meditation. It's not bravado. It's trained composure under real pressure.

Mind coolness comes from repetition in real cornering environments, not parking lots. The moment your tires load, suspension compresses, vision locks on, and your brain enters that flow state—that's where focus and awareness fuse. That's the training ground for staying cool when a deer jumps out or a car swerves into your lane.

Because here's the truth: you can't fake focus. You can't breathe yourself out of panic once it's already taken over. You need to replace panic with something stronger—competence, understanding, and controlled aggression.

That's why every drill I teach—braking, throttle control, trail braking, counter-steering—feeds the same goal: building a rider who doesn't flinch when it matters most.

A cone in a parking lot won't give you that. But a properly designed cornering program—that challenges your mental bandwidth—will. You might think I'm trying to sell you a ticket?! Think what you will. Just don't forget to see that I'm right, no matter what.

Psychological Takeaway

This search for cognitive certainty is displacement behavior that avoids the hard work of building comprehensive crisis response skills.

Asking "What if a deer jumps out?" is lethal specificity. You're seeking a memorized rule to prevent panic, but this is merely avoiding the hard work of building comprehensive skills. In a real crisis, ten invisible variables (speed, lean, panic, etc.) overwhelm your brain's cognitive load. The solution isn't more information; it's higher processing power, achieved through mind coolness.

Cornering is Your Universal Skill

Cornering is the ultimate brain training and your universal skillset because it demands the highest cognitive bandwidth. It forces you to integrate braking, throttle, body positioning, and vision simultaneously. Master corners, and you master everything.

Training cornering mastery builds proactive confidence. You replace panic with precision: you substitute your brain's ingrained panic template with an execution template. So when a crisis occurs, your brain defaults to a trained cornering sequence (brake, steer, look) instead of freezing or target fixation.

The fusion of focused attention and elastic awareness—mind coolness—is the goal of all this training. This is the psychological state where your brain precisely processes the immediate task while staying aware of escape routes.

Your safety depends on abandoning the illusion of certainty for the undeniable power of a universal, trained skillset.

Paradox of Speed and Control

Have you ever noticed the fundamental paradox that exists across all levels of two-wheeled competition, from street riding to high level racing?

Did it ever occur to you that the front runners of all high-level racing categories are the least likely to crash? This is true even though they're operating at the absolute razor-edge of friction, locked in a brutal dogfight for victory, while the riders crashing are often the ones further back in the field, going slower.

I remember being a professional racer and seeing repeated crashes behind me at Assen. I couldn't comprehend why slower racers were binning their bikes while I was laying down perfect black lines, pushing to take home a trophy.

This observation points to a truth that defies simple logic: Control isn't proportional to slowness; control is proportional to stability, and speed often generates stability.

Mechanics of the Paradox

The lack of control for a less experienced rider is often physical and mechanical, not just mental:

Beginner riders struggle with low-speed maneuvers precisely because they're going so slow. Their tires lose the gyroscopic rotational force—the basic physics that creates a massive amount of stability. The bike feels heavy and wants to flop. A subtle increase in speed often makes the bike *easier* to manage.

For less experienced riders, speed triggers a "protective reaction." This decision-making, almost always wrong, is triggered by the feeling of being "too fast." The rider tenses up, cuts the throttle, and makes a sudden, incorrect input that sends them into the dirt for a reason that was entirely self-inflicted.

Cognitive Gap

The danger of the velocity paradox is most clearly seen when a rider has the speed but lacks the necessary protocol to manage it.

Consider track day Joe, pulled to an advanced pace by an instructor. He memorizes the speed, but when he goes back out, the matching line for that pace is gone. Without the required entry speed, arc, and exit point, his muscle-memorized pace is instantly excessive. The result is a corner entry or mid-corner maneuver that's fast enough to exceed his skills but slow enough to be unstable given his incorrect line.

Or consider the rider who "read about" counter-steering and decided they "got this." They get faster and faster on the straightaways, but they struggle to hold the line mid-turn and feel perpetually in danger. Why? Because the clumsy, muscle-driven way they used to steer the bike can't keep up with their current mid-turn pace anymore. Only the precise, minimal input of effective counter-steering can manage the bike's physics at speed.

The two elements, speed and control, find each other paradoxically at a certain rider level. It isn't always the obvious cause you should point out; the instability is often the result of being almost fast enough, but missing a fundamental input that the speed now demands.

Invitation to Mastery

This is absolutely not an invitation to just go faster. It's an invitation to master the elements that make speed safe. We need to understand that a certain momentum is needed to create stability—a paradoxical truth for a beginner.

To master this paradox, you need patience and structure:

We need to take the time and patience to let our eyes and brain fully adapt to higher paces, removing the "Protective Reaction."

We need the knowledge of correct line geometry, the skill to execute subtle counter-steering inputs, and the experience to trust the bike's stability at lean.

Examples of Speed Delivering Stability

This is the most crucial example for two-wheeled vehicles. A stationary motorcycle is inherently unstable and will fall over instantly without support. The moment the wheels start spinning, they become gyroscopes.

A gyroscope resists any force trying to change its plane of rotation. The faster the wheel spins, the stronger its angular momentum and the greater its resistance to tipping over. This force actively works to keep the motorcycle's rotational axis (the wheel) upright.

At very low speeds (like beginner maneuvers), the gyroscopic effect is weak. The bike feels heavy and unstable, forcing the rider to constantly make large, exhausting steering and body corrections. Once the rider achieves a moderate speed (around 15–20 mph), the gyroscopic effect stabilizes the bike, making it feel lighter and more controllable—even though it's moving faster.

Aerodynamic Stability

While a minor factor at street speeds, it becomes significant at the velocities you see in racing, especially MotoGP.

When moving slowly, a bike is easily buffeted by crosswinds or turbulent air, which destabilizes it. As speed increases, the air resistance (drag) creates a constant, high-pressure force against the bike's front surfaces. This acts like the feathers on a dart, keeping the entire assembly aligned and pointing straight ahead with less effort from the rider.

The higher-speed riders are actually less susceptible to minor destabilizing forces because the air itself is pushing the machine straight.

Counter-Steering Effectiveness

The essential technique for turning a motorcycle—counter-steering—relies directly on speed for its effectiveness.

You turn the handlebar slightly *away* from the direction you want to go (steer left to go right). This momentary input causes the gyroscopic forces to lean the bike into the turn. The higher the speed, the smaller and quicker the steering input needed to initiate a deep, stable lean.

At low speed, you have to turn the bars wide to lean the bike, which feels clumsy and unstable. At high speed, the system is so responsive that a light tap is all it takes to achieve a stable, deep lean angle, which is the only way to balance centrifugal force in a corner. The fast rider's seemingly effortless turn is a product of speed-amplified control.

True Edge

However, when we truly examine this paradox—where the slower rider crashes and the faster rider doesn't—the biggest issue isn't the technical limit of the machine; it's the mental limit of the rider.

The rider crashing well before the bike's actual capacity is overwhelmed because they're mentally on the limit.

This state of saturation triggers the worst possible chain reaction:

Instead of executing a calculated counter-steer or throttle adjustment, the rider's primal brain takes over, leading to counter-productive, desperate actions like chopping the throttle, freezing up, or standing the bike up mid-corner.

The rider is already using 100% of their cognitive bandwidth just to maintain that pace. When an unexpected event occurs (a ripple in the asphalt, another bike's shadow), they have zero mental processing time left to react correctly.

The rider effectively runs out of instinctive intelligence before they run out of tire grip. The crash isn't a technical failure; it's a failure of bandwidth and self-control.

The goal, therefore, is to expand your mental comfort zone until your physical skill set can be accessed without triggering that panic. Mastery isn't about reaching the physical limit; it's about making your mind's limit far exceed the demands of your speed.

Psychological Takeaway

Controlled speed is a stabilizing resource that frees up mental energy. For beginners, a bike feels unstable and "heavy" at low speeds due to a weak gyroscopic effect. This feeling of instability instantly triggers insecurity and a low "panic bar." Conversely, speed is a stabilizing resource. For master riders, increasing speed (within safe limits) isn't fear-inducing; it's a resource that settles the machine, making it feel predictable and freeing up cognitive energy otherwise spent fighting instability.

Danger of Bandwidth Collapse

Riders lose control because they're mentally at their limit, using 100% of their cognitive bandwidth just to maintain an unskilled pace. When insecurity flickers, they have zero mental processing time left to execute the correct counter-measure. This is the protective reaction loop in action: any perceived speed threshold triggers the primitive tense-up, target fixation, and panic inputs sequence, instead of the required full protocol of f'n smooth execution. Losing control is fundamentally a failure of bandwidth and self-control, not the bike's capability. The clumsy, muscle-driven inputs of the counter-steering deficit are simply too slow for the forces at speed.

Expand Your Mental Comfort Zone

The solution is to acquire the full protocol by replacing primitive "instinctive intelligence" with instinctive precision (unconscious competence). The core objective is to develop cognitive lag time: Intentionally practice creating mental processing time between perceiving a problem and executing a response.

By training your brain to adapt to higher paces and trusting the bike's inherent stability, you expand your mental comfort zone. This ensures that "too fast" triggers precision, not panic, giving you control and adaptive decision-making.

Controlled speed (legally of course) brings stability. Expand your mental limit until it far exceeds your physical demands, and achieve true, unconscious performance on any road.

Getting Lost in Electronic Riding Aids

Cost of False Confidence

I remember testing one of the first traction control systems and it was horrible. Back then, a TC would cut any rear-wheel spin instantly. Not gradually, but like someone hit a light switch. For a less experienced rider, that might have been comforting, but for those of us who purposely spin the rear a little faster than the front on corner exits, it worked against us. Power sliding takes smoothness and a committed, steady throttle hand. That kind of abrupt interference from the TC nearly got me into trouble more than once.

Of course, things have changed since those days. Modern systems are far more refined. Electronic rider aids have come a long way and most of that progress came from motorsports. What started as crude traction control evolved into a complex ecosystem of rider-assist systems: wheelie control, launch control, slide control, cornering ABS, active suspension, quick shifters, and auto-blip. The racing world has become the R&D lab for all that.

But that raises a question: how much of this takes away from the rider's raw skill and at what cost?

ABS and the F1 Parallel

Take ABS for example. It's the one electronic system that statistically saves lives. Studies show that ABS-equipped motorcycles are involved in roughly 20%–35% fewer fatal crashes than those without it. That's a big win for safety, but it doesn't tell the full story. In racing, ABS is banned because it increases braking distance. You'd have to brake earlier, which means slower lap times. That should already tell you something, shouldn't it?

In MotoGP, traction control and wheelie control changed the game. Gone are the days when a rider could draw black lines out of every corner, sliding on the edge of control—that visceral proof of throttle mastery. Now, you can pin it open and let the computer manage grip. Sure, the rider still has to know how to work with those systems, but it's not the same. It's a different kind of skill—more about interpreting data and managing electronics than pure mechanical feel.

And that's not just a MotoGP thing. Formula One is the perfect mirror. When computers began to dominate that sport, they transformed it. Tons of sensors started reading everything—throttle position, tire temperature, lateral G, suspension movement—feeding it all to the engineers. Suddenly, car setup was no longer about the driver's "seat-of-the-pants" feedback; it became about data logs and algorithms.

Remember when Jacques Villeneuve was the only one who could take Eau Rouge at Spa flat-out? The man was flying on pure guts and precision. But as traction control and downforce systems advanced, every car could do it. Electronics made what used to separate great drivers from good ones accessible to almost anyone. Launch control made every start perfect, traction control made every exit flawless, and active suspension smoothed out the worst bumps. It got to the point where the FIA had to ban many of those aids just to bring human skill back into the equation.

And here's the irony: most of those systems eventually made their way to the street to our cars and motorcycles. Things like power steering with active feedback, stability control, cornering ABS, adaptive suspension, and even "backing-in" control. It's all in our hands now. Don't get me wrong, today's MotoGP and Formula One racers are incredibly skilled. Mastering these new systems takes a whole new kind of intelligence. But the question remains: does the tech serve the rider, or does the rider serve the tech?

The Dark Side

When it comes to street riding, the story gets complicated. Electronic rider aids can absolutely help in panic situations. ABS prevents lockups. Traction control can prevent a high-side. Stability control can stop a tank slapper before it begins. But there's a dark side that nobody likes to talk about—false confidence.

Let me tell you something I heard straight from the source. I once coached a CHP motorcycle officer who told me something shocking:

after they switched from Harley patrol bikes to BMWs with more electronics, their injury rates went up. The department's own study found that the new electronics gave officers more confidence—too much confidence—and they started riding beyond their old limits. The result? More crashes. It's the classic case of risk compensation: when you feel safer, you often behave less safely.

Now think about today's sportbikes. A kid can walk into a dealership and buy a 230-horsepower machine with traction control, slide control, and cornering ABS. He'll think, "I'm safe—the computer's got me." But slide control doesn't mean you can slide. It just helps manage one, if you're fast enough to even trigger it. In other words, the tech doesn't make him Rossi, it just makes him believe he could be.

I've been looking at data from 1965 up through now, and the truth is hard to ignore. Despite all these advances—better tires, better suspension, rider aids, track days, rider education programs—motorcycle fatalities are still climbing. Even with all this technology meant to keep us alive, riders keep dying. That's not a tech problem; that's a human problem.

Maybe riders aren't much more reckless than before. Well, maybe just a little. Maybe the electronics make them more risk-friendly. Maybe riders with fewer aids are pushing harder to keep up with those who have them. Maybe the bikes themselves are so powerful now that even with all the aids, you're still dancing with physics at the edge of what's survivable.

I'm not here to be the bad guy. I'm not anti-tech. I'm anti-complacency. What I'm saying is this: electronics don't replace skill or mental discipline. They don't teach you to read a corner or control your panic in a split second. They just give you another margin—one that's too easy to burn through if you never learned to ride without it.

Fatal Question

When I look at those fatality numbers, I can't help but wonder:

How can deaths still rise when we have more safety tools than ever?

How can riders still crash this often when traction control, cornering ABS, and advanced tires exist? How is it possible, when chassis, tires and suspensions got a whole lot better?

Maybe the answer isn't about the bikes, maybe it's about us. The confidence that comes from electronics is false if it replaces awareness, training, and respect for limits.

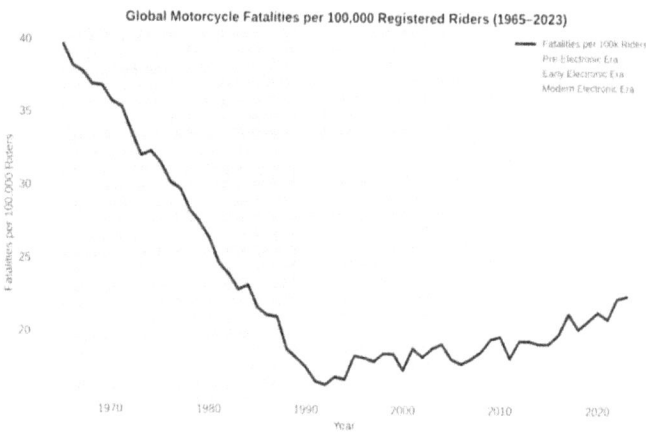

Not to mention that at least in the U.S., the education system hasn't changed, and from my perspective, is equally responsible for these horrible numbers.

Psychological Takeaway

You're falling for risk compensation, and your brain perceives electronic aids (ABS, TC) as a safety net, automatically adjusting your "risk dial" upwards.

This is the safety net lie. It encourages false confidence, pushing you beyond your actual skill limit. This isn't safer; it just moves the crash point further out, making inevitable failure more catastrophic.

Electronics provide a small, technical margin of error. Your brain, operating under false confidence, immediately burns through that margin by increasing speed or aggression. The technology helps the bike go faster, but it simultaneously sabotages your skill development.

Stop delegating survival to a computer. Understand that electronic aids enable you to ride faster, but they erode your accountability and skill margin through risk compensation.

PART III: Intelligence

Competitiveness

Do you remember all those races up the stairs you've had against your bigger brother? You lost badly, 'cuz he could run up there skipping on one step. You got him good, though, playing chess over Christmas. Remember all those little competitive 'games' you guys had going? Some ended up in verbal or even physical fights. Even though you loved him, there was nothing above the relieving call of: "I'm first!" Mom was tired of hearing it, while Dad just said, "you'll get him next time."

It was a daily, ongoing thing, wasn't it? Did it ever slow down? Oh yeah, the moment your legs got longer and you could also skip a step up those stairs. That was the moment your brother couldn't win that easy anymore, and you hear the first 'excuses.'

Competitiveness is in all of us. I believe it's part of shaping individuals from the day of birth. Recognition is what we actually seek, isn't it?!

Was it really fun? Maybe in the very beginning, but later, only for the 'winner.' You remember when it was easier for you to lose, when there was no direct comparison? When you knew you had the shorter legs and the race was already decided because of it, but it helped you gain acceptance? That acceptance kind of allowed you to still have fun.

It's in our DNA. For some more and for some less. Triggers throughout life can boost that gene up to a napalm-peeing, full-blown apex competitor who would go over dead bodies—or keep it asleep, and it comes out as needed. Life, environment, opportunities, and experiences are all triggers for it.

Marquez Paradox

The Marquez brothers are a great example here. Can you only imagine what was going on in that home on a daily basis? Oh boy! Marc, the older one, had 'the longer legs' because he could grasp and create the skills earlier than Alex, taught by their dad. That's a head start for Marc that's still intact, but fading.

Well, I actually believe that Marc also has a killer instinct that Alex doesn't have (yet). That killer instinct might have been created by constantly winning their races, and on the other hand, it helped Alex to find acceptance in his 'loser position,' and so to keep the fun with it anyway. This in-comparison was probably the healthy balance for their relationship.

I wonder what that would have looked like for them otherwise. It's gonna shift, though, because Marc has proved everything, and the decline is there. He knows. Alex's 'legs' are growing out soon, and he'll be able to skip steps of that staircase.

I think also here they will be lucky, because the 'shift of power' will create in-comparison again. Alex picks up Thor's hammer and Marc will be able to live in peace with it.

Competitiveness is a dilemma. It can trigger hopes, dreams, and an undeniable will to overcome holdbacks. But competitiveness can also kill fun, relationships, and much more. It can literally kill YOU! What a bridge, huh?

Average Rider's Dilemma

I see it pretty much every day. We have students in all kinds of our programs that are reeking of competitiveness. Their 'I need to be fastest' appearance shines through in no time. Body language, the questions they ask—and for the most part—there is an arrogance shining through their eyes.

That's how we know what's coming:

That rider probably has an ego driven personality. Low listening abilities, which then leads to him possibly saying "I didn't get much out of it" after all. Because he's an 'all about balls' thinker, he'll be more likely to go down during class. That could be the chance of hurting someone else, and there's also a fair chance of losing that rider to track days anyway.

So now we're trying to 'reach' that rider, and make him aware that this isn't a competition, nor a fair comparison. Some of them, we actually can 'wake up', some not. Those are the ones we'll be telling that they're a danger to themselves and others, because they're competing the shit during their group rides up and down Hwy 9, where ambulances are out in a frequency of an hour.

There is a competitiveness in some that makes them not think logically anymore, just for chasing the chance of declaring a 'win.' Imagine you coach someone on a track. You go way below your capabilities for that rider and all of a sudden, the guy makes an inside pass on you. just to have his moment in space and time. Needless to say that we're sending such personalities right home.

Outcome Shift

Competitiveness can be THE key element for huge success, when in the right and skilled hands!!!

Competitiveness can be THE element that kills people, when in <u>mentally unstable</u>, or lack of physically skilled hands!!!

Psychological Takeaway

Competitiveness is hardwired into your DNA, but in the wrong hands, it's a death sentence. The toxic competitor is driven entirely by external validation. You aren't riding for yourself; you're riding to hear the "relieving call" of being first.

When your goal is to be perceived as the fastest guy in the group, your brain prioritizes the ego-hit of a "win" over the actual process of learning.

This creates a dangerous "all about balls" mindset where you override logic just to make a pass. Because your self-worth is tied to your position on the road, you become resistant to instruction and blind to the ambulances waiting at the bottom of the hill.

Trap of Outcome over Process

When you compete against others, you're at the mercy of their skill level, not your own. If you're faster than a slow group, you develop a false sense of mastery, but if you're slower than a fast group, your confidence shreds. This is the outcome shift. By focusing on the result—the win, the lap time, the "inside pass"—you introduce chaos into your riding. You're no longer a pilot; you're a gambler. Toxic competitiveness kills the fun for everyone else and eventually kills the rider because it demands 100% risk for 0% technical gain.

An apex competitor flips the script by mastering internal motivation. Your only real opponent is the gap between your ideal performance and your actual performance. The goal shifts from "beating that guy" to perfecting your entry, your line, and your vision.

The true test of your mindset is how you ride when no one is watching. If your discipline drops when there's no one to impress, you're still a slave to your ego.

※ **Mind Note – Coach's take**

"Competitiveness is in all of us. I believe it's part of shaping individuals from the day of birth. Recognition is what we actually seek!"

— *Can Akkaya*

Beast Mode

The Awakening

We've all been 18-year-old idiots once. We all know that this period is marked by significant instability, identity exploration, and challenges, rather than just foolishness. The inexperience and underdeveloped brain function of a young kid can lead to impulsive decisions, and so to a wide range of f-ups. Honestly speaking.

And so was I. This was at a time before I even knew about racing. Oh man, riding my street bike was all that I had on my mind back then, and when I was riding, I was out of my mind. Literally. There was something else about riding though. That's the 'something' that made my frontal brain cortex pop like a balloon. If there was some kind of risk assessment left in there, it must have been evaporated by an adrenaline rush when it all switched to 'beast mode,' willingly or not.

It wasn't about the actual act of riding a motorcycle, but about looking for dogfights! No matter if I was on a ride out with riding buddies or all alone—when I spied another rider or group... holy crap. Hell broke loose and all I wanted was to beat them real hard and bad, ASAP. As if there was no tomorrow. Going up and down my favorite canyon, hoping there will be more 'prey' to mess with. There were times when I was just standing there, waiting for the next sportbike rider to come by. Oh boy!

Sounds sick? Kinda is, right? But don't you tell me you wouldn't even know what this is and that you never had that going as a kid. Also, it was a different time in Europe back then. There was no such thing as 'track days,' where I just could go like nowadays, so don't blame me for

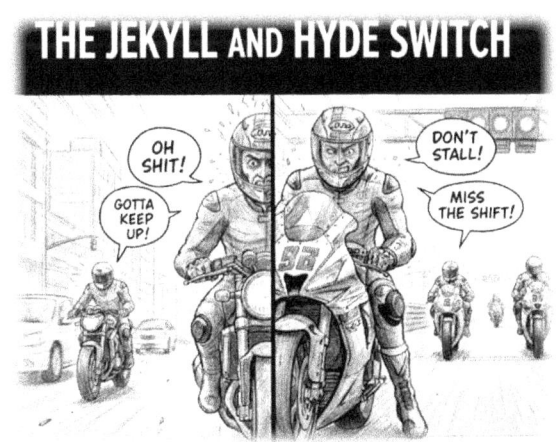

being irresponsible. Messing around is a whole lotta gray zone and part of growing up and finding identity. I found mine as a competitor, and it was calling me to battle.

Fatal Flaw

When I finally arrived in amateur racing, dogfights were all what I was going for. That was the picture, the vision of what racing is all about. It was so deeply manifested that this dogfighter attitude had followed me up to early semi-pro racing level.

This is where it began to work against me. Let me break my agenda of a race weekend down for you:

Free practice = beast mode on

Practice = beast mode on

Free practice 2 = beast mode on

Qualifying = beast mode on

Race = beast mode on

Don't get this all wrong. Sure, I did my work to make things better throughout and I also like to believe that I'm not stupid. But there was always that question around, of why I was not that strong in Qualifying sessions and why I couldn't grab a strategically solid grid position. I also questioned why I was having such a hard time managing my tires, trying to get them to perform for a race distance.

It was after a Qualifying session at the Nürburgring GP track in Germany, when one of the title contenders walked up to me very angry and said "Why the hell did you try to shake me out of your slipstream? I gave you plenty of slipstream to do a good lap time!" I remember it as if it happened just yesterday. (Sorry Juergen)

This split me in half when I realized that I wouldn't be able to perform that way on a higher stage. I had to rewrite and rewire everything.

Finding the Mixture

Well, I did rewire. To a certain extent, because then I also realized that I needed dogfights to actually 'wake up.' I found a mixture.

Do you notice that Marc Marquez waits in the pitlane for someone to tow him? How's that even necessary for an 8-time world champion?! Well, obviously also he needs that 'something' to make his blood start boiling up to operation temperature!

I think that being a dogfighter is a necessity, and part of becoming a competitor. But where does this become a necessity for you, the street rider?

Here and there, when I finally have some time to take my street bike out for a little ride, there's that guy who's looking for a dogfight. I gotta smile, remembering all of this. Well, sometimes I take his 'invite,' and sometimes I just let it go.

Both of you—the dogfighter and the one who just got 'invited'—both have the choice to bring it to the track. Nowadays it's quite easy. I've learned it the hard way as that got me injured a hell of a lot of times. Now, I 'invite' you to learn with me!

Psychological Takeaway

When you go "Beast Mode" in a canyon or on the track, you're letting a hostile takeover happen inside your head. Your primal lizard brain—the part that only knows how to attack or run away—shoves your strategic mind out of the pilot's seat. It feels like focus, but it's actually an adrenaline-soaked blindness. You aren't riding a motorcycle anymore; you're just hunting "prey." This might win you a dogfight, but it evaporates your risk assessment and leaves your frontal cortex popping like a balloon. You're trading your survival for a momentary surge of ego.

Dopamine Trap

If you need a fight just to "wake up," you're a dopamine addict. Keeping the beast switched on for every practice and every street ride is a fatal flaw. While you're busy trying to "beat them real hard and bad," you're failing at the things that actually matter—like managing your tires or hitting a solid line. The damn lizard brain doesn't care about the oil patch in the next turn or your grid position; it only cares about the kill. Relying on pure aggression makes disciplined riding impossible and turns every corner into a high-stakes gamble you're eventually going to lose.

Champion's Ignition Switch

Real pros don't live in the dogfight; they use it as a deliberate ignition switch to bring their blood up to "operating temperature." They might use a rival's slipstream to sharpen their focus, but they keep their strategic brain in control of the throttle. They aren't reacting to the invitation; they're using it. It's the difference between being a mindless animal and a calculated warrior. You have to learn to trigger that focus without surrendering your mind to the adrenaline.

You need to recognize the exact second that the lizard starts reaching for the controls. On the street, that "beast" is what gets you injured. Every time you spy a group and feel that "hell break loose" sensation, remind yourself that you're about to sacrifice your skill for a short-term high. Use the presence of other riders to sharpen your own precision, not to start a battle that ends in a dark room of frustration. Tame the beast, or it will eventually run you off the road.

❖ Mind Note – Locked Doors

"The fact of being an underdog changes people in ways that we often fail to appreciate. It opens doors and creates opportunities and permits things that might otherwise have seemed unthinkable."

— *Malcolm Gladwell*

Being Gung-Ho

Necessary Phase of the Over-Thinker

You know, when you start racing, you figure there are two primary types of amateur racers around you: one is the over-thinker, and the other is the Gung-Ho kind of racer. That doesn't mean the over-thinkers are much slower, especially if they have that sickness going on—the one called 'speed junkie.' That was me right there.

Before racing, I was hauling ass on street bikes. I was pretty much a gung-ho kind of guy. Everything was just happening, and it seemed to come easy to me. The only thing I knew for sure was that nobody could even get close to me.

When I got to racing, though, it immediately made me an over-thinker. Confused? So was I.

My simple analysis for the change is this: race bikes are a different breed, tracks are intimidating and, even worse, and I had to deal with opponents who could actually beat me. All of this forces you to start thinking.

Problem with Premature Aggression

During my early years as an amateur, I was chasing myself—trying to be the gung-ho guy I used to be, yearning for that kind of 'freedom' that comes with pure instinct. Trust me, I tried. When that old feeling did surface... I crashed.

It quickly became clear that this sport has far more facets than I believed, and that racing is much more than just about how big your balls are. I felt bad about myself, but I eventually understood that being an over-thinker is a necessary phase to go through. There's a massive list of variables you're suddenly up against:

Tracks, race bikes, race tires, and engine management.
Suspensions, fears, exploring limits, and crashing.
Opponents, strategies, psychological games, and yourself.

You have to dedicate mental bandwidth to master all of this before you can take the next major step forward.

Birth of Race Intelligence

I was a semi-pro when that time came. I was a quantum leap ahead of the racer I once was. It all came together—the pain, blood, and sweat paid off. This struggle creates what I call 'race intelligence,' but that happens to only a few, I believe.

As a full-pro racer, I was tough as nails, and I even found 'that guy' in me again—that gung-ho kind of guy. By then, though, I was able to let that gung-ho guy off the leash only when I was in control of all those variables. The over-thinker did the necessary intellectual work to create the framework, and the gung-ho instinct became the weapon within that framework.

The Slower, Smarter Way

If you couldn't understand what I'm saying here:

Being Gung-Ho makes you maybe faster in the beginning, but you'll hurt more, which will likely break your learning curve and cost a lot.

Don't feel bad being an over-thinker. It might take you longer to 'arrive,' but once you do, your competence is built on a solid intellectual foundation.

Marc Márquez is a great example of the final evolution: controlled aggression built on supreme control. And by the way, some racers only get their aggressive nicknames *during* their gung-ho era—it's a phase, not the final state.

Relax, and don't over-think why you're not 'like that guy' who seems so confident. You can't leave your skin, but just thinking about this transition should relax you. And hey, that gung-ho guy might be thinking the exact same thing about you right there.

Mental Freedoms of Being Gung-Ho

The initial appeal and power of the gung-ho mindset come from its simplicity and aggressive focus:

The gung-ho rider operates purely on instinct and impulse. There's no room for the internal debate that plagues the over-thinker. When a gap appears, or a turn comes up, the gung-ho rider simply commits.

Result. This decisiveness translates to faster initial reactions and a powerful, unwavering confidence in their *immediate* action, even if the action is technically flawed. They don't waste time on the "what if" scenarios that cripple the over-thinker.

Freedom from the 'Contract of Commitment'

The gung-ho rider operates with a temporary psychological blind spot to the consequences.

Result. They're not consciously worrying about "Hurt, Pain, and Dying" or the cost of the "Nuts n' Bolts." This lack of inhibition allows them to push the bike physically harder, faster, and earlier than their mental development justifies. They're not paralyzed by the fear of failure because they're too focused on aggressive action.

Freedom from the System

The gung-ho rider is operating without a complex system of patterns, strategies, or opponent analysis.

Result. Riding is a simple, singular goal: Go fast. This simplicity can lead to moments of genuine, effortless flow. While it's unsustainable for mastery, the feeling of the bike "just happening" (as you described in your youth) is the purest form of riding—it's riding as an unburdened, pure act of aggression and speed.

Necessary Synthesis

The ultimate goal, as outlined in the chapter, is to synthesize these freedoms with control. The professional racer achieves the mental freedom of the gung-ho rider (pure commitment and decisiveness) but only by first building the necessary intellectual control of the over-thinker (the mastery of all the system variables). The fully-evolved racer is gung-ho by choice, not by accident.

The Over-Thinker's Advantage

While the gung-ho rider enjoys the initial freedom of impulse, it's the over-thinker who builds the foundation for long-term, sustainable mastery. Your "over-thinking" isn't a problem; it's a superior mental operating system. Here are the critical advantages the over-thinker develops:

The over-thinker is constantly analyzing and categorizing every input. This rigorous intellectual work is the only way to build defined competence (the core of the "Yin & Yang" chapter).

When the over-thinker eventually gains speed, their confidence isn't based on a feeling or a gamble; it's based on proof. They know *why* they're fast. This intellectual certainty makes their confidence unshakeable and immune to the temporary setbacks that derail the gung-ho rider.

Built-in Risk Management

The gung-ho rider only learns by repeated, often costly, crashes. The over-thinker learns by anticipation. They process the complexity of the variables (tires, track conditions, suspension setup) and mentally run the scenarios.

Sustainable and Evolving Patterns

The core discipline of the over-thinker is the focus on patterning (Chaos Control). They're obsessed with *how* the bike works, *where* the shift point should be, and *why* the line is correct.

The gung-ho rider relies on one fixed style, but the over-thinker creates adaptable intelligence. When conditions change—wet track, worn tires, or a faster opponent—the over-thinker can intellectually adjust the entire system of patterns to compensate. This makes them a more complete, more durable, and ultimately, a much faster competitor in the long run.

The over-thinker's journey maybe slower, but every step is reinforced with knowledge. They're building a fortress of competence that, once complete, allows them to wield the necessary aggression with surgical precision. Intelligence is the only path to controlled, ultimate speed.

Are you disappointed again that this lecture is 'all about racing' and less useful for you as a street rider?! But is it really? OK, this is for you then:

Safety is the Over-Thinker's Domain

The gung-ho attitude is built on a dangerous premise: "Trust the impulse." On the street, impulse is the enemy of survival. The over-thinker's approach directly translates to maximum safety for the average rider:

The over-thinker trains the mind to anticipate and analyze the variables you can control (your shifting pattern, your braking point, your line) rather than relying on pure instinct for what you can't (the deer, the car pulling out).

The over-thinker's slow, analytical learning creates unshakeable confidence because they know why their inputs work. This prevents the "confidence crack" when a complex scenario arises.

The over-thinker learns from mental simulation and small, manageable errors. The gung-ho rider learns from costly, traumatic crashes. The over-thinker's method is the only sustainable way to build skill without frequent, debilitating resets.

When to Use the Gung-Ho Mentality

The street rider should never ride gung-ho by default, but they must be able to tap into its most valuable mental freedom: Decisive action.

The gung-ho mindset is powerful because it bypasses second-guessing. On the street, a momentary lapse in attention requires immediate, smooth, and aggressive correction (braking, counter-steering).

You should use your over-thinker brain to establish the correct smooth patterns. Then, in an emergency, you use the gung-ho's commitment to execute that pattern instantly and fully, without hesitation or "protective reactions."

The ultimate goal for the street rider is to be an over-thinker who acts gung-ho when the established, correct pattern demands it.

Being gung-ho shouldn't be you at all on the street, but there's something in your DNA which makes it come out. You need to be aware of it and tame it. Then you'll be able to use it more like an 'explorer nature', and things come easier to you.

Psychological Takeaway

When the stakes get real—like moving from the street to the track or facing faster opponents—you'll likely shift from being a "natural" to an over-thinker. Don't feel bad about it. This is a necessary phase where your brain is trying to categorize a massive list of new variables, from tire management to psychological games. You're dedicating mental bandwidth to build an intellectual foundation. While the gung-ho guy might look faster initially, he is likely riding on borrowed time and a blind spot for consequences. Your over-thinking isn't a weakness; it's the birth of your race intelligence.

Freedoms and Flaws of Going Gung-Ho

The gung-ho mindset is seductive because it offers freedom from second-guessing and the fear of failure. It's pure, unburdened aggression. But if you try to be that guy before you've mastered the variables, you'll crash hard. Relying on instinct before you've built a darn good framework is a fatal flaw that shatters your learning curve with injuries and repair bills. The goal is to reach a level where you're gung-ho by choice, not by accident. You want to be tough as nails because you're in control, not because you're ignoring the risks.

Over-Thinker's Advantage

As an over-thinker, your confidence is built on proof, not a gamble. You know exactly why you're fast, which makes your confidence unshakeable. You have the ability to "crash the bike in your head first," using mental simulation to find limits without the blood and broken plastic. While the gung-ho rider relies on a fixed style, you're creating an Adaptable Intelligence that can adjust to wet tracks or worn tires. You're building a fortress of competence that eventually allows you to let the "beast" off the leash with surgical precision.

Being Intelligently Gung-Ho

On the street, being gung-ho by default is a death wish; impulse is the enemy of survival. Your job is to use your over-thinker brain to establish perfect, smooth patterns for braking and steering. Then, when an emergency hits, you tap into that gung-ho decisiveness to execute those patterns instantly without a second thought. You use the over-thinker to build the framework and the gung-ho instinct as the weapon inside it.

Relax and stop worrying that you aren't "that guy" yet. Build the foundation— slower, smarter, and far more durable.

▓ Mind Note – A Chess Game

"Don't worry about being faster than the other guy. Worry about knowing exactly what the other guy is going to do."

— *Bobby Unser (Three-time Indy 500 Winner)*

Mental or Physical Aggression

It's actually kind of funny when I say this, because I've always been a very physical rider- on and off the track. Being physical, in my opinion, isn't far away from being physically aggressive and it doesn't take a lot to get soaked into it. How about we define it first:

Right Way

Being physical means using your body as a precise input device to manage the bike's weight distribution, chassis geometry, and center of gravity. It's about timing, leverage and balance. Think of a gymnast on the balance beam. They're very strong and physical, but their movements are precise, and executed with minimal visible effort.

Wrong Way

Being physically aggressive means using tension and excessive force to *fight* the bike. It's a sign that the rider is out of sync with the machine and is trying to solve a finesse problem with brute strength. Think of an unskilled driver yanking the steering wheel violently when they realize they missed a turn. They're being aggressive, not physical.

Tension vs. Core

The difference boils down to where the effort is applied:

The physical rider uses the core and lower body for stable, intentional movement. The upper body is loose for feedback.

The physically aggressive rider uses the arms and shoulders to muscle the bike, creating rigidity and resistance.

If your forearms are pumped and your hands are sore, you're physically aggressive. If your core is tired but your hands are relaxed, you were physical—and you were riding correctly. In other words, the more aggressive you ride, the more and sooner you're wearing yourself out. Consequences are lack of performance, stamina, making more and more mistakes because a tired body is also a tired mind.

That is the most important transition a rider can make. To shift from being an aggressive fighter to a physical master, you have to train your body to relax your hands and engage your core. Here are three focused techniques to help a rider move from physical aggression to being effectively physical on the bike:

Three Core Techniques

The goal is to move the work from your shoulders (tension) to your legs and core (leverage). Physical aggression starts with the hands. A tight grip prevents the bike from steering naturally and locks up the chassis.

The drill. During your warm-up, practice riding with your middle finger, ring finger, and pinky finger barely touching the handgrips. The only fingers with firm contact should be your thumb and index finger, used for braking/throttle.

The intent. Your hands should feel featherlight. If you hit a bump and your grip tightens instinctively, you're relying on arm strength instead of your core. This forces your body to find stability elsewhere—which leads to the next technique.

Inner Thigh Clamp

The single most effective way to become a "physical" rider is by using your lower body to support your weight and initiate direction change.

The drill. Focus on clamping your inner thighs against the tank at all times, especially under braking and through the corners.

The intent. Your legs are the anchor. When your legs are working, your upper body can relax. Clamping the tank allows you to support your weight through your core, freeing your hands to simply *guide* the handlebars, rather than *wrestle* them. If you feel your hands tiring, you've lost the clamp.

Breathing Synchronization

Physical aggression is a manifestation of mental panic. Breathing is your control switch.

The drill. Before a critical section—like corner entry—consciously take a deep breath in through your nose and exhale fully through your mouth as you tip the bike into the corner.

The intent. Synchronize your breath with the start of the action. The deliberate exhale forces a release of tension in your shoulders and core, breaking the panic loop. This is the mental aggression winning: you're deliberately choosing to relax and execute your plan, rather than allowing your fear to dictate a violent, physically aggressive input.

By consistently applying these drills, you rewire your body to use leverage and precision (physical) instead of force and tension (aggressive). Not just that. Being 60 years old today demands that I manage my energy even better. This technique still helps me on that side, but also to be still consistently fast.

Power of Intent

Mental aggression is arguably the most valuable trait in high-performance riding. It's the opposite of panic and it's what allows a rider to be fast, smooth, and consistent without burning energy. In short, mental aggression is the absolute commitment to a precise plan. Here is a breakdown of what mental aggression is, how it works, and how it translates to the bike:

Mental aggression isn't *about pushing harder; it's about eliminating doubt and maximizing focus. It's the clarity of thought required to execute an input at the precise moment it needs to happen.*

Commitment Over Force

Mental aggression means being 100% committed to your planned action, regardless of the perceived risk or external pressure.

It's the absence of hesitation. When a marker flashes by—your visual cue to brake or turn in—a mentally aggressive rider immediately executes the plan. A hesitant rider suffers a fractional delay, forcing them to use physical aggression (brute force) to correct the line they just blew.

It's a deliberate choice. Unlike physical aggression, which is a *reaction* driven by panic, mental aggression is a *proactive choice* driven by confidence in your preparation.

Training Mental Aggression

You can't do push-ups for mental aggression; you have to train the mind to be decisive under pressure.

The go/no-go rule. Before you enter a corner or a passing zone, establish a clear rule: "If X happens, I go. If Y happens, I don't." Once the decision is made, you must execute it with zero inner debate. The failure isn't in choosing the wrong action, but in hesitating between two actions.

External focus. Mental aggression is maintained by focusing on external targets, not internal feelings. The mind should be locked onto the brake marker, the apex, and the exit curb. The moment you start focusing on the feeling in your hands or the fear in your stomach, you lose your mental edge and start using physical aggression.

Mental aggression is the quiet strength that makes speed look easy. It's the difference between a rider who knows what they're doing and a rider who is desperately trying to make up their mind.

Weaponizing Aggression

We've established that constant physical aggression is a mistake that makes you slow. However, there's a critical distinction: the difference between a panicked reaction and a calculated tactical move. There were moments in my own racing career where I went into full-out physical aggressive mode. This wasn't because I was scared; it was because I was on a mission to intensify pressure and to break confidence.

Psychological Tool

Don't confuse being tense and panicked with being committed. Most riders mistake physical aggression for the mental aggression they actually need. The essential transition is shifting from being a "physically aggressive fighter" to a "physical master" using core strength and leverage.

Physical aggression is a manifestation of mental panic. It's the rigid, unskilled reaction of using your arms and shoulders to "muscle the bike," signifying you're out of sync and fighting for control. This rigidity creates rapid physical burnout ("a tired body is also a tired mind"), guaranteeing a continuous flow of mistakes.

Mental aggression is arguably your most valuable trait, as it's the opposite of panic. It isn't about pushing harder, but about achieving clarity of thought and executing inputs at the precise moment they need to happen. This aggression is defined by the absence of hesitation. A mentally aggressive rider immediately executes the planned action; a hesitant rider delays, forcing them to use brute force (physical aggression) to correct the line they just blew.

While the amateur uses physical aggression as a permanent, self-sabotaging riding style, professionals use it as a calculated psychological tool—a temporary, decisive, and loud "shock-and-awe" tactical maneuver intended to sabotage an opponent's mental aggression. Knowing the distinction and when to switch it off is the mark of mastery.

On the street, you need to trade that violence for smoothness, elegance, and grace. Think about it: a truly meaningful input is one that doesn't upset the bike's balance. When you move with grace, you're working *with* the physics of the machine, not against them.

By using the Inner thigh clamp and keeping your hands featherlight, you turn your body into a secondary shock absorber. You aren't just saving energy; you're staying "meaningful" in your actions so the bike can handle the chaos you didn't see coming.

Train your decisiveness and use external focus. This is the path to a calm, and controlled performance.

Mama Bear Effect

This piece is primarily aimed at female riders. I'm sure, however, that many of you will recognize yourselves in most of the other psychological twists we've discussed throughout this book. Where I'm going with this might seem counterproductive at first glance, but my intention is that it can also be a huge relief if you grasp it correctly. My understanding of female riders is based on working with them over multiple decades, on and off the track.

I know very well that this section (just like all the others) might not apply to all women. I knew about this phenomenon, but I finally considered 'saying it' when my own daughter's competitiveness started getting in her way. Let me approach this as sensitively as I possibly can.

Have you noticed that there are no women at the highest levels of motorsports, neither in Formula One nor, especially, in MotoGP? That's exactly what I asked my daughter, Jill, when she started getting confused about where she stood and where she was headed. I truly hesitated to tell her what I believe the reason is, because I knew it could deeply impact her.

Jill's cautious nature makes a papercut a subject for an entire week. At the same time, she's an internal competitor. Now, since I work with her constantly and she literally joined every single class, she made immense progress in an impressively short amount of time. That progress, though, also unleashed her external competitor. Meanwhile, I taught someone else to ride, just like Jill, but he was progressing through all the classes at an even faster pace – and I saw it coming.

She never said anything, but her eyes, body language, and motivation levels were speaking volumes. So I asked— "Are you comparing yourself with him?!"—demanding 101% honesty. She knew I already knew, and she confirmed it. Now I was in a dilemma. I didn't want to hurt my girl in any way, so I tried a couple of different approaches, but they didn't help her break free from it. It took me half a day to finally articulate the actual issue.

I tried to help her find the answer herself by asking the right questions about motorsports and the differences between female and male riders. Jill admitted, "There is obviously a physical difference, but also a mental one," but she couldn't define that mental part. The difference is that males possess something that's 'present' all the time – a 'killer instinct' – which females often only access situationally.

Think of it this way: a male caveman hunter might jump on the back of a mammoth just to be *that guy* in the cave tonight. A cavewoman, however, would typically only access that kind of killer instinct state if her baby was in danger. I like to call this the 'Mama Bear Effect.' This is the mental state where she would kill – or die – for whatever gets in the way. So yes, males often have this and will 'go for it' for more primitive, ego-driven reasons. That's pretty much it, isn't it?!

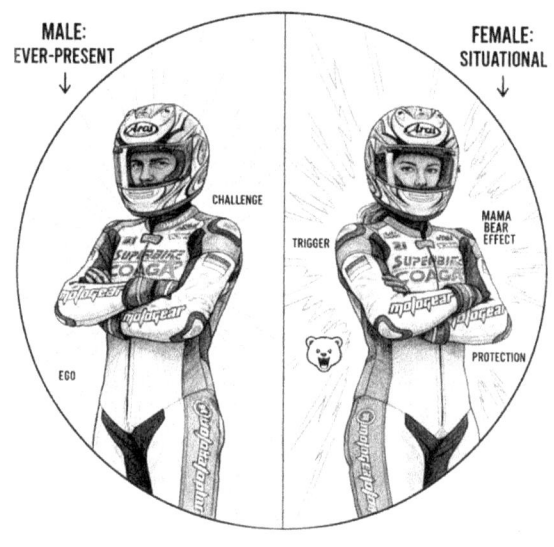

So now I'm watching Jill's physical responses to see how she's taking this, and I ask if this smashes her motivation. Her eyes wandered through the room, and she confirmed it had. Then I asked her to consider if comparing herself with a 'caveman who is just going for it' was, in fact, a fair comparison or not. From there, I let her go through the thinking process herself, looking for a resolution. All of a sudden, I saw light coming back in her eyes, which brought a smile, and she dropped her shoulders.

I saw new perspectives, motivation, and new goals sparkle in her when I told her that she needs to search for fair and realistic comparisons only among other female riders. To open her eyes and truly see where she stands compared to them. She recognized that there are not a whole lot who actually level with her at all. Pressure faded, relief took over, motivation recovered, goals reset!

Look... I'm not slandering your hopes and dreams, just speaking realistically. I'm also NOT saying that the highest levels of motorsports are forever unreachable for women. Sooner or later, it will happen. But that woman is going to be a quite different type – inside and out.

Triggering the Mama Bear Effect

Now, if you desperately want to reach out to the stars – you'll have my fullest support. But you'll have to find triggers that make that Mama Bear scream a battle cry that makes the track shake up. Controlled aggression, channeled energies. They're in you, but you need to find them.

But there are even more mental blocks affecting female riders when they're around male riders, which, in fact, make them stay away from education in the first place:

Being observed by males.
Taking orders from males.
Accepting critique from males.
(Add yours!)

I guess in here you might find yourself as the street rider, because all this and more leads to feelings of helplessness, smallness, being overwhelmed, feeling set up for embarrassment, and ultimately... failure. This is where Jill and I decided to offer female-only cornering classes, and she's now running them as a head coach.

Psychological Takeaway

No use, torturing yourself with the idea that you should "naturally" want to hunt like the guys. For most men, that reckless, ego-driven aggression is an always-on default. For you, that level of intensity is usually situational, the Mama Bear Effect. You don't jump on the mammoth just to brag; you do it when there's a reason that matters. When you compare your measured, technical progress to a guy who is simply "going for it" on raw impulse, you're losing a game you shouldn't even be playing. It's an unfair comparison that robs you of your motivation.

The moment you stop looking for validation in a "caveman" environment, the weight falls off your shoulders. Painful to watch, when my daughter Jill was drowning in frustration until she looked at a realistic peer group and realized she was actually elite. If you're feeling small or overwhelmed, it's usually because you're measuring your worth against a different biological blueprint. Resetting your goals to a fair standard isn't "settling"—it's clearing the mental clutter so you can actually focus on your own mastery.

If you want to reach the top, you have to find the "triggers" that pull that protective ferocity out of you and put it into the tires. It's about taking that energy you'd use for a loved one and aiming it at the apex. It's a deliberate rewiring. You have the fire; you just don't waste it on ego-trips.

The biggest barrier for many women isn't the bike; it's the audience. Feeling watched or judged by men creates a mental block that makes you stay away from the training you need. Unlike men, they don't need nor want attention of that kind, and I get it.

▩ Mind Note – It's there!

"A woman is like a tea bag; you never know how strong it is until it's in hot water."

- Eleanor Roosevelt

Race Intelligence

Mastering the Future

Most professional racers have developed a 'race intelligence' which helps them on multiple levels. Basically, it makes you have an instinct on what's going on around you momentarily, AND can picture what's gonna happen next. There's a lot to it though.

This has more or less, something to do with 'spatial thinking' and human knowledge. Additionally for our sport, you need a deep understanding and feel for physics, technical grip levels, and the ability to make decisions in a split second for always changing variables and conditions. An instinct for the consequences of a wrong decision must also exist. That's quite a mental load, isn't it?!

Manning Analogy

NFL star Peyton Manning had an enormous 'game intelligence.' Was he that good at throwing the ball? No. Other QB's were better than him at this. Was he that good at running the ball? No, he wasn't. He compensated all this with a game intelligence like no other. He could read a defender's mind. I believe he could see the pass and what's gonna happen in front of his eyes, right before calling 'Omaha.' He could think like his receiver did, just in that certain moment on his route. Like a 'what would I do' triple scenario vs. consequences rundown in just a split second. Try to imagine that!

Race Intelligence in Action

A race intelligence can help you run down several start scenarios, depending on your grid position. This isn't like the 'what/if' thing. This is more like a look into the future and comparison, where you can literally see yourself and the entire field as if you're sitting on the grandstand.

I could literally see what would happen if I'd attack the first turn on the inside, then rewind and attack on the outside. How would my opponents react and where would that take them. Don't know if you can imagine what the first turn looks like when ten racers throw themselves into every open gap right after start, but that's pretty much the most frightening thing you can do to yourself. Now here is you, who had all those different scenarios running like a video through your head. This means, you've already seen the outcomes and it's less shocking when it actually happens. Cool, huh?!

That race intelligence helped you setting up an overall strategy for the entire race.

That includes facts like:

How many laps remain.

Your momentary stamina.

The championship point standings.

The tire compound decision you made on the grid.

If you're in a start-to-finish dog-fight or leading the field.

During the race, race intelligence makes you have an instinct of when and where your opponent is going to ride an attack. You think 'like him' in his position. If you're required to attack, your instinct is to play it through before you actually physically do. Instead of punching around, you literally lay him up for a confidence-breaking attack.

Now you're leading, and your race intelligence allows you to switch on risk management. Every time you zip down the finish straight, your team shows you the gap on the board. You go just as fast as you have to in order to save tire life.

Race intelligence isn't a magical sixth sense. It's the result of turning high-stakes, real-time chaos into a series of pre-processed, automatic choices.

Pattern Compression

Your brain can't process raw, novel information in a split second. What race intelligence does is simple: it compresses millions of past decisions (from practice laps, supermoto, mountain biking, and race mistakes) into immediately recognizable patterns.

When you "see" the first-turn scenarios run like a video through your head, you're not seeing the future; you're accessing the closest relevant historical files in your brain's memory bank.

The "Omaha" call from Manning or the sudden braking by a racer isn't a fresh decision. It's the automatic output of a pattern matcher: "This situation right now is 98% identical to the crash/success I had three years ago, therefore, the required action is X."

This compression frees up your conscious brain. The instinct takes over the heavy lifting, allowing your limited mental bandwidth to focus only on the 2% of information that's actually *new* (like a flick of an opponent's elbow or a sudden tire slide).

Illusion of Control

You've already seen the outcomes and it's less shocking when it actually happens:

Panic occurs when the brain encounters a situation with no clear, pre-programmed response. It freezes, wasting precious time.

By running the "what-if" video ahead of time, the racer ensures that no first-turn pile-up or aggressive overtake is truly novel. The conscious mind accepts the chaos because the subconscious has already rehearsed a response.

This creates the powerful psychological illusion that the racer is controlling the environment, when in reality, they're merely controlling their *reaction* to the environment. They've shifted from reacting to responding, and that difference is the gap between the field and the champion.

Decoupling Body and Mind

When you reach this level, the intelligence decouples from the physical act. The body rides, using its own motor memory, while the intelligence floats above, analyzing the future and managing risk.

The body handles the physical inputs (throttle, lean angle, shifting) on autopilot.

The mind calculates the strategy (tire life, gap management, opponent's weak spot) and runs the video ahead of the action.

The result is that the professional racer isn't just in the present moment; they're simultaneously living in the past (providing the instinct) and the immediate future (managing the risk).

Takeaway for the Street Rider

Yeah, I know this one is tight for an average street rider. All I can say to this is that I could transfer these abilities to my street riding and that THIS is what saved my butt more than many times. You're just not dealing with opponents, but with traffic. Also here are natural response patterns to find.

Race intelligence on the street becomes survival intelligence. Instead of running scenarios for passing a rival, you're running scenarios for avoiding a disaster:

"Where will that driver pull out without looking?". You're predicting the movement of the four vehicles around you based on their speed, brake light patterns, and body language etc.

The goal remains the same: By constantly observing and processing the tiny clues in traffic (the swerve, the brake flash, the wheel turning), you build a compressed mental library of predictable errors. This lets your "instinct" take over and execute the correct counter-move while the average driver is still processing the initial threat.

Psychological Takeaway

Race intelligence isn't a psychic gift; it's a high-speed filing system. Your brain can't actually think fast enough to handle raw, brand-new chaos in a split second. To survive, it uses pattern compression, turning years of practice and close calls into a "compressed mental library." When you see a gap or a slide, you aren't making a fresh decision, you're instantly matching the current moment to a file from three years ago. This frees up your conscious mind to stop worrying about the basics and focus on the tiny details that actually matter.

Living in the Immediate Future

The ultimate weapon of the champion is the ability to pre-process chaos. By running "what-if" scenarios through your head before the lights go out, you ensure that no pile-up or aggressive pass is truly a surprise. Panic only happens when the brain sees something it hasn't rehearsed.

When you tell yourself "I've been here already," you kill the panic before it starts. This creates an illusion of control where you aren't just reacting to what's happening, you're responding to what you already knew was coming.

Split Mind

At this level, your body and mind decouple. Your body is a machine running on motor memory, handling the throttle and lean angle on autopilot. Meanwhile, your mind "floats" above the bike, living five seconds in the future. You aren't thinking about the turn you're in; you're managing tire life, calculating the gap to the guy behind you, and setting up the pass three corners away. You're simultaneously using instinct to manage the present so you can dictate the future.

Survival Intelligence for the Street

On the street, this translates into survival intelligence. You aren't hunting a racer; you're hunting the tiny clues that give away a disaster before it happens. You're watching the front wheel of a parked car, the tilt of a driver's head, or the rhythm of traffic.

By building a library of "predictable errors," your instinct can execute a counter-move while the average rider is still trying to figure out why they're in a panic. Don't just ride in the "now", but start building the library that lets you live in the "next."

The Mastery Loop

Suck, Click, Reset, Repeat

Know this fundamental truth: Every step up you take is also a complete reset of your foundation.

This ascension puts you back into a place you might not be used to anymore, a place of temporary incompetence and uncertainty. That's the brutal reality you must mentally accept and work with while you analyze how to master this higher step.

Cyclical Journey

The journey of the racer isn't a straight line up a ladder; it's a series of cyclical phases, each beginning with a collapse of competence:

Street riding. You start riding motorcycles, and you suck. You drop the bike just because of a loss of balance. You learn the right things, and all of a sudden, it clicks. Years later, you find out you're too fast for public roads and literally smoke everyone.

Track days. You find passion in riding on race tracks, and you suck. You learn the right things, and all of a sudden, it clicks. Despite the crashes, you move through C and B groups and literally smoke everyone in A group.

Amateur racing. You start attending amateur racing, and you suck. You learn the right things, and all of a sudden, it clicks. You learn to beat people on the brakes and win the amateur championship after years of effort.

Semi-pro/national level. Sponsorships come in, and you start in a racing league on a semi-pro level. Surprisingly... you suck. You learn to deal with the pressure of success, and the competition is so tough that it begins to toughen you. Despite the bleeding and walking sideways out of hospitals, you've made it to the professional team.

International level. You're competing on the international stage, and you suck. You learn the right things. Physical and mental pain makes you fight harder than ever. The clock is your worst enemy. Tears, sweat, and blood are shed to find the missing tenth of a second for your first international pole position.

The elite challenge. Years of success lead to the next milestone: the European Championship. You're now racing against former champions from around the planet, and you suck. You learn the right things. The word 'retreat' doesn't exist for you anymore. Your physical commitment compensates for equipment differences, and you fight your way into the top five.

MotoGP. Your phone rings. You're invited to join a MotoGP team because their number two rider got injured. They let you test their prototype race bike, and you suck.

Lesson of the Reset

The rider who fails is the one who refuses to accept the initial sucking phase at the next level. They mistakenly believe that their prior success guarantees competence. The mastery loop requires you to check your ego at the door of every new opportunity. You must embrace that initial, humbling phase of incompetence, because it's the only necessary prerequisite to the next "click." Your strength as a rider isn't measured by your current competence, but by your willingness to start over.

Psychological Takeaway

Every time you level up, you have to get comfortable with being incompetent again. Whether you're moving from the street to track days, or from track days to racing, your prior success doesn't guarantee a damn thing at the next level. In fact, your ego is your biggest enemy here. If you walk into a faster group thinking you're already the man, you'll stop learning. You have to accept the "suck phase" as a mandatory tax for entry. The moment you stop being willing to look like a beginner is the moment your growth hits a dead end.

A professional career isn't a ladder; it's a series of circles. You struggle, you learn, it finally "clicks," and you dominate. Then—the moment you reach the top of that hill—the phone rings or you sign a new contract, and you're right back at the bottom of a much bigger mountain. This collapse of competence is the only way to shed old, limited habits and build a foundation for the next level of speed. If you don't "suck" at the beginning of a new phase, you aren't actually moving up; you're just plateauing in your comfort zone.

Riders who fail at a higher level are usually the ones who refuse to be humbled. They try to "muscle" their way through with their old skill set instead of adapting. You have to check your ego at the door of every new opportunity. Your strength as a rider isn't measured by how fast you're right now, but by how quickly you can swallow your pride, admit you don't know your shit in this new environment, and start the work of "clicking" again.

Enjoying Incompetence

This isn't a character flaw; it's just a temporary state required for growth. By mentally embracing the uncertainty of the reset phase, you keep your learning journey alive. Whether you're a street rider hitting your first track day or a pro jumping on a MotoGP prototype, the process is the same. Don't fear the reset—see the chances in it. It also means you've officially outgrown your old self.

See it this way… You can be the 'rookie' again and find some freedoms.

※ **Mind Note – Coach's take**

"Where there's an up- there must be a down. Hot means- there's a cold. If there's a bad- there must be a good."

— *Can Akkaya*

A Child's Heart

Imagine you could race like there's no tomorrow. You would exist in a mental state where there are no regrets and no worries. Not even the subconsciousness of pain or even death. A world in a different time zone in space, where you're seven feet tall and f*cking bulletproof. No remorse, no regret that might hurt yourselves or others. A state of pure invincibility. Total freedom on the inside, which makes you glare on the outside for your opponents to feel and to weaken. You feel like a napalm-peeing beast. This is actually truly happening for those few who are about to become 'truly good at it.' That's a short phase in a racing career where you're just like that kid who doesn't know what pain is (yet). A child's heart which hasn't been confronted with the term DEATH is free, and can fly up high as it wants. A heart like this isn't restricted by natural survival instincts.

By the way... maybe next time you see a real young kid racing and conclude 'how talented and fearless it is'—you might ask yourself if that older racer with all those open wounds, scars, and twisted bones is actually the braver one—the one who has faced all those facets of mental and physical pain. Anyway, that's not my point. You might also say that racing kids go down many times. I agree, but they don't consider long term consequences a whole lot. I know that this is maybe an extreme example, but there's one more. One which separates the boys from the man at the end of this phase.

Marc Márquez Equation

Marc Márquez was racing with a 'child's heart' pretty much all his life. That made him what he has become—or let's say what he once was. See where this is going? Oh, yeah—he always got physically hurt. For years, actually, and pretty much twice per weekend. It actually has become part of it and his life to be bandaged up and to have the smell of pain-relieving lotion on him for weeks. Nothing he couldn't smile away and to be even more badass than he ever was.

With all that being said, this isn't even about the physical hurt, sweat, blood, and broken bones. This is about the subconscious realization that you actually have an expiration date, and that you're not invincible. Go ask me how I know. Don't get this wrong. It's not that a racer on this high level grows much more fears of getting hurt or dying. This type of fear goes much deeper. It's a career-deciding fear for most, which is why I mentioned in the beginning that only a few make it through this kind of phase. This is about 'thinking.'

Breakage of Momentum

Time isn't always a good healer. This operates against you. Here is Marc. He was absolutely dominant, especially the day when he crashed out—twice. The second one was physically quite extreme, and it was over. His fighter heart refused to give up, but a surgery didn't help his ability to do pushups in front of the commissioners. Now you take the embarrassment of crashing twice into a very long healing phase... and that's a lot of time to think about things.

Besides the frustration of seeing your opponent's sharing 'your' championship points, anger arouses because you can't do what you're supposed to be born for... to race. That's out for months to come and you can't even do your daily gym chores. Everything seems wrong because your routine—your momentum—is f*cked up. But also, the healing period has an end and you can't wait to get back on track to kick ass again. It takes a while and some tests to get back to your lap times, but even only half a second short on it makes you worry. While others are impressed with you, you just can't accept it because you subconsciously knew that this is going to happen again, and this was exactly what you were so afraid of all the time. You're now fighting a mental fight with yourself.

You start to hold back to keep from crashing or bending those titanium plates in your arm which would take you off the roster for months again. These are feelings you never even knew till you arrived in this dark place. You're confused and you race under deep aggression, and you wonder about it, because you never had to perform like that to be dominant.

You start leading races again here and there, but 'something' is holding you back. You reject that these are fears of getting hurt, because you never have been worried so much about it. Sometimes you're successful with it and sometimes you aren't, and you feel embarrassed of not being the big dog anymore. You don't feel like you're the one who sets the bar, and you realize that your opponents know now that you're not unbeatable—that even you have an expiration date, and so your aura fades. Subconsciously, you're actually afraid that all this could happen again in the very next race.

The child's heart is broken. From here, you won't ever be the same again, even if you're able to win championships. You've lost that immense portion of absolute freedom. You might not like this article for reasons even I understand. There will be the time where you will though, and when you don't have to ask me how I knew. Don't worry if you're in this state, because you can adjust to it.

Final Trade

The truth is, you will never get the "Child's Heart" back. The moment that subconscious realization of your fragility sinks in, the absolute freedom is gone. The professional racer who makes the comeback—the one with the titanium and the new, guarded focus—didn't find the old freedom. They achieved something far more valuable sometimes: Calculated control.

The amateur rider's goal isn't to try and recapture that reckless state of bulletproof invincibility. Your goal is to use the pain of that realization to become a better machine.

You trade the unthinking, naive freedom of a child for the conscious, tactical control of a warrior. Accept that the heart is broken, and then use the pieces to build a better, stronger commitment. The mental fight begins when the crash compilation stops, and the purposeful, disciplined work starts.

Psychological Takeaway

There is a short, beautiful window where you ride like a god because you haven't truly met pain yet. You feel seven feet tall and f*cking bulletproof. This "child's heart" gives you a glare that makes opponents flinch and keeps your hands off the panic button. You think you're invincible, but you're really just naive. On the street, this is that dangerous "honeymoon phase" where you're hauling ass, thinking you've mastered the world because you haven't tasted the asphalt or seen the inside of an ICU. It's not talent—it's just an absence of consequence.

The heart breaks the second you realize you have an expiration date. Time isn't always a healer; sometimes it's a parasite. When you're off the bike, your mind starts doing "what-if" math. You stop thinking about the line and start thinking about the titanium plates in your arm or the debt on your bike. That absolute freedom is gone, replaced by a ghost that sits on your shoulder and whispers about everything that can go wrong.

When you finally get back on the bike, you aren't the same. You try to force it. You ride with a weird, desperate aggression because you're trying to fake the dominance that used to be effortless. You're frustrated because you're half a second slow, or you're hesitating where you used to pinned it. This is the mental fight. You're no longer the "big dog," and your riding buddies can see the confidence has faded. You're scared it's going to happen again, and that fear turns you into a passenger instead of a pilot.

Warrior's Trade

The kid in you who didn't know pain is dead. Stop trying to find it. You will never get that reckless, unthinking freedom back, and frankly, you shouldn't want it. The survivors make the final trade: They exchange the naive heart of a child for the calculated control of a warrior. You stop relying on being "fearless" and start relying on being disciplined.

You use the scars and the broken pieces of that heart to build a better machine. You aren't "bulletproof" anymore. You're just too smart to get hit. Accept that you're vulnerable, then use that knowledge to become a tactical master who rides on purpose, not on luck.

When Learning Too Fast

Learning fast sounds good. In domains like mathematics or low-risk, non-physical sports, rapid progress is unequivocally positive. But let's shed some critical light on our arena, where the price of error is measured in bones and blood. In motorcycle riding and racing, it's not always good to learn fast. In fact, learning "too fast" can be a dangerous, high-velocity trap.

I have witnessed this paradox repeatedly, where a rider's eagerness to absorb information creates an imbalance that their body and instinct simply can't handle.

Self-Sabotage Accelerators

There are several common ways riders unconsciously accelerate into this danger zone:

Instructor tow. Being pulled for a session by a coach can instantly put you on a pace you've never touched. The problem is, that newfound muscle memory can cause you to maintain that pace when the instructor—and their perfect matching line—is gone. You're riding the speed, but not the skill.

Hunger for speed. Your personal, unchecked drive pushes you to constantly filter the internet, read the books, and watch the videos—all good things so far. But if the theoretical input far outstrips the physical integration, you're setting yourself up for failure.

Yes, even riding schools, including one like my own, can expose riders to the danger of learning too quickly.

Skills vs. Instincts Imbalance

Take my long-time student, Michael H., for example. Michael is a smart, middle-aged guy who only started riding last year. He dove headfirst, progressing from Cornering School Day 1 through Day 3 in the same year. He devoured Road Skills and even managed to drag a knee in the Knee Down class. His passion and eye-hand coordination made him soak it all up like a new sponge, driving him straight into the A-Group faster than almost anyone.

It sounds all positive, doesn't it? But there were also three crashes and a surgery down the road.

I won't take all of the credit because Michael has an animal in his soul. He is a former skiing and cycling competitor who brought that unmanaged, aggressive spirit to the track. I can prepare a rider mentally for 'the moment,' but my options to tame a pure animal nature are limited.

The deal here is a lack of simple, critical BALANCE.

Imagine I taught you the technique to brake so late that your bike steps out like Marc Márquez in MotoGP. A guy like Michael would absolutely have the guts to apply it. But that doesn't mean he would have the instinctive capacity to save a bike

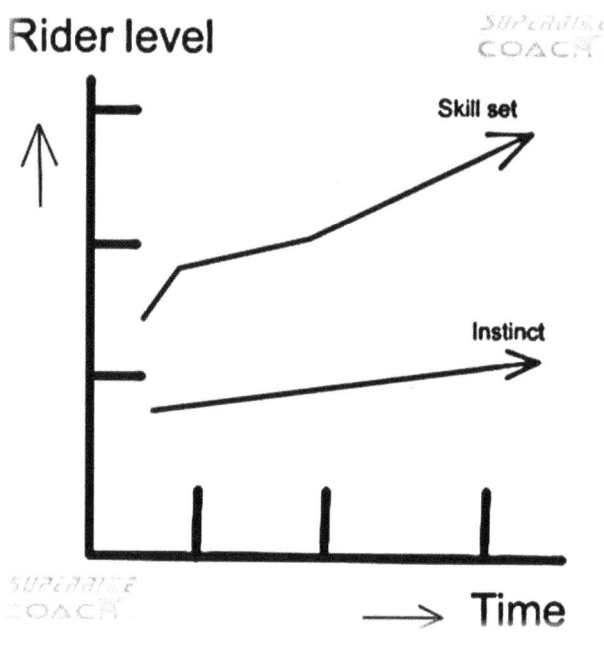

that's sideways, or catch a locked-up front wheel.

What I'm saying is that the pace at which he was picking up SKILLS was putting him far ahead of his INSTINCTS, which need to be developed to 'catch the shit up' when it goes wrong. If this deep, subconscious development can't keep pace with the skill line's acceleration, the rider is wildly out of balance.

Instincts grow slower. Their substance is fed by situations you're actively trying to avoid. True muscle memory is forged not in theory, but in the repeated, physical doing of things. It's the difference between knowing the theory of friction and knowing what a sliding tire actually *feels* like in your hands.

This brings me to my own accountability: A new rider, like a kid with new toys, wants to play immediately. My challenge is to identify that 'animal nature' quicker and deliver instruction piece by piece, step by step, giving the system time to integrate.

See? I'm also still learning, and that's positive. The negative only occurs when you fail to see the need for this BALANCE and try to skip necessary steps in order to learn fast. Trust me: you won't be fast for long.

Psychological Takeaway

Learning too fast is just another way of saying you're borrowing speed from your ego that your instincts can't pay for. You've devoured the books and the videos, and maybe you've even got the balls to apply a pro-level braking technique, but your brain is currently over-clocked. This is cognitive debt. You have the technical 'how-to' in your damn head, but your subconscious lacks the survival files to handle it when the front tire actually tucks. You're riding a pace you don't own, and when the bill comes due, it's paid in blood and broken plastic.

When you force yourself into the A-group through sheer grit, your brain hits a sensory shutdown. Because you're 100% occupied with not dying, you stop 'feeling' the bike. This is the accelerated plateau. You hit a wall where you can't get faster because your tension has created a firewall against the feedback from the tires. You aren't learning; you're just f'n surviving.

This leads to evasive riding, a state where you're so busy avoiding a crash that you've stopped building competence. You're white-knuckling the bars, and that chronic tension ensures your skills never become the effortless instinct you need to actually be fast.

The shortcut is the longest route to mastery because fear is a much better architect than logic. A single high-consequence 'f-up' doesn't just teach you a lesson; it rewrites your wiring with a hesitation program that takes years to delete. While the 'gung-ho' rider is busy walking sideways out of a hospital and trying to relearn how to trust his tires, the steady rider is busy stacking layers of actual skill. The irony of the 'fast track' is that it's full of forced restarts. You don't save time by rushing; you just spend more time in the reset phase.

Taming the Animal

Mastery requires a balance between your ambition and your 'seat-of-the-pants' reality. If you've got an 'animal in your soul' pushing you to skip the basics, recognize it as a trap. You aren't being a badass; you're just being impatient.

True performance comes from the slow, messy, repetitive 'boring' phases where you can actually observe the physics instead of just reacting to them. Stop trying to 'over-clock' your nervous system. Deliver the instruction to yourself piece by piece, let it sink into your marrow, and give your instincts a chance to catch up to your ego.

※ Mind Note – Acceptance

"Progress is a timeline with acceleration to a pivot point where it slows and narrows to its end. That's gotta find acceptance."

— *Coach Akkaya*

Yin and Yang

Can you imagine why true racers—even semi-pro riders—are often much easier to teach than most street riders? It's not just that they already possess an elevated mindset; it's that they're masters of definition. They can articulate, with surgical precision, exactly what they need. In 99% of cases, the average street rider cannot.

Sure, you have goals just like racers do, but you still can't define the substance of those goals. Racers, particularly at a high level, know their weak spots and their strengths down to the millimeter. More importantly, they understand the Yin and Yang of their performance: where there's black, there must be white. Where there's a weakness, there's an inherent or latent strength. The two are inseparable, and understanding this duality is the key to true optimization.

Defining the Enemy, Defining the Weapon

Racers grasp this concept because they apply it externally to their opponents. They don't just use a lump term to describe a competitor—they define his strengths and weaknesses to the bone and everything that comes with them. They seek granular detail.

I have a perfect, deeply personal example of this duality. When I was moving up the ranks, I had a specific characteristic—a habit—when I was studying an opponent in a dogfight. I was subconsciously always off the ideal line, maybe one or two feet. I'd be slightly wider on entry, a tad tighter mid-corner, and so on.

I thought of this as a strength. I was calculating distance and speed, constantly adjusting my angle to set up an aggressive, opportunistic pass at the precise right time. And it worked. For a while, I felt safe and sound with this weapon.

The following year, when I was in a full professional racing league, this strength flipped into a devastating weakness. The moment those top Pros figured out my habit, they stopped fighting me on the *ideal* line. They simply closed the gap when I was following, recognizing my deliberate offset as a predictable move. I became easy prey. This predictable pattern led to numerous passes throughout the dogfights and cost me up to ten seconds over a race distance. Worse still, when they knew I was following to study them, they would deliberately run 'funky lines', which immediately confused my calculations and broke my focus. They neutralized my strength by reading its vulnerability.

I quickly identified that I was too easy to read, and I fixed it. I could provide deep examples like this all day—the process of identifying a vulnerability and eliminating it. But that's not the point. The point is the importance of knowing both sides—your strength and the weakness it generates—in order to efficiently seek and destroy the problem.

Vagueness Trap

Good racers can define things. You, the street rider, often cannot. That's because you likely never thought of a thing like this existing in the first place, and you certainly don't know what your actual strengths are. You know oh-so-well all about your weaknesses, but even then, you cover the problem with a lump term that stops the investigation cold: "I need more confidence." Period.

What the hell does that exactly mean? Are you using a fancy word for saying, "I'm peeing in my pants"'?

We need to start from the ground up and define the substance of the word 'confidence.' Confidence isn't a feeling you acquire by magic; it's the direct result of having competence in defined areas. Confidence is knowing that you know your sh*t.

Your assignment for mastering the Yin and Yang of your riding is simple, but requires brutal honesty:

Define your strengths. Learn to define and describe, with specificity, what you believe you're strong with (e.g., "My braking point consistency is perfect because I hit that marker on the spot" or "My low-throttle control in the wet is excellent because of my smoothness").

Define your weaknesses. Define the specific, granular weakness (e.g., not "I corner poorly," but "I am consistently two feet wide of the apex because I initiate the turn too late").

See, not just plain. There's always a 'because...' to define. Consequently, you do have strengths, as well as weaknesses. If you're acutely aware of both, you might be able to find a way to compensate for a defined weak spot with a defined strength. This is the duality of mastery. Maybe these examples here give you an idea of what defining Yan and Yang and possible solutions can look like:

The power of the Yin and Yang concept lies in this: Your strength, when over-relied upon or executed without counter-balance, is your weakness. Every time you compensate with a strength, you're leaving a vulnerability open to be exploited, either by an opponent, or by the track itself.

Brake Point Hunter

A rider known for aggressive, late braking often develops a complementary weakness that limits overall speed:

Strength late braking. The ability to carry maximum speed deeper into the corner than anyone else, maximizing straight-line velocity (Yang).

Weakness compromised entry speed. Because the rider spends so long and so much mental energy focused on the braking zone, they often rush the bike past the turn-in point or overuse the front tire, forcing them to bleed off speed *after* turn-in. They win the entry but lose the corner, sacrificing valuable mid-corner velocity (Yin).

The duality. The late brake is a confidence weapon, but it creates a predictable window where the bike is slow to turn and is easily passed on exit.

Throttle Addict

This rider loves to feel the drive of the engine, but their eagerness often costs them stability and grip:

Strength early throttle application. The guts to open the throttle aggressively and early (Yang).

Weakness over-rotation/apex exit. The rider's eagerness causes them to pick up the throttle before the bike is fully set on its line. This often forces the bike wide on exit or induces a slide, prematurely using up the rear tire's grip. They get power down early but at the expense of exit consistency and stability (Yin).

The duality. The strength delivers a rush, but the resulting unstable exit compromises the setup for the next straight, leading to poor overall lap time despite feeling fast.

Perfect Line Calculator

This is common among technically oriented riders who prioritize line perfection above all else:

Line precision strength. The ability to consistently hit perfect apexes and utilize the exact maximum width of the track (Yang).

Lack of adaptability weakness (flexibility). Because they're so focused on the *ideal* line, they become completely lost and vulnerable when the line is blocked, the pavement changes, or they're forced onto an alternative trajectory (Yin).

The duality. Their strength only works in a vacuum. The moment a variable is introduced—a slower rider, a damp patch, or a purposeful disruption by an opponent—their rigidity turns into confusion, shattering their focus and forcing a "protective reaction."

I'm certain that this can be helpful to riders on certain levels, no matter if you're a racer or a street rider- while the less experienced rider isn't 'there yet' to comprehend, so wait it out if this is you.

Psychological Takeaway

Every strength you have is also a target for your opponent. If you don't recognize the Yin and Yang of your riding, you're leaving yourself wide open.

Your strength is your vulnerability. Aggressive late braking, which you might think is good, might compromise your entries. Being good with line precision, might create a lack of adaptability. This is the vulnerability trap.

Strategic Compensation

Self-correction requires escaping the Vagueness Trap. By knowing what your Yin & Yang's are, you might find a way to compensate for a weakness with a strength of yours. Like, knowing your braking strength is compromised by slow turn-in, allows you to focus precisely on the fix.

There's also a lot for the regular street rider in there. A strong belief-system could compensate for lack of confidence, the moment when needed (running into 'protective reactions'). The list is long, but I skip on writing this up because I want YOU to take that over from here. This might let you actually begin to identify YOUR Yin & Yang's.

That's the art of strategic self-awareness. Understand your duality, pinpoint your vulnerabilities, and use your strengths to compensate.

▓ Mind Note – Coach's take

"You know… sometimes it's better to go down on the attempt to save it, instead of going down entirely senselessly just because you simply gave up."

— Can Akkaya

Addicted to Perfection

The Illusion

I want to describe scenes from professional racing. That doesn't mean this is all about racing and doesn't apply to you, so go grab a beer and listen closely, because you might find yourself in here as well.

For the most professional racers I know—and that included myself—EVERYTHING needs to be 100% in order. In the right place, at the right time, and in a complete, rigid routine. Only then can it channel positive energy to make the moment count and also to be 'perfect'. Then comes the moment when your team leaves the starting grid, and you're all on your own with all of it.

This routine literally restarts after a race—winding back up for the next one. It doesn't feel this way, but it's there. While the racer goes for some Supermoto and lots of mountain biking, he already dials towards that moment of perfection next Sunday. He's talking to his friends and laughing. It doesn't feel like it, but it's there. The reset has begun already. The bike gets prepared down to the core and every single bolt is looked at. The office works to organize travels for each member. The team arrives in the paddock and sets everything up. There is fun—lots of fun so that it doesn't feel like it—but it's there. Practice sessions, qualifying sessions, and warm-up… it all feels different every time, but everyone and everything is following a specific routine. A routine which chases perfection.

Now you're standing on your starting grid again. The warm-up sign comes up and the pace car leaves, and so do your team members. You're on your own and all you think—all you feel is "...everything is perfect. I'm ready!" The finish flag falls, and you're relieved for a couple of hours before it all restarts. The strive for perfection—for that particular moment.

Perfection is a Dilemma

It's almost like solid OCD, isn't it? But do you see what I'm pointing out here? It all comes down to 'a perfect moment'.

Nothing is Ever Perfect

Once you or someone else decides they have 'reached perfection,' that's the end of the journey. But that's something most of you're chasing... to be perfect forever. There's always something better you could do or have done. There's always the next bike you want to have, the ice cream you eat, the helmet you wear. I could go on forever on this because this one goes in all life directions. Let me tell you the philosophy I decided to follow:

Perfection is an illusion! Don't ever decide to have reached perfection, because where else do you go when already you're there? Unless you have the urge of a professional racer to chase and to channel positive energy up to THAT MOMENT, which allows you to snap into the competitor you HAVE TO BE. For you, my friends, I hope you never reach perfection.

Danger of The Perfect Moment

Because the moment you think you did—that moment is dangerous because you stop searching, you stop striving. Your journey is over.

Just make sure you keep that strive in a healthy balance with 'fun', because too much chasing and the feeling to never be 'like that guy' (or whatever you categorize to be perfect) can lead you mentally right into dark rooms. I've been there, which is why I know. A room enriched with frustration, confidence-breaking energies, and not knowing where the f*cking door is to get you out of the darkness.

Trade-Off

When you chase 'perfection' in riding or in life, you're usually operating from a fixed mindset. You believe skill is a fixed talent—you either *have it* or you *don't*. If you don't instantly look like a 'rock star' or hit the perfect apex, failure isn't seen as a chance to learn; it's seen as proof of your fundamental lack of talent.

This is why the constant chase is so frustrating: Perfectionism is just a fear of being seen as incompetent. When you fail to be perfect, your brain instantly shifts to self-protection, freezing your ability to adapt or try again. You become rigid, and rigidity is what causes you to crash.

Value of "Good Enough"

The alternative is the growth mindset. This is the philosophy of the amateur rider who actually gets faster. They aren't chasing a flawless *result*; they're chasing flawless *effort*.

The goal is to focus on mastery, not perfection. Mastery means: I accept that the turn will never be exactly the same twice, but I commit to being 1% better at adapting to the change next time. This releases the pressure. When you accept that "good enough is great" for a non-professional, you turn your focus from what you *can't* control (perfection) to what you *can* control (effort and continuous adjustment). You become fluid instead of rigid.

Ritual vs. Result

The pro racer's "addiction" isn't to the perfect result—it's to the perfect ritual. That meticulous routine (bike prep, travel, warm-up) is actually a psychological tool to manage the massive stress of competition. It gives them a feeling of control over the chaos.

For the amateur, you should adopt the ritual but drop the obsession with results. The ritual is your friend: clean your helmet, check your tire pressures, walk the track in your mind. This focused preparation channels that positive energy you mentioned, but without the lethal pressure of needing the outcome to be flawless. It allows you to feel "ready," which is the only perfection you need.

'Perfect' is a closing word

It is psychologically final. Once something is labeled 'perfect,' it carries the implicit message:

The work is done. No more effort, analysis, or creativity is required.

The goal is met, and there's nowhere left to go.

Because it's perfect, it can only be damaged, criticized, or lost.

That is precisely why the professional racer only aims for a 'perfect moment' (a temporary, fleeting state), while the amateur who chases perpetual perfection stops their own growth.

'Perfect' seals the door on growth, while 'better' leaves it wide open.

It is the mental signal that the journey—which is the entire point of riding—is over. So don't chase perfection that much, because you never reach it anyway. It's a dilemma. In terms of riding itself—for you, the regular street rider— 'perfection' is a whole lotta gray zone. Instead, enjoy your imperfections. Actually, learn from your imperfections. Learn to laugh about yourself, because perfection means pressure!

Psychological Takeaway

If you're obsessed with being 'perfect' on the street, you're riding in a mental cage. Perfectionism isn't about high standards; it's a Fixed Mindset fueled by the fear of looking like an amateur. When you miss an apex or flub a downshift, a perfectionist doesn't see a lesson—they see proof that they suck.

This triggers a self-protection mechanism in your brain that makes you rigid. And on a bike, rigidity is the precursor to a crash. You stop riding the road and start fighting your own ego.

Pros are addicted to the ritual, not the result. The obsessive bike prep, the gear cleaning, the specific warm-up. This is all a psychological anchor to handle the chaos. For you, the ritual is your best friend. Checking your pressures, cleaning your visor, and visualizing the route are tools to make you feel 'ready'.

But here's the trade: adopt the pro's discipline in the garage, but dump their pressure on the pavement. The pro needs that "perfect moment" to win a title; you just need to be 'better' than you were yesterday to stay alive and enjoy the ride.

'Perfect' is a dangerous word because it's final. Once you decide a corner or a ride is perfect, you've hit a dead end. There's nowhere to go but down. 'Perfect' is fragile. It can only be ruined or lost. 'Better', however, is resilient. If you aim to be 1% better at adapting, you leave the door wide open for growth. Mastery isn't about hitting a flawless result every time; it's about having a growth mindset where you're fluid enough to handle the 1,000 things that *won't* be perfect on a public road.

Street Rider's Grace

On the street, 'perfect' is a gray zone that doesn't exist. There will always be gravel, wind, or a driver who didn't see you. If you're chasing a flawless lap on a canyon road, you're inviting a dark room full of frustration and broken confidence. Mastery is flawless effort, not a flawless outcome.

Learn to laugh at your sloppy shifts. Use your imperfections as data points, not insults. When you trade the pressure of 'perfect' for the fluidity of "better," you actually become the rider you were trying to fake being in the first place.

※ **Mind Note – Coach's take**

"Know that the guide you've picked is actually able to hold your ropes up that Eiger North Wall."

- *Can Akkaya*

Own the Damn Candy Store

I know this might sound like I'm promoting our school. Try not to see it that way, and you'll get to see the much bigger picture into the rider's psyche.

Our Superbike-Coach Cornering School is extremely popular, and we have riders coming from all over the United States and even overseas. The fact that riders commit to Day 1, and then return for Days 2 and 3, speaks to the value of a structured, slow-burn approach. Spreading the days out over a manageable period of time makes sense in multiple ways:

It forces a 'slower manner' of learning, preventing the Velocity Paradox.

It's less overwhelming, giving the student time to absorb complex concepts.

It provides a decent amount of time to practice drills and allow skills to mentally settle.

The logical order of subjects ensures the student efficiently builds a true foundation.

It allows me to see if a student is genuinely ready to attack the next step.

I was already aware of what could come when I designed this program, so I chose the title thoughtfully 'Cornering Day 1, etc'. That should clearly indicate that this is not to be seen as a 'level' of education, but part one of three of an entire program. What you're about to experience is how blind wish-thinking and denial one can make.

A La Carte Trap

This class offers a full spectrum of cornering, from A to Z. Yet, we frequently receive emails from experienced riders (or from those who believe they are) who want to skip Day 1, which they often incorrectly dismiss as 'beginner level.'

The typical track rider, focused on a perceived deficiency, might have Body Positioning at the top of their wish list. They'll ask, "Can't you just teach me that?" or say, "I suck at counter-steering, but I don't want to do the other subjects!"

This is exactly where my logic kicks in: "If you don't have counter-steering down, then you can't be very good at all the other stuff either, can you?!"

In fact, once this rider is in class, we often expose subjects they didn't even know existed, or skills that were wrongly taught to them via the superficial copying process used by other schools.

This reveals the core mistake: you should not try to skip foundational subjects and just grab the single skill you think you might need—like a piece of candy in a damn store. You actually hurt yourself because you're skipping out on something extremely powerful. You wouldn't fly to Hawaii for a vacation and skip Day 1 of the trip, would you?

Philosophy of the Complete System

The reason you can't skip the foundational steps is simple: I'm not just teaching skills. I'm teaching philosophy.

I can help you put your mindset in the right place. I teach you how to keep ego and emotion in check. I know the mental state of a rider because I've been there. Even if you lack confidence, you don't need to be ashamed of it—we will define what that means. I'll change the way you look at things, which often goes way beyond riding bikes.

This is a complete working system. To try to cherry-pick a single skill makes no sense when the true reward is available. You don't want to get a single piece of candy; you want the Master Key that allows you, one day, to OWN THE WHOLE DAMN CANDY STORE.

Ownership means complete control, complete understanding of the system, and the confidence to choose any sweet treat you want, at any time, without being overwhelmed by its complexity. Mastery is the Store Key.

The Non-Negotiable

Again, this isn't about promoting our cornering program, but to throw light on what most riders believe to know and what they believe they need next. To clarify the mindset, stop thinking of Day 1 as 'beginner stuff' and start seeing it as prerequisite knowledge.

The core issue with trying to 'just grab one skill' is that skills in riding are cumulative and interdependent. When you try to isolate a skill like body positioning:

You don't just skip the subject; you skip the safety net. For example, the confidence to shift your body comes directly from having mastered throttle control and the subtle inputs of counter-steering (the prerequisites).

If you attempt advanced Body Positioning without those fundamental systems in place, your body position becomes a vulnerability, not a strength. You have moved your weight to the edge of the tire, but you lack the skill to stabilize it.

Systemic Risk Management

This isn't about money or time; it's about systemic risk management. A professional racer knows that the bike is a complete system. You don't install a turbocharger without upgrading the fuel pump, the brakes, and the cooling system.

Similarly, you can't install a high-performance skill—like late braking or deep lean angles—without upgrading your personal operating system first. The philosophy you're buying is the insurance policy that ensures every new 'candy' you acquire is fully integrated into a stable, functional, and safe machine.

You're not just buying classes; you're buying the essential structural steel that keeps your whole performance stable when you push the speed envelope.

Psychological Takeaway

Stop cherry-picking the 'sexy' skills like knee-dragging while ignoring the basics. This isn't efficiency; it's a lack of Systemic Risk Management. You can't build a house without the foundational structural steel to support it. That becomes a liability quickly.

Vulnerability, Not Strength

Skipping prerequisites deletes your safety net. If you hang off the bike like a champ while you still can't even shift right, you're probably only giving away lean angle resources with no plan for when the bike gets upset. You wouldn't walk into a damn good movie half way into it, or would you?!

Owning the System

Mastery is about building a personal operating system, not collecting tricks. When you 'Own the Candy Store,' you have the master key and the ability to integrate any skill at will because you understand the underlying physics. You aren't just doing things; you own the system.

Settle Time Rule

Your brain needs a slow-burn approach to turn skills into unconscious competence. Rushing the process triggers cognitive overload, forcing you back into old, shitty habits the moment things get hairy. A structured foundation is your insurance policy.

※ **Mind Note – Coach's take**

"If I have a favorite track, it only means I f*ck something up on all the other tracks!"

— *Can Akkaya*

Being the Underdog

Freedom of Low Expectation

There is something to it and that makes us all want to be… the 'big dog.' That rider who seems like they can't be caught on canyon roads. The guy who sets the bar at track days. That pro rider who is dominating international podiums. Being the big dog!

So did I, so you know where this one is coming from. This is kind of also similar to the 'The Rookie Effect' we already discussed, but it has its small differences, so let's discover them.

Remember, we talked about Marc Marquez being put on the spot as a top contender. After all the incidents and setbacks throughout many racing seasons, he was pretty much stripped of the "big dog" title, which effectively made that eight-time world champion an 'underdog.' Almost hard to believe, but the interesting part is that this was the trigger for what happened next: the biggest comeback in all of sports history.

Weight of Success

I remember when I finally had the chance to throw my leg over factory-supported equipment. Oh man, I was so proud, but also under extreme pressure. This time not just self-imposed, but also from all those who believed in me and gave me that chance. Furthermore, also from fans and the press. Damn, it took a long time to get out of that tight prison cell.

However, when we went to do tests and practice sessions somewhere in France between the races, I also took my 'old' race bike out just to get more laps on my belt. That bike was quite a bit slower, it wasn't dialed in that well, its suspension components were more limited, and it was quite heavier than the factory-supported GP bike.

Despite this, I was half a second faster with it!

My team members tried to help, of course, thinking that I was just afraid to break their stuff, telling me that there were a ton of spare parts on that truck to give me a hall pass. But no… that's not it. It's that everyone is watching you now. All other teams have a stopwatch running on you as well. The trust investor's eyes are burning on your neck when you come out of that chair. It's the expectations that come along with being a big dog.

The Underdog Experiment

Thinking this through, made me do an experiment.

Each time I came out of the chair and took the old race bike out, I was another guy! That was a guy who wanted to show that I could kick your butt even on a less powered bike. A guy who was striving to show what's possible even when not sitting on top-level equipment.

The pressure for success was gone. The game didn't ask me for a specific outcome. I felt like the cameras turned away from me. Heading out the pit lane, I was just an underdog racer whose 'never surrender' attitude makes the cameras just turn on him. There was a fire in that helmet. A fire that I'd have to replicate.

You know… it's like you're standing in front of a locked door, but you have about 10 keys on that ring. Most of the time you'll have to try them all. But there will be the one that opens the damn door.

Guess what I found behind that door? One second!

Psychological Takeaway

When you start thinking you're the 'big dog'—the fast guy in the group or the rider with the top-tier gear—you walk into a mental trap. External expectations turn the ride into a performance review. This creates physical tension that kills your feelings for the bike. You stop riding to improve and start riding to defend your ego.

Underdog Advantage

Underdogs are faster because nobody is watching them and the expectations are low. When I rode my 'old' bike, the pressure vanished, and I found a full second of pace. This "nothing to lose" mentality provides a massive relief from the weight of being perfect. On the track or the street, being the underdog allows you to focus 100% on the job instead of worrying about how you look to everyone else.

Finding Your Triggers

The goal is to find your own mental triggers to get back into that underdog state on command. You have to learn how to ignore the imaginary cameras in your head. For me, it was switching to less capable equipment to lower the stakes. For you, it might help to lower your expectations and to not to want to, nor to ask for high-end equipment. Have a 'let's see what it can do' attitude.

Freedom to be Fast

When you find the switch that lets you ride like you have zero reputation to protect, you unlock a fluidity that tension usually smothers. Don't try so hard to be the big dog and start hunting for that underdog mindset. It's the only way to stay loose enough and to actually have fun on the bike again.

※ Mind Note – Coach's take

"Confidence isn't a feeling you acquire by magic; it's the direct result of having competence in defined areas. Confidence is knowing that you know your sh*t."

— *Can Akkaya*

Favoritism

Let me show off a little

There is a track in Belgium, the Zolder Circuit. This track was not designed on a computer where corner speeds are pre-simulated for crash zones. Oh no. Zolder was one of the last dinosaurs. The curbs were ramps that launched you toward a wall of death. When it was built, someone with a tractor probably just decided, "...and here, we'll put a jump hill."

Zolder was my absolute favorite track to go to. It's where I set records on the cracked asphalt, grabbed pole positions, and won races—and yeah, I crashed there too. But it was the place where my mind and soul let out a battle cry that I never felt anywhere else. My preparation was different. I woke up earlier with a smile on my face. My confidence level was so high, it was bursting signals to my competitors: *don't even try.* They knew it. At Zolder Circuit, I was a force.

Before race day, I had a ritual: I'd go out at night on the start/finish line and sit down for a few minutes. Just me, looking down the straight toward the first turn. Strategies and hole-shot scenarios were flowing. I was turning on race mode. So I'm sitting under the stars at Zolder, and a thought popped up: I wished I *only* had to race here! That led to the single most important question of my career: WHY? The answer to that question put my racing game up to the next level: If I have a favorite track, it only means I f*ck something up on all the other tracks!

As simple as that conclusion sounds, the outcome was huge. It immediately led to the next question: What am I doing wrong or different everywhere else? Why can't I 'be like that' at every circuit, when Zolder is actually the most intimidating of them all? The answer wasn't primarily physical riding skill. No, the answer was clearly something else...

The Hunger

It was about the attitude of a hungry apex predator. The ice-melting look of an eagle's eyes, burning on the back of its prey. The body language that makes others step aside. Every interview I gave, the words came out, but what I meant was: This is MY HOUSE!

That night under the stars was a genuine revelation. I was so taken away by it that I barely slept, and I actually messed up the start the next day. The entire race was a mess. But when it was over, I was not disappointed. I was in total peace because I knew I had found a huge key to a massive door. I just needed to find a way to trigger that kind of hunger wherever I showed up. And I did.

To whatever track we headed out to compete, mentally, I was heading back to Zolder Circuit in Belgium!

I decided not to have 'favorites' anymore. The feeling of having a favorite now signaled that something was fundamentally wrong. This new principle went into everything: riding techniques, fitness training, even what I was eating. I found a new tool for everything.

Street Rider's Blind Spot

Now, where does this picture fit for the average street and track rider? You don't see it? Let me throw a light into the darkness for you. We all have favorites for everything: colors, bikes, cars, vacation spots. Even a favorite child, under brutal honesty, is kind of true, right?! It's human nature. Having a favorite sounds so positive, doesn't it?

BUT… besides defining your personal taste (food, colors, etc.), is it really always a benefit? For example: If you favor going to Hawaii's Big Island, you're running low RPMs on your explorer spirit. You might never find out how awesome Kauai Island is. Shaky example, I know, but you get it. Let's move that over to the regular motorcycle rider, shall we?

I bet you have a favor for left turns, do you? Most riders do. Maybe you favor right-handers? What about riding uphill sections throughout a nice canyon road? I actually bet you hate going downhill because the bike feels so damn head-heavy… right?! The list goes on and on. Lean back and make your own list about it. I believe, having a favorite automatically signals issues on the 'other end.' Just like Ying and Yang, remember?! There must be at least a mental or, for the less experienced, a physical riding skill issue that needs some fixing. It starts right here: with a change of mindset.

There is also something coming along once you decide to have a favorite, for example left turns. Because that will have in most of the time an 'I let it go' effect, and find acceptance to suck on right turns. This acceptance—the mental surrender to a weakness—is the real problem. You've placed a ceiling on your potential and told your brain, "This is good enough; we'll focus on the fun stuff."

Avoidance Anchor

The reason you have a 'favorite' corner, track, or riding condition is because your brain is using it as an avoidance anchor. Your favorite side is where your existing skill set provides the most cognitive ease. You don't have to work hard, your brain is under less stress, and the experience is rewarding. This comfort is what the brain seeks to repeat.

The disliked side (the right-hander, the downhill section) requires maximum cognitive load and exposes your incomplete skill. Instead of facing the difficulty, your brain employs a psychological defense called acceptance through avoidance:

Reward (left turn). Your brain grants you a "win" for the easy part, creating a surplus of self-esteem.

Surrender (right turn). You use that surplus as currency, telling yourself, "I'm great at the other nine corners, so it's okay that I miss this one." You actively choose the path of least mental resistance, deciding to "let it go" rather than spending the intense focus needed for improvement.

The overall emotional stability gained from succeeding in one area is used to justify the failure in the other. Your body language and preparation unconsciously shift because your ego knows it can get a score on the left, which grants it permission to be lazy on the right.

The only way to smash that ceiling is to recognize the dislike not as a flaw, but as a diagnostic tool pointing directly to the 100% focus area needed for growth. The path to becoming a complete rider runs directly through the corners you hate.

Just by deciding you don't have a favorite anymore, you open yourself up to actually start improving the dislike. This reduces discomfort and possible frustration with yourself. You might even finally begin to see the mistakes you've been making on those damn tight downhill turns. So, next time you fly to Kauai Island, put in the effort to get there.

Psychological Takeaway

Having a 'favorite' track or corner sounds positive, but it's actually a diagnostic tool for your weaknesses. If you have a favorite, it means you're failing somewhere else. Favoritism is a self-imposed ceiling; it's your ego's way of staying in a comfort zone where the cognitive load is low. You're giving yourself mental permission to suck.

Your brain uses your strengths as an avoidance anchor. You take the 'easy stuff' to mirror your performance and use that confidence to justify being lazy where you're weak. This is acceptance through avoidance. You trade the frustration of a difficult downhill section for the easy reward of an uphill one. By 'letting it go,' you stop growing.

For a street rider, favoritism is often a physical red flag. If you hate downhill hairpins, it's usually because your vision is dropping or you're bracing against the dang bars. You probably are only half as focused on turns you hate. It's time to clean that up and to use some Yin & Yang wisdom.

Smashing the Ceiling

Growth lives exactly where your discomfort is. The path to becoming a complete rider runs directly through the sections you usually hate. Once you decide you no longer have a favorite, you stop surrendering to your weaknesses. You force your brain to apply 100% focus to the "other end." Identify your favorites, recognize them as the anchors holding you back, and lean into the discomfort.

Track Days Make Better Riders

Psychology of Overload

I was debating with myself if this chapter should be in this book or not, but as you can see, it's here. The reason is simple. Even brand-new riders are looking into this tempting 'thing' everyone is talking about. So here is what I see is happening and what that does to you.

Ever heard the slogan: "Doing one track day replaces one year of riding on the street," or similar claims? What about statements like, "Riding on a race track makes you feel your bike on the limit," or something similar?

Sounds exciting, right? Well... the excitement is real, but the idea that this alone makes you a better rider is dangerously misleading. Where the hell should all that skill come from all of a sudden? I'm here to tell you that nothing will change overnight just because you have a track day ticket in your pocket. Straight up: The only thing that's going to move "on the limit" are your guts.

Reality of Cognitive Overload

Here is what actually happens in reality. You probably couldn't sleep the night before your first track day. You don't feel tired, though, because adrenaline is pumping through your veins. As you listen to the obligatory riders' meeting, you feel the early signs of performance anxiety, which only freaks you out more.

You attend the beginner (C group) orientation classroom. You're told about the racing lines, information that's immediately forgotten the moment you step out of the room. Why? Because the amount of new data—track layout, flags, etiquette, speed—creates a state of severe cognitive overload. Your brain's processing capacity is completely saturated. Additionally, you've been struggling to find the line anyway, no matter where you go.

Then you head out for your first session. You cling to the hope that the 'beginner sightseeing lap' will make a huge difference. It doesn't. You're riding in a massive convoy at 30 mph on lines that are darn pretty funny, and everyone is all over the place. It's largely senseless, because the moment you're on your own, your brain reverts to fear and you still have no clue where you actually are.

Myth of the Quick Fix

You realize how desperately you need help. After the lunch break, you approach an instructor. After likely entertaining the entire crew with your pronounced 'chicken strips' (the unused edges of your tires), one agrees to follow you. Twenty minutes later, he offers some vague advice about your body positioning and sends you off with a plain, "...other than that—good enough."

Don't harbor the illusion that a three-minute chat with an instructor fixes anything. To hear a "you're looking good" is designed primarily to engage the rider's confirmation bias and to make you feel good, encouraging you to say "...I like him". This brief, generic feedback serves the venue's economics, not your skill development.

Naturally, you're alone again in your very next session, and you're doing the same B.S. you did before. While riding, you constantly think about why everyone is passing you so easily. This engages your Ego and competitive bias, causing you to start pushing and making your first ill-advised passing attempts. You still don't remember where it goes behind that blind crest and you almost run off the track.

Psychological Aftermath and Delusion

You refuse to admit your confusion and the fact that you were overwhelmed pretty much the entire time. You might finish the day early by deciding to skip the last two sessions without a good reason. In truth, your entire body feels like you got hit by a truck. You're physically exhausted and mentally hurt because you just realized how much you suck. Admitting this... different story!

You are tired and weak, caused by hours of being physically tensed up and mentally overloaded. And then comes the final act of confirmation bias: You spend an hour staring at a monitor to find 'the perfect shot' the photographer took of you—all high-res and awesomely tilted—but none of them show much lean angle, not even in your last session when you truly felt best.

So you attack one track day after another for the next three years. A five-second drop-in lap time, and two crashes is the total outcome. You still don't know why those "A" riders are faster per lap or why you're still not dragging the damn knee. I might sound harsh, but I don't think every rider is the same. I know you're excited, and I'm totally on your page, but excitement and the feeling of being scared to death is all you're really going home with.

Looking back, you're probably loaded with wishful thinking that your riding performance felt "so much better than usual." You felt faster because you were mentally on the limit, and operating at your psychological ceiling. In reality, you're probably only marginally more confident on your favorite canyon road. I've even heard riders talking themselves into a 'better world' by deciding that the photographer must have messed up and didn't capture their deepest lean angle. Maybe even the shutter settings are at fault. This is delusional self-reinforcement.

How do I know all of this? Well, four decades of riding, pro racing, teaching, and dealing with massive egos should give me some experience in what people go through when they hit the big track too early. It's also backed up by riders who have had the guts to admit their failure—which, to me, is the real evidence.

It seems that some riders become 'blind' after a track day, seeing themselves as 'grown up now' in terms of bike mastery. This is a deadly psychological error, because again: nothing is better all of a sudden. If you're going to do a track day, then do it for fun, and don't fool yourself into believing you've gained skill you haven't earned.

A track day doesn't make you immediately a better rider; it merely highlights where you're failing. Cognitive overload, confirmation bias, wishful thinking, and the ego. It's a critical deconstruction of a common rider experience.

Psychological Takeaway

The claim that "one track day equals a year of street riding" is a myth. In reality, the flood of new data—lines, flags, and high speeds—immediately triggers cognitive overload. Your brain's processing capacity hits a wall, and you default to survival instincts. You aren't learning; you're just surviving. The exhaustion you feel afterward isn't from "working hard"—it's the result of hours of uncontrolled mental stress and physical tension.

Most track day instruction is built for volume, not skill. When an instructor tells you that you 'look good,' they're often just feeding your f'n confirmation bias. It makes you feel better, but it doesn't fix your riding. If you rely on three-minute chats and cool high-res photos to measure your progress, you're practicing delusional self-reinforcement. You're chasing a visual outcome instead of objective competence.

There is a massive difference between the experience of going fast and the *mastery* of it. Because you're operating at your psychological ceiling, you feel like you're flying. In reality, you're likely just as shaky as you were on the street, just with more adrenaline. This creates a 'blindness' where you think you've grown as a rider simply because you survived the day.

High-Pressure Diagnostic

An unstructured track day is a diagnostic tool, not a shortcut to goodness. It highlights exactly where you suck, but it doesn't provide the tools to fix it. True growth requires structured repetition and targeted feedback that keeps you below the level of panic. Don't confuse excitement with improvement. If you go to the track, go for the fun, but don't fool yourself into thinking you've gained skills you haven't actually earned.

(A word to Instructors: Don't think I don't respect what you guys do. I do know your workload very well and what you get for the job, which limits your abilities to help. My hope is that all this might help you as well to find better ways.)

PART IV: The Long Game

Expectations Are Good

Self-Inflicted Trap

If I had titled this chapter 'Expectations vs. Capabilities,' you'd probably already nod and think, "Yeah, I know where this is going." Because you've lived it. You've felt that tension before.

And yes, I just started with a sentence that actually belongs at the end. But that's how this stuff works: it loops back on itself. Every time.

Here's the hard truth: *Your frustrations are usually nothing but the echo of your expectations.*

That's tough to admit, isn't it? Because the moment you do, you have to admit that you built the very thing that's now beating you up.

Expectations can be beautiful. They give you vision, drive, motivation. They make you train harder, invest more, dream bigger. But they're also a trap. They can blind you to what your current capabilities actually are. And that's when frustration walks in the door.

Ground Level vs. Sky High

Let's use a practical example that I see every week.

You just passed your DMV parking-lot test and got that shiny new M1 license. You feel good—like you unlocked something. Next thing you know, you've signed up for a wheelie class.

Expectations? Sky high.

Capabilities? Ground level.

How's that supposed to work?

Success in that situation is almost impossible, yet you'll probably still demand it from yourself. When it doesn't happen, your ego gets embarrassed, and instead of accepting that maybe you jumped a few steps (violating 'The Right Order'), you get frustrated. Maybe at yourself, maybe at the course, maybe at the coach.

"Why didn't this class make me better?"

Because, my friend, no one can bend physics or biology for you. Your brain and body need time, exposure, and calibration.

Expectation–Frustration Loop

The moment that internal crash happens—when expectation hits reality—is purely psychological and biochemical.

The human brain builds emotional 'contracts' without telling you. You imagine success, your brain releases dopamine as if it already happened. When reality doesn't meet the image, dopamine drops, cortisol spikes (the stress hormone)—and that's frustration. It's not even ego yet; it's just chemistry.

Admitting a gap between expectation and ability threatens the ego's self-image. So the mind looks for external blame to rebalance itself—the weather, the tires, the coach, the bike setup. Anything but self-reflection. That's how growth gets delayed.

This is where wish-thinking replaces feedback. You *feel* ready because you *want* to be ready. But skill progression doesn't care how you feel. It only responds to what you've proven to yourself under pressure.

Knowing Your Place

This isn't about humility in the moral sense. It's about awareness. Tactical awareness.

Just because you shot a gun once doesn't make you SWAT material. You'd never even think that way, because your context awareness is intact. But for some reason, with motorcycles, people lose that sense completely. They mix fun, freedom, and adrenaline—and out goes judgment. The same tool that can give you joy can kill you if you handle it out of sequence.

Knowing your place doesn't make you small. It makes you free.

You're not performing for anyone. You're not proving anything. You're simply learning at your pace, safely, sustainably. That kind of grounded expectation also keeps you off other people's radar, especially those who love to compare, judge, or compete.

When your 'pro-level expectations' shine too bright, others subconsciously project their own onto you. Now their expectations become your pressure.

See how the trap builds? Don't let your beautiful expectations become a weapon your ego uses against your own progress.

Psychological Takeaway

Frustration is a chemical failure. When you imagine success before you've earned it, your brain signs a 'dopamine contract.' You feel the reward upfront, but when reality falls short, dopamine drops and cortisol spikes. That 'hit' of frustration is proof that your expectations were uncalibrated. It isn't a lack of talent; it's a math error in your head.

The Blame Exit

To protect your ego from this crash, your mind looks for an external excuse. You blame the bike, the tires, or the instructor. This external blame strategy is a dead end. By refusing to admit your expectations were irrational, you block the self-reflection needed to actually improve. You trade growth for a temporary sense of being right.

Tactical Awareness

'Knowing your place' is a survival tactic. It means matching your mental goals to your current, proven capability. Many riders get into trouble because they let adrenaline override their judgment, attempting 'pro-level' moves on a beginner foundation. This gap between expectation and skill creates a high-risk environment. Grounding your expectations isn't about being slow; it's about staying within your mental and physical limits.

Power of Realism

Grounded expectations protect you from the dopamine trap and keep the 'stress hormones' at bay. By admitting where you actually stand, you remove the pressure to fake it. This clarity allows you to build mastery in the right sequence, safely and sustainably.

※ Mind Note – Coach's take

"Anxieties are imaginations. It plays a 'what-if' movie in your head, scripted by yourself."

— *Can Akkaya*

Living in Denial

The Abyss of Self-Delusion

Straight up... the power of denial can kill you. Do you understand that?! Denial goes from wish-thinking right into stupidity. Some riders live in this state of mind and just can't see it anymore. Sure, that might be a 'happy world' for a while, but this is a slide into the abyss.

Before it gets really bad, denial causes you to pretty much lie to yourself—living in excuses—and lying to others about your performance and abilities. You're only polishing up your ego. Denial is a powerful, self-imposed delusion that creates a dangerous gap between your perception and objective reality.

Ego's Defense Mechanism

Denial isn't just foolishness; it's a fundamental defense mechanism of your ego.

To admit "I am not fast enough" or "I am riding above my skill level" is emotionally painful. Denial provides an immediate shield against that reality. It maintains your self-image of the "competitor" even when your performance says otherwise.

When you're in denial, you selectively focus on data that supports your delusion. If you beat one slow guy in a session, you replay that victory repeatedly, completely ignoring the ten faster riders who blew past you. This bias keeps the 'slide into the abyss' invisible until you hit the bottom.

The abyss isn't the crash itself; the abyss is the conscious choice to ignore the warning signs leading up to it.

Paralyzed Learner

Denial acts as a powerful defense mechanism that actively paralyzes your learning process.

You shift blame away from your own skill and effort and onto external factors (e.g., "The tires were cold," "The bike has a head shake," "The track surface is bad"). This creates an external locus of control, meaning you believe results are determined by luck or circumstances, not your actions.

Your mind aggressively seeks information that confirms your existing delusion ("I am fast and talented"). It filters out all contradictory evidence—the near-misses, the slow lap times, the faster riders passing you. You might only remember the one clean overtake you made, not the ten corners where you almost ran off the track.

In the face of undeniable proof (e.g., being consistently passed), your ego panics. Instead of slowing down and reassessing, you take irrational risks (late braking, aggressive overtakes) to protect your fragile self-image of being a "competitor." The move isn't strategic; it's an emotional reaction.

Let me describe a scenario that constantly loops at track days:

Here is "Joe," a B group rider, who just got passed by a high-level coach. That pass was safe, but the speed difference, elegance, and precision—like a brain surgeon's touch—was a quantum leap beyond Joe's level. It clearly screams, "Don't try. You only hurt yourself!"

Next, that coach runs up on a couple of way slower riders and holds back as he should. But now, Joe arrives and instead of living in peace with the reality that this almost surreal pass should have been released, Joe's denial sees the opportunity to put his ego to shine. He passes that coach, 'fights' his way through the rest of that slow group of riders, and makes one of them almost go off track. All of this… just to finally give his soul a space upon stage.

In fact, this is stealing, but he disappears in the paddock, and his denial makes him lie to his friends that he just passed a professional. This isn't fiction… This happens all the time.

Now, if Joe wouldn't have been steered by denial into stupidity, he might have had the chance to follow that coach for a few turns to learn something. But no, now he's just seeing a real mad coach who leaves him in a split second.

Another example: In our cornering classes, we do some lead and follow laps. Now here are you, coming up on that 1-on-1 duo. Would you make a pass on them or would you add yourself to it and learn something from it as well?! It's easy to detect the level of denial; some can't see that they can also learn something even if it's below their pace. Needless to say, we let these riders know that they just lost their part of 1-on-1. Am I sounding frustrated to you? Yes, I am! I hate to see when people who are actually smart as shit are in a free fall right into stupidity.

Anti-Denial Strategy

The only cure for denial is introducing objective reality in a measurable, undeniable way. When the brutal difference in pace isn't enough to pop out of a delusion, maybe a stopwatch is?

The clock is the ultimate truth. It doesn't care about your feelings, your excuses, or your ego. It's impossible to deny a clear, objective lap time. Watching a video may force you to see the mechanical truth of your riding—your delayed lean-in, your early throttle-cut, your nervous braking—with the emotional distance necessary to actually learn from it.

In summary, if the stopwatch, a coach, and a video all agree you have a problem, but your mind argues against them, you're living in denial.

Denial on the Street

Look, the track gives you immediate, brutal feedback—a clock, a coach, and a wall. The street? The street lets your bullshit simmer. That's why denial is even more dangerous out there; it has room to grow into a full-blown goddamn death wish.

Street Rider's "Joe" Moment

On the track, Joe risked a fairing. On the street, the risk is a coffin.

The street rider's delusion isn't about beating a fast guy; it's about making ego moves in traffic. That insane, high-speed lane-split through rush hour? That blind-corner pass where you assumed the coast was clear? That wasn't skill; that was wish-thinking fueled by pure ego.

You tell yourself, "I'm the ultimate talent out here." The denial is that you're only responsible for 5% of the safety equation—your own riding. The other 95%? That's the uncontrolled chaos of some idiot in a minivan texting his ex. Yet, you use the small 'win' (making the light) to feed your denial, ignoring the ten times you should have been flattened.

Blame the World

The rider in denial is a professional blamer. After every close call—which he'll call a 'near-miss' instead of a 'self-inflicted screw-up'—it's always, "That driver is a complete moron." He never looks at his own speed, his own proximity, or his own choice to ride like the world is his personal track day.

This is the ultimate self-betrayal: you reject the one truth that saves lives on the street: Assume everyone else is trying to kill you. By blaming the car, you avoid the only thing that matters: bringing your own risk level back down to reality.

Street's Hardest Lesson

You said denial leads to the abyss. For the street rider, that abyss is right there in the guardrail.

On the track, failure is expensive. On the street, failure is permanent. The denial gap trades a few seconds of saved commute time for an infinite, immediate increase in risk. You can lie to your buddies about your lap times, but you can't lie to the asphalt. The ultimate cost of denial on the street is paid in blood, and there's no refund.

Psychological Takeaway

Denial is a hard stop for your progress. By refusing to see your own mistakes, you trap yourself at your current skill level. You can't fix a problem you won't admit exists. This just leads to a dang stagnation loop: you repeat the same sloppy habits for years, wondering why you aren't getting faster, while your ego tells you that you've already peaked. When you lie to yourself about your ability, you lose the capacity to judge danger.

Social Cost

In the riding community, denial makes you an unsafe bet. Whether it's a coach on the track or buddies on a group ride, people stop wanting to ride with the guy who can't admit to riding over his head. You lose access to the people who could actually help you, but your ego is too busy protecting a lie to listen to the truth.

Price of Truth

Eventually, the physical world provides a 'reality check' that the ego can't ignore. On the track, it's the stopwatch or a low-side. On the street, it's the guardrail.

Break free from denial. Confront your self-delusions with objective reality, accept brutal honesty, and reclaim responsibility for your actions. On the street, this isn't just about mastery; it's about survival.

※ **Mind Note – Delusional**

"The Easiest Way to Solve a Problem is to deny it exists."

- Isaac Asimov

Celebrate You

Yea, I'm also opening this one up referring to racing, but trust me, this one goes right to you as well. Have you noticed that the celebrations of the Grand Prix winning team are quite crazy? Sure, winning a GP or even the championship is quite an achievement, but there are teams or individual racers who have been there a hundred times, but they're celebrating it as if it's their very first victory? They also get paid to be successful, so this might make an excessive celebration a tiny bit questionable, right?! But is it though?

Psychology of Hidden Happiness

No. It's not questionable. That celebration is mandatory mental hygiene. Those professional teams aren't just celebrating the finish line; they're celebrating the thousands of failures, the near-misses, the budget fights, the sleepless nights of mechanical engineering, and the physical pain that went into finding that final hundredth of a second (remember the Inverse law of progress?). For them, the celebration is a ritual of emotional accounting. It's the moment they deposit the full value of the achievement back into their psychological bank account, giving them the emotional capital necessary to face the next week of grueling, non-glamorous work.

But before we dive into why you need to celebrate, let's explore why you might be holding back. There's a fascinating and common psychological phenomenon at play: hiding happiness after a success, or downplaying it, can stem from several different psychological roots. It's often not about the happiness itself, but about the perceived consequences of expressing that happiness. Here's a breakdown of the psyche behind it:

Worry that celebrating success invites resentment or bad luck. Manifestation: "Oh, it was nothing, really."

Believing success is a fluke or deception, not deserved. Manifestation: Attributing success to luck, fearing exposure.

Cultural or personal value against appearing arrogant. Manifestation: Quiet satisfaction, redirecting praise.

Success brings pressure for future performance. Manifestation: Downplaying achievement, focusing on the next challenge.

Personal standards are higher than the achieved outcome. Manifestation: Immediately pointing out flaws.

Discomfort with being in the spotlight. Manifestation: Changing the subject, deflecting praise.

Unwillingness to express joy when others are suffering. Manifestation: Subtle happiness, acknowledging others' difficulties.

In many cases, it's a combination of these factors, influenced by personal history, cultural background, and the specific context of the success. It highlights the complex interplay between internal emotional states and external social dynamics.

Why *You* Must Celebrate

Do you see yourself in this?! You might take all those little tiny steps in progress forward you take for granted. The first shift into 2nd gear you successfully made, that line on your favorite canyon road you finally hit right, that bad-ass counter steer that made you hit the escaping gap to avoid the car, that sliding front wheel you mastered not to go down on gravel. All these, and a thousand more moments you should have for celebration and to boost your brain with a dopamine shot!

This is the psychological core: Your brain is a machine driven by rewards. When you successfully execute a complex task—like hitting the perfect apex, holding a consistent throttle through a series of turns, or finding that tiny, incremental improvement—your brain releases dopamine. This neurotransmitter doesn't just make you feel good; it's the chemical currency of learning. Dopamine is what says, "This worked. Remember it. Do it again."

Celebrating successes, no matter how small, is crucial for sustained motivation, psychological well-being, and reinforcing positive neural pathways. When we hide or downplay achievements, we deny our brains the vital dopamine release that solidifies learning and drives future effort. This self-denial can lead to burnout, imposter syndrome, and a diminished sense of self-worth.

Celebrating validates our efforts, builds confidence (linking back to "competence-defined confidence"), and creates a positive feedback loop that says, "What I did worked, I'm capable, and I can do it again." It's not about arrogance; it's about honoring the journey, acknowledging growth, and fueling the tank for the challenges ahead.

One Tiny Win at a Time

Remember our talk about the vagueness trap? Riders often say, "I need more confidence." We defined confidence as the direct result of competence in defined areas. You build that rock-solid competence by celebrating the small victories that prove your skill is increasing. Your challenge is to shift from the negative spiral (always focusing on the gap) to the positive reinforcement loop (always focusing on the gain). You don't have to dump champagne on your head, but you do have to own the moment of victory.

Non-Negotiable Assignment

I want you to make celebrating small, tiny successes a non-negotiable part of your riding protocol. This is the counter-ego discipline applied to self-reward. Every time you execute a difficult maneuver correctly—a smooth downshift, a precise line through a tricky intersection, or a disciplined throttle hold—I want you to create an internal checkpoint:

Silence the inner critic that is already pointing out the next flaw.

Even if it's just a mental fist pump, or a whispered "Nailed it" inside your helmet, give yourself the reward.

Explicitly define what worked: "My eyes stayed up!" or "My hands were loose!"

This is the fastest, safest, and most sustainable way to build the deep, unshakeable confidence that separates the master from the mediocre. You aren't just getting better; you're training your brain to reward the right behaviors. So, the next time you see a GP winner going crazy on the podium, remember: that frenzy isn't just for the crowd. It's an essential psychological requirement for them to return next week and do it all again. Now go find your own champagne moments.

Psychological Takeaway

Celebration isn't about being loud; it's about mental hygiene. When you execute a skill correctly—a smooth downshift or hitting a perfect line—your brain releases dopamine. This isn't just a 'feel-good' moment; it's the chemical currency of learning. It signals your brain to remember the specific neural pathway you just used. If you ignore these tiny wins, you starve your brain of the reward it needs to solidify that new skill.

Downplay Trap

Many riders downplay their progress due to imposter syndrome or a fear of looking arrogant. This is a mistake. When you say, "It was just luck," or immediately focus on your next flaw, you trigger a negative spiral. You're training your brain that even when you do something right, the result is stress or a higher expectation. This leads directly to burnout and stagnation because the effort never feels "worth it" to your subconscious.

Internal Checkpoints

To build competence-defined confidence, you need a 'non-negotiable' protocol for self-reward. Every time you nail a maneuver, create an internal checkpoint. Stop the inner critic, acknowledge the success with a mental "nailed it," and specifically define what worked (e.g., "I kept my eyes up"). This reinforces the correct behavior and builds a psychological bank account you can draw from when things get difficult.

Fuel for the Journey

By celebrating the small victories on your favorite road or at the track, you provide the fuel necessary to push through plateaus. Stop waiting for the "big" win; start rewarding the tiny steps that actually make you a master.

Don't be afraid to yell out an echoing "YEAH" once in a while. It's a relief for your soul.

The Decline

Let's take a moment here…

Um, I've put this subject pretty much last in this book for several reasons. Some are personal, but mainly, I'm doing this for you. Why? Because you might be in the middle of your riding career and you don't want—nor should you—read this one here before the time is right for you.

Just trust me on this for now. Take a bookmark, write a note on it like 'Read when ready!', and place it right here. Put the book away, or skip to the 'Final Word' (283). Talk to you later!

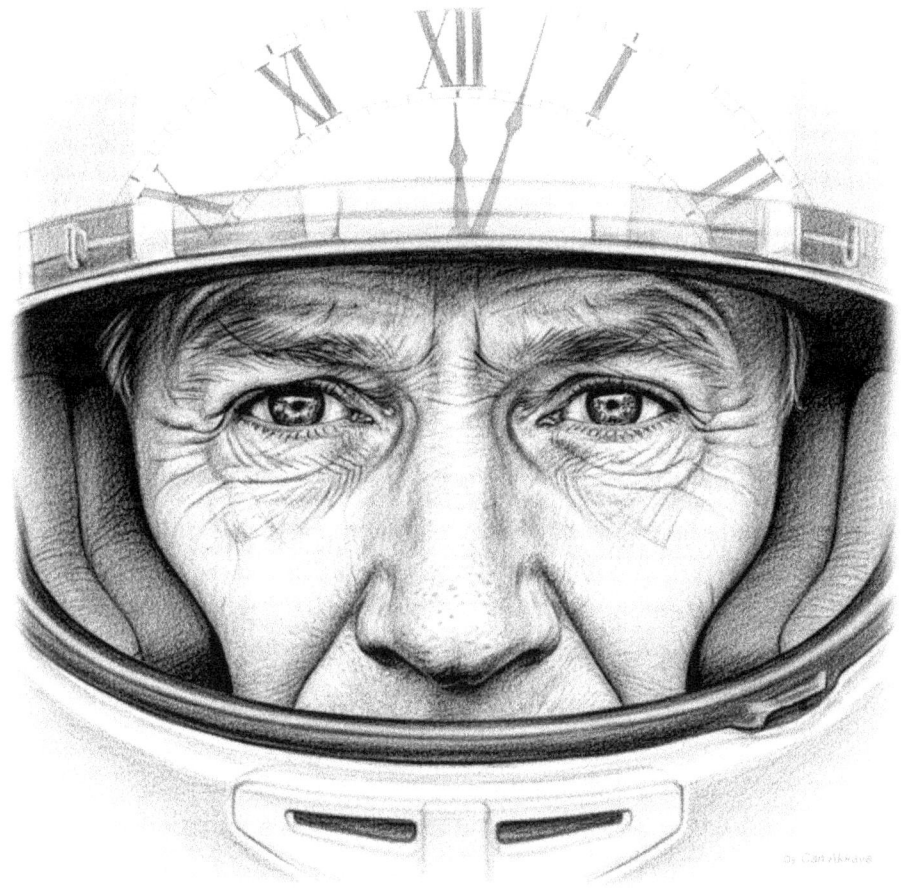

You know, when you're young, you live in a total vacuum of denial. Life is great. Nothing seems to bother you really. You're onto something, and you feel invincible, even immortal. You look at the older guys with arrogance, smiling at them when their performance lags. You think you're better than them. Are you, though?! Maybe you're faster, but maybe that's just because they're declining in fact. This is a reverse reality you reject to see, just like you also reject that your own time is ticking. Go ask me how I know!

We are like comets, shining bright for only a moment in time. Your way up that ladder is about to come to a stop. Every cell in your body is fighting to believe that, but subconsciously, you do know that there's nothing you could do about it. Sure, if you stay physically in shape and keep riding a lot, you're able to extend the final destiny. But you won't ever be able to prevent what's coming to each and all of us.

It's just like with the best set of tires money can buy. They reach their peak performance, and from there… they're declining. Lap by lap, mile after mile, until the wires are showing.

When I retired from pro racing, I was 31 years old. I stopped racing and riding because of the beginning of a decline. Today, I'm almost 61 years old, still declining of course and I feel like there's only a thin layer of rubber left on that tire set, covering the wires. Sure, I still rip lap times that make most people regret their existence, but that doesn't mean that I'm not suffering, because I know what I was capable of more than 30 years ago. It hurts.

Decline happens on the mental, as well as on the physical side. I can say that I'm still in okay shape, as there was an athlete once, but my body is also past peak performance and runs down its own set of tires. Soon, my eyesight will be narrowing, and my judgment for distance and speed will falter. My reaction times will be longer, and the ability to make multiple decisions in a split second will be gone.

However, something good comes with age—wisdom. You see everything more from a distance and look at it with a smile on your face. You can see the unnecessary drama and cut the shit. I still have reflexes like a f'n Ninja, but I also have more control over my ego and emotions. That makes me, even with the high pace I'm still able to maintain, not crashing anymore, unless it's because of a technical issue or caused by someone else. I'm in control of my body and mind.

Marc Marquez made a remarkable comment just recently. He feels the decline and seems not to hide nor deny it. Finding that out made him live a little bit more in peace with it. He said, "I'm not the racer I once was, but I have different strengths now."

So, what I'm saying right now is that you will need to let things go. The harder you try to hold on to that 'time straw,' the harder the wake-up call will be. You might be able to stop your wristwatch, but you can't stop the universe from spinning. Keep riding till the wires are showing, but pick your fights wisely. I'm actually kind of delighted that I don't have to be a rock star on a bike 'that much' anymore.

When You Know It's Over

Don't know if you can lie to yourself that well, but the moment you identify the decline, and that's when it has already begun. The beginning of the end. This is mostly noticeable in your eyes, body language, and preparation routines. There are time phases you're going through…

The Beginning

Your riding performances are getting more and more inconsistent. You can't even describe it, nor are you 'really' trying hard to understand it. You try to be pickier, but you're kind of hiding something. You have more social contact—something you used to prevent distractions. Now, you kind of need that. You consider starting to play golf more often.

The Middle

Your lack of riding performance is showing now. Which is good, because this sport has a ton of excuses to pick from. Your desperation is showing, especially on the brakes. You're a beast there, but overshooting lines on entries becomes a habit. You can blame the bike for only a short time. Your preparation routines seem to change. You're not on time anymore. You kind of know why you're not waiting for a call from teams anymore, but you've actually started playing golf now.

The End

Your riding performance is way off now. Each time something happens, thoughts go through your head: "…why am I still doing this?!". When you wake up, your first thought is about something else. You're showing up late, but you don't even care. The entire circus feels like a huge drama, and every time you swing your leg over the bike it triggers a '…let's just not crash anymore'. You're now having a VIP Golf course membership.

Simply put, you can wrap this up in denial, rejection, and realization. I think it's needless to say that the middle—the rejection phase—is the hardest and also the most dangerous.

Don't you dare think that this is 'just a pro level thing'. Oh no. This is going to happen to all of us. No matter what your level is or what category of rider you are. The occasions may differ, but the signs of time are the same.

Besides, a pro can't just pull the plug as there are more factors in play, I hope for you that you see the signs of time towards the end of the 'beginning phase'. If you do…

Don't be afraid to make the call… It's OK!

❈ Mind Note – So true!

"We delight in the beauty of the butterfly, but rarely admit the changes it has gone through to achieve that beauty."

— *Maya Angelou*

Final Word

As we reach the end of this journey, I hope you've found not just answers, but perhaps more importantly, the right questions to ask yourself. My work sheds a necessary light on the mental and psychological side of motorcycling. It's essential for every rider—from the absolute beginner to the high-level racing professional—regardless of age or bike choice.

If you were hoping for more straight-lined resolutions, man, they're actually laying within the 'knowing all about the Psychology of Riding Motorcycles.' This isn't about quick fixes; it's about the profound process of discovering where you see yourself in all this mess, and only then do you open yourself up for healing. It's just like going to a therapist. They hear your stories, go in-depth, and have you discovering how f'd up you are yourself, and then the healing process can be triggered. I think I gave you plenty of stories to 'find yourself' in this lecture, so don't be disappointed.

This book, I believe, gives all riders—no matter on the road or on the track—a ton of keys to a whole lot of doors. Searching for the right one is entirely up to you, because that can be very individual. The road to true mastery, both on the bike and in life, is less about innate talent and more about a relentless pursuit of self-awareness, honest feedback, and the courage to challenge ingrained beliefs. We've peeled back the layers to reveal the psychological blueprints that truly govern our performance, safety, and enjoyment on two wheels.

My ultimate hope is that this book empowers you to ride with greater confidence, deeper understanding, safer and an unshakeable sense of calm, allowing you to truly own the candy store that is the open road. May every ride be a testament to your growing awareness and an enjoyable expression of your evolving skill.

This book wouldn't have been possible without the dedication and support of many. My deepest gratitude goes to the entire Superbike-Coach Corp team, whose selfless work and unwavering commitment to each student's growth and safety truly make true mastery possible. I love you guys!

I also want to extend my thanks to all those who believed in this project, contributed their insights, and helped refine this manuscript—especially my editor and collaborators—into the powerful guide it has become.

Thank you for allowing me to share this passion with you. Now, go ride. And ride smart and remember… This is all part of a long 'road trip'! :-)

Can Akkaya, *Headcoach of the Superbike-Coach Corp*

Free Bonus Material

Thank you and Congratulations!

You've proven you have the Mindset for mastery.

Your journey doesn't end here. Two additional chapters—too intense and specialized for the main book—have been reserved exclusively for you, the committed reader.

Scan the QR code. Upon sign-up, you will receive an email with the link and password to instantly claim your exclusive and free chapters.

Your Review

Thank you for reading my book! If this book helped you change your mindset or improve your riding, I ask for one final action: To share your opinion on Amazon.

Scan this QR Code or visit the Amazon product page now. Your honest feedback is highly appreciated. Thank You!

Be safe out there!

www.ingramcontent.com/pod-product-compliance
Ingram Content Group UK Ltd
Pitfield, Milton Keynes, MK11 3LW, UK
UKHW022238230426
12048UKWH00018BA/1332